Romantic Conventions

Romantic Conventions

Anne K. Kaler

and

Rosemary E. Johnson-Kurek

editors

Bowling Green State University Popular Press
Bowling Green, OH 43403

Library of Congress Cataloging-in-Publication Data
Romantic conventions / [edited by] Anne K. Kaler / Rosemary E. Johnson-Kurek.

      p.   cm.
      Includes bibliographical references.
      Contents: Conventions of the romantic genre / Anne K. Kaler / -- The good provider in romance novels / Pamela Marks -- From bodice-ripper to baby-sitter : the new hero in mass-market romance / Abby Zidle -- Persona, promotion, and the fabulous Fabio / Rosemary E. Johnson-Kurek -- This is not your mother's Cinderella : the romance novel as feminist fairy tale / Jennifer Crusie Smith -- Cavewoman impulses : the Jungian shadow archetype in popular romantic fiction / Amber Botts -- Medieval magic and witchcraft in the popular romance novel / Carol Ann Breslin -- Conventions of captivity in romance novels / Anne K. Kaler -- Time-travel and related phenomena in contemporary popular romance fiction / Diane M. Calhoun-French -- Leading us into temptation : the language of sex and the power of love / Rosemary E. Johnson-Kurek -- Postmodern identity (crisis) : confessions of a linguistic historiographer and romance writer / Julie Tetel Andresen -- Hero, heroine, or Hera? Anne K. Kaler.
      ISBN 0-87972-777-2. -- ISBN 0-87972-778-0 (pbk.)
      1. Love stories--History and criticism. 2. Love in literature.
I. Kaler, Anne K. / Rosemary E. Johnson-Kurek
P3448.L67R66   1998
809.3'85--dc21   98-25221
                                                            CIP

Cover design by Dumm Art

Contents

Language and Love

Introduction

Conventions of the Romance Genre

Anne K. Kaler

> Telling a story's an art, writing's a craft.
> —Nora Roberts (*Second Nature* 99)

Just when does the craft of writing become the art of storytelling?
Just when does a rosebud become a rose?

Within the popular genre of romance, craft becomes art when the story unfolds seamlessly, the conclusion ties all loose ends together in a happy ending, and the conventions blend so perfectly that the romance is completely satisfying to our expectations, like a rosebud opening to its full glory.

Critics unravel the apparent mystery of the art of the romance by inspecting the crafts and techniques which authors use to create it. In order to understand the means by which a complex art has been created, we often explicate the tale via a process of studying what elements or factors determined the author's use of various conventions or literary devices. The critics in this book believe that the romance genre is an important part of the literary scene, not only because it has captured nearly fifty percent of the paperback market, but also because it employs sympathetic values and identifiable conventions of its own. Like the genetic makeup of the rose, these sympathetic values—literary, challenging, and socially redeeming values—are actually encoded in the themes, conventions, patterns, or familiar images that are the very tools of the craft of romance writing. How well each author uses those tools determines how well she tells her story, her tale, her art.

When I was a youngster, I wept when I could find no new fairy tales to read. I rejoiced when I found them again in the myths. When I was a teenager, I wept when there were no more romances to read after *Jane Eyre, Wuthering Heights,* and *The Sheik.* Later, I rejoiced when I discovered category romances; however, because of years spent in the scholarly pursuit of distinguishing the finer points of literary worth, I approached these romances with reserve even as I consumed them. Why was I consuming these bits of "marshmallow fluff" so heartily and hardily?

1

Eventually I came to understand why I hungered for this particular genre, why I craved the happy ending like the cherry on top of the sundae: it satisfied me. Romances are a lot like sundaes. The specific ingredients vary, but do not deviate much from the basics of ice cream and topping. A sundae is recognized as such by the conventional arrangement of these basic ingredients. Even the bowls used to "serve up" sundaes are generally of a certain style—within a prescribed range of design to allow for variety—that conventionally identifies them as sundae dishes. (Book covers for romance serve a similar function.) Neither all sundaes, nor all romances, are equal.

Some writers emerge as great because they "work" the formula, shaping it to their particular vision. This "reworking" is why I found, and still find, the romance genre as satisfying as chocolate and a lot less fattening. Fortunately for me, good romances abound and some great romances exist as well. The great authors work current topics into the old forms, or invent new combinations of forms for the old ideas I had relished so in myths and fairy tales.

Like Alice, I became curiouser and curiouser about these combinations and recombinations, about the comfort of convention and the exhilaration of invention in this genre. I found my own curiosity about romances duplicated in the writings of other scholars. I met many other romance readers who enjoyed writing about them, talking about them, and questioning them as much as I did. That's why we assembled this book. We believe we can contribute to the romance genre by analyzing what we read. Our arguments are simple. Some authors write romances. Some romance writers write better romances (plots, themes, and conventions); some write romances better (style); and some get better (development). When we read an author who consistently writes better romances and writes them increasingly better, our scholarly instincts rise to the challenge to discover why. This discovery process is our job and our joy.

As critics we bring to the genre various modes of critical analysis by which any literature may be judged. Critics do more than criticize. Some critics judge or compare the way individual authors use words to get their stylistic effects. Some critics ponder how a popular idea is developed by several authors to meet the demands of a particular time period. Some critics investigate how the plot patterns and themes from earlier literature are echoed in modern writings. We explicate, explain, dissect, analyze, and research to make our enjoyment of reading the romance greater.

Despite academic wariness of popular culture in general and feminist concern for romances in particular, some researchers and romance writers have already analyzed the romance genre for its sociological and economic impact. The first line of criticism includes critics such as Janice Radway in *Reading the Romance,* Tania Modleski in *Loving with a Vengeance,* Kay Mussell in *Fantasy and Reconciliation,* Carol Thurston in *The Romance Revolution,* and Margaret Jensen in *Love's Sweet Return.* Some critics judge the romance genre as an amusing literary phenomenon rather than as a separate genre with its own set of conventions. However, in *Dangerous Men and Adventurous Women,* editor Jayne Ann Krentz and sister romance writers defend the genre and attempt to explain it. A special issue of *Paradoxa* has a similar goal and also includes analysis of the genre from an academic and literary perspective. In addition, organizations such as the 8000-member Romance Writers of America enable the authors themselves to discuss their craft by holding conferences, workshops, and critique groups. Publications such as *Romantic Times* and *Affaire de Coeur,* along with a bevy of particularized newsletters, websites, and chat rooms provide information and feedback for both romance writers and readers through reviews, feature interviews, and regular columns.

Our book centers on the analysis of a limited number of aspects of the romance genre and attempts to pinpoint the specific conventions, patterns, themes, and images that make it work. We follow the strands of convention back to the origins of the story in folklore or fairy tale or forward into a newer style an author may use to tell her stories and achieve her effects. A critic may study the grafting of the romance's cultivated rose onto the wild rambler genres and forms of old stories and older myths. What was the original tale? How is the new bloom better than the older rose? What bound the graft together? What vision pushed the simple form of the tale into the complicated romance? These are the types of questions we try to answer—in detail, in specifics, in depth, and in variety.

Writers of genre fiction are often accused of writing hackneyed revisions of old tales using flat, two-dimensional characters, while serious writers write original works peopled with round or three-dimensional characters. Sometimes it seems as if the writers of romance—more so than writers in any other genre—are more apt to be required to defend themselves against this accusation and less apt to be considered exempt from it. High praise for a romance author may sometimes include the observation that she has "risen above her genre." If she has risen above her genre, is she then outside of it? Nowhere is it dictated that formula fiction be poorly written. A successful "formula" is not only a challenge to authors, but a challenge for critics as well. Critics look not only to the work of individual authors, but to the collective works of the genre itself. Romance, despite presumptuous assumptions that it is froth and frills, is a sturdily constructed form whose component parts must be correctly mixed to achieve its intended effect. Mastery means that everything comes together—art, craft, tools, techniques—all in one splendid burst of passion where the pattern set down by art is frequently changed —by one or all—to create new, different, and sometimes better patterns. Many of the romance authors we have critiqued have "broken" the pattern to make a new one in order to take the reader into a realm beyond the expected story, transcending the very form of the art. In a way, this ability to make art mean something bigger than itself takes on a mystical, magical quality. Whether a work of art is a natural one like a red rose or a stunning sunset, or a man-made one like music, it creates a sympathetic response in those who encounter it. Word artists are able to capture a sympathetic essence, to recreate it in a story, and to transmit it with an intensity that enables the reader to transcend everyday feelings.

Why then would a happy romance reader turn critic and seek to demystify the mystery of an author's creation of a new world? Let me cite my own example. I feel better after I read romance. As a critic I want to understand why this is so. I've always liked stories. I've hungered for them so badly that I've devoted my life to telling students about them. Because romance satisfied this hunger, I wanted to examine the cause of this satisfaction. My years of analyzing other literature came in handy and led me to the answer. Romance satisfies me for the simplest of reasons—it has a happy ending, always and in all ways. This endearing ending is the most critical and enduring convention of the romance genre and, if its inclusion means it has been written to a familiar "formula," then so be it. Amen, I say, and hallelujah as well. Although I am a romantic trapped in a real world, I have always been a determined optimist. I feel good when I read romances because they reinforce, reiterate, and restate my beliefs.

I even use romances as spiritual reading because to me they have a salvation myth that repeats the good news that, if I am faithful and try my best, there is a better world somewhere. Like Dorothy, somewhere over the rainbow of romances, I know bluebirds sing. Like Alice, the looking glass holds many wonders for me. Like the nursery rhyme character, I will "sit on a cushion and sew a fine seam and [I] will be fed on strawberries and cream" and read romances because, as Nora Roberts has her hero advise the heroine in *Second Nature,* "they're good for you" (149).

However, my formal education drummed into me the traditional literary values and analytical tools—those approaches we call the masculine virtues—of reason, logic, coherence, symmetry, order, etc. Those of us who are teachers know how little of formal education actually sticks.

My real education took place around teacups on kitchen tables, late-night pizza in dorm rooms, and hasty meals in college snack bars. At the same time as formal and informal education vyed for my attention, the rhetoric of the feminist revolution sensitized my ears to the roar of women's voices and to the whisper of a woman's voice. But feminism generally decries the values of the romance genre. So, having been trained to value masculine virtues and to listen for women's voices, I arrived at a critical age (and mass) for explosion into writing—critical writing about romance.

Between the excesses of extremely biased male criticism and rampant feminist theory, there exists a middle ground from which I view the romance genre—a ground so sacred, so special that I hesitated to tread on it until I was impelled by genuine concern. It is that spirit that I seek in my critical writings.

The conventions of popular genre literature may be likened to the vowels in our language. A . . . e . . . i . . . o . . . u . . . are the simple carriers of human breath out of the body until harsh consonants form them into words. They are the simple building blocks of words, a primal glue between packets of energy we call sound. Analogously, popular conventions are the primal glue, the building blocks, the carriers which shape a human story into a recognizable form or genre. What are the conventional vowels of the romance genre and what do they mean to its readers, writers, and devotees?

"A" stands for aestheticism—the love of beautiful words, of lyrical phrases, of singing sounds that transmit their delight to the reading eye. "A" also implies asceticism, that necessary restraint in words, the sparsity of adverbs, adjectives and ablative absolutes.

"E" suggests eroticism. It does not suggest pornography, but rather the sense of fun that good sex should convey. It is an eroticism where actions should speak louder than words describing such action, where less is better, and where anatomy should take second place to commitment. "E" is also rooted in exoticism, in the traveling of the mind to new continents, new worlds, new adventures. The older romances called them travelogues; we call it escape.

"I" represents the identity we connect with in skilled writing, that central personality whom the reader sees mirrored in the main character. "I" is also the impetus toward imagination, innovation, and imagery— extravagantly lush islands, inward journeys toward the soul, dusty safaris into Africa, or innocent flirtations in Greece.

"O" represents the outsized characters in romances, those oafs or ogres, those hunks or heroes, those outlandish larger-than-life characters who make us go "O" or "Ooooo" or "Oh, no!"

"U" tells of the u-turns in love, the sharp veering ironies of human conditions, the coincidences of chance, the luck of the draw, the "cute-meet." "U" speaks of Utopias promised between the book's covers but never experienced in reality. But then romance and its vowels are not reality.

Or are they?

And sometimes "Y." Why?

Realistic fiction, biography, even autobiography, often dwell on the darker issues of the dichotomy of life and death—war, in which men kill other women's sons and call it glory. (I can read the *Odyssey* but not the *Iliad*. I may have to live in a world where such actions take place, but I don't have to read about them or write about them.) That is why I choose romances to read and critique. The spirit of romance is the invigorating spirit in the truest sense of the "breath of life," the muse, the life-force, the essence, the Sophia, the Shekinah, the "come tell me a story over a cup of tea" syndrome, the womanliness of writing, if you will.

This spirit of romance energizes me in a way no other genre does. For example, Jane Austen makes me think but Charlotte and Emily Bronte make me feel—Heathcliff and Rochester will always be more tempting (intellectually, at least) than the comfortable Mr. Knightly or Mr. Darcy. So when a critic such as Northrup Frye claims that Austen wrote novels while the Brontes wrote romances, he praises the masculine virtues of order and reason while ignoring the feminine virtues of passion and sensibility, which are so essential to the Brontes' work.

Romance is an old genre and the curious critic is interested in discerning why it is so timelessly popular. Romance originally meant the matter of Rome, those stories of Caesar, Antony, Cleopatra that have spanned the centuries—the exoticism, the fantasy, the larger-than-life characters, the adventure, the breathless excitement. Thus romance pervades and includes all categories—mysteries, horror, thrillers, western, adventure, fantasy, science fiction, gothic, and, of course, love stories. So inspiring is this spirit of romance that categories now leap across boundaries to borrow conventions, themes, patterns, images, and plots from each other.

Why? How? Which ones?

When I approach any piece of art—a book, a play, a painting, a movie—my first response is immediate—I either like it or I don't like it. Then I indulge my tendency to take things apart to see how they work. At this analysis stage with a romance novel, I ask three questions: How do I feel toward the novel, why does it affect me this way, and what devices were used to make me feel this way? Since the critics have gone through a similar process, the variety of the essays in this volume should give further clues as to why the conventions of romance and its particular brand of genre fiction works.

The essays for this book fell quite naturally into three groupings of familiar conventions. *Archetypes and Stereotypes* investigates commonly held images of men and women in the romance genre—as diverse as the witch and Fabio, the "new hero" and "good old provider," Cinderella and Prince Charming. The second section, *Time and Place,* looks at the exotic as integral to the genre, and the final section, *Language and Love,* delves into the words that capture the essence of our fascination with romance.

In the first section, Pamela Marks traces the shift of economic and emotional needs as they relate to the hero's role as a good provider in both current and early American romances. It is a provocative look at the modern relationship in light of past literary examples. "The providing that is done by men and women alike . . . guarantees that human society will continue in its most basic unit."

Abby Zidle looks at the romance's construction of a stereotype of the New Hero as a combination of elements of the playboy and the wild-man, resulting in the "mass market romance hero" that is popular today. If the New Hero is a composite of every woman's dreams, then, according to Rosemary Johnson-Kurek, Fabio may be his image and likeness. Her account of her fascination and pursuit of the Fabulous Fabio ends in a face-to-gorgeous-face meeting which left her to sigh that "no man had ever affected me like this before."

On the other side of the romantic stereotype spectrum is the hero-ine. Jennifer Crusie Smith, a romance writer and academic, analyzes why the Cinderella myth must be altered to fit today's romance heroine, since the shoe simply doesn't seem to fit anymore. The persistence of the myth, however, demands that the romance writer rethink the elements of the fairy-tale and "recast" them to create a heroine with which the modern reader can identify.

Amber Botts's essay claims that the appeal of romance is that it "reflects a cavewoman impulse deep in the heterosexual female psyche that wants to tie the primary Alpha Male to her." Her argument is that the true goal of the romance writer is to "give other women a safe place to experience these [primal] urges, to deal with them, and to ultimately accept and integrate them." Carol Breslin's article takes these primal urges one step farther with her identification of the concept of a "witch" as used in romances, as one who is a "breaker of stereotypes who challenges male pride . . . to create a landscape where women of special gifts and powers can work out their destinies unencumbered by structures of patriarchy."

An integral element in early romance novels was the travelogue because it provided escape to women trapped by circumstance or economics. Although the historical novel gives women readers the sense of escaping time itself, conventions of time and place continue to be the bedrock of romance novels. Diane Calhoun-French's essay on time travel shows how writers capitalize on both elements by placing the hero and the heroine in dangerous, fantastic, and provocative situations. Dealing with the element of place in a somewhat different way, my article closes this section by detailing how a woman can be made physically powerless but emotionally powerful through her captivity by the hero.

Critics have long noted that one characteristic of romance lies in its use of euphemistic language. My co-editor Rosemary Johnson-Kurek deals with the problems of such language where "conventionally understood euphemisms . . . are a definitive aspect of the romance genre and critical to maintaining the balance between esthetic and erotic sensitivities."

Dawn Heinecken details how the romance genre has evolved from a male-dominated stance into a kinder, gentler form more acceptable to feminist beliefs. As a romance novelist and academic, Julie Tetel Andresen addresses the problem of "negative prejudice" which such a combination stirs up in both circles. She addresses the issue of how her two lives—as a linguistic historian and romance writer—intersect and thus provides insight into the process of the human mind in general.

An allied problem exists in the terminology used to describe the central character of a romance: she's not a "hero" since that is a term used for the male character, yet she's not truly a "heroine" because she controls her own destiny. So what term is suitable to describe the female hero? My article offers a solution.

So, just as the familiar symbol of eternal love, the red rose, opens its petals to reveal its full glory, so, too, does the romance novel open its pages to welcome the reader into the comfort of the old story of love made eternally new. Only then does the craft of romance writing become the art of storytelling in its full glory.

Bibliography

Jensen, Margaret Ann. *Love's Sweet Return*. Bowling Green, OH: Bowling Green State University Popular Press, 1984.

Krentz, Jayne Ann. *Dangerous Men and Adventurous Women*. Philadelphia: U of Pennsylvania P, 1993.

Modleski, Tania. *Loving with a Vengeance: Mass-Produced Fantasies for Women*. Hamden, CT: Shoe String, 1982. Reprinted, New York: Routledge, 1990.

Mussell, Kay. *Fantasy and Reconciliation: Contemporary Formulas in Women's Romance Fiction*. London: Greenwood, 1984.

Radway, Janice. *Reading the Romance: Women, Patriarchy and Popular Literature*. Chapel Hill: U of North Carolina P, 1984.

Roberts, Nora. *Second Nature*. Silhouette, 1991.

Thurston, Carol. *The Romance Revolution*. Chicago: U of Illinois, 1987.

"Where's Love Gone? Transformations in the Romance Genre." *Paradoxa: Studies in World Literary Genres* 3.1-2 (1997).

The Good Provider in Romance Novels

Pamela Marks

[The relationship of husband and wife] is one of mutual esteem, mutual dependence . . . [Their] affection shows itself by practical kindness. They know that life goes more smoothly and cheerfully to each for the other's aid; they are grateful and content. The wife praises her husband as a "good provider."
—Margaret Fuller (*The Great Lawsuit,* 1843)

The readership of novels in which the explicitly stated objective is copulation with the blessing of society must be reckoned with; no one would buy such works unless they filled a need. And they apparently do: these books sell, and do so by the millions. Recent statistics show that fifty-percent of the paperback books sold are romances. According to Jeanne Dubino, thirty-one percent of women who *read,* read romance fiction (qtd. in Mann 103). If we are to believe the statistics reported by even the harshest judges of romance novels, works whose primary focus is love and marriage are read by 25 million in the United States alone. When expanded to include readers around the world, the number reaches a quarter of a billion (103).

Therein lies the rub, particularly with regard to those of us who struggle to teach "good" literature. We're puzzled: we want to find a reason for the huge popularity of these books. And we're scornful, for the most part. Most academic criticism of romance novels seems filled with thinly veiled contempt: for the works themselves, for the publishing houses that print them, and—implicitly—for the readers who consume them as quickly as they appear on booksellers' shelves. This disdain appears to be fed by the notion among academic critics that the only acts of acceptable reading by women are those which require the reader to take a critical stance—preferably one with a Marxist-feminist orientation—and that a woman who spends her leisure time and money on romance novels is an unwitting pawn of some vast patriarchal conspiracy to keep her in her domestic place. Janice Radway, among others, has declared that the romance always follows a standard and completely predictable pattern, a system of narrative logic that begins with the heroine's social identity being thrown into question. It then meanders through mutual antagonism between the heroine and an Aristocratic Male (AM); separation; tenderness; and disclosure of the AM's previous hurt or betrayal. It ends with the heroine's stated or implied sexual response to the AM, and the restoration of her identity, always in the form of marriage (150). Radway goes on to observe that "[in] learning how to read male behavior from the romance, a woman insulates herself from the need to demand that such behavior change . . . [A]ll popular romantic fiction originates in the failure of patriarchal culture to satisfy its female members" (151); finally, Radway affirms that "the romance continues to *justify the social placement of women* that has led to the very discontent that is the source of their desire to read romances" (217) [emphasis mine]. I will probably draw fire from my colleagues for saying it, but this attitude is not far from the stance taken by eighteenth- and nineteenth-century male critics of domestic novels, who "have in general affected contempt for this kind of writing, and looked upon romances, as proper furniture for a lady's library," as Clara Reeves wrote in 1785 (qtd. in Dubino 117).

But why should it matter to us? In America, millions of women are reading in a time and place often described as post-literate; as academics, we ought to be enraptured by that fact alone. And since literature itself, oral or written, is an integral part of the human experience, the modern romance novel must fill some niche of human necessity. Further, works which transport readers to imagined fulfillment of needs and pleasure, however defined, are not currently limited to female readership, and have not been so historically: *Utopia* springs to mind, or *The Faerie Queene*. Closer to the point, *Pamela's* adventures surely gave contemporary readers a vicarious thrill, and her tale of virginity preserved sold in huge numbers. It strikes me that the romance's taproot must go far deeper into the collective unconscious of literate humanity than has been commonly thought.

Yet despite some necessary historical backtracking, my purpose here is not to trace the modern romance's roots from eighteenth-century novels of sexual virtue richly rewarded by patriarchy. Neither do I wish to attack the romance itself as a running-dog of phallic imperialism, for my forays into romance novels—a genre in which I had no previous experience before I began the research for this article—have opened my eyes to the fact that all of the heroines I have met there are superficially self-sufficient women. I merely wish to ruminate for a bit upon what I perceive to be the dominant theme of the modern romance, which I believe is the nineteenth-century domestic novel's natural descendant. This central focus is the heroine's—and by extension the reader's—desire for a protector who will shield her from the slings and arrows of the struggles of everyday life. She is not necessarily looking for a rich man, but a "Good Provider"—that fine and manly figure whose presence resonates throughout the pages of romance novels. Sometimes he may appear in the disguise of a man of bad temper or indifference; he may even appear to be a villain in his early manifestations. But by the novel's *denouement* the reader is certain that he would never condemn the heroine to a life of cheese-paring or drudgery. We know that Jenny or Claire or Maddy will not spend the days of her married life waiting tables at a truck stop, endlessly scrubbing toilet bowls or dirty diapers or the kitchen floor of a single-wide trailer in some dreary desert town. There may not be wealth, but there will be comfort. Yet more importantly, there will be emotional security, for the Good Provider will never leave the heroine stranded. His passionate concern for her well-being, whether it be economic or psychological, will be the main focus of his existence from the novel's end to the fictive end of time. Far more than the acquisition of big money, the moving target of romance novels is the man who will provide the heroine with a source of emotional stability—while simultaneously heating up her libido. The Good Provider's primary function is as a reliever and preventer of the kind of stress that comes from living in a world fraught with assaults on a woman's desire for a quiet, peaceful, and secure life.

A Short but Necessary Historical Digression

Peace of mind is central to the convention of romance (*nee* domestic) literature, and has been since its conception in the eighteenth century and its fetal development in the nineteenth. This is particularly true in the United States, for if there is any one motif which runs through popular American literature as the Mississippi runs through the heartland, it is the theme of prosperity after tribulation, fair weather after foul, reward after struggle. After all, this is a nation founded on material opportunity coupled with spiritual conviction, both of which are usually attained after considerable hardship, if not outright mistreatment. As every schoolchild knows, the Separatists and Puritans who landed in Massachusetts were fleeing religious persecution. And though their religious polity had largely petered out by 1700, their heritage of hard work, perseverance in the face of setbacks, and intellectual and spiritual self-scrutiny has continued to inform American culture ever since. So has the Calvinist insistence upon the ability to read the Bible (later resulting in a bookworm citizenry), as well as the affirmation that Providence will heap substantial material benefits on the Elect. Such a mind-set is fertile ground for hope of Heaven, whether couched in spiritual or material terms.

The industrial revolution, from the early decades of the nineteenth century, had laid the groundwork for the birth and development of an ever-expanding consumerist society. But it is certainly no secret that in the decades following the birth of the American nation, the largest piece of the material action went to men, even though some education—that almost certain ticket to a more affluent lifestyle—did become available to women as well. America's agricultural economy was evolving into that of commercial capitalism, and its future adult citizens had to be trained to accept the terms of a new world view: American education was training prospective members of a new middle class to aspire to success.

If educators in the nineteenth century presented as paramount the goal of attaining and maintaining placement within the ranks of the mushrooming middle class, they frequently displayed that objective as resting squarely upon the ability to read well. Ebenezer Porter, D.D., president of the Andover Theological Seminary, published his *Rhetorical Reader* in 1831, and addressed his students' parents in the preface:

Every intelligent father, who would have his son or daughter qualified to hold a respectable rank in well-bred society, will regard reading as among the very first of polite accomplishments, that they should be able to read well. . . . In this country then, where the advantages of education are open to all, and where it is a primary object with parents of all classes, to have their children well-instructed, it would seem reasonable to presume that nearly all youth, of both sexes, must be good readers. (2)

Despite such desired outcomes, apparently for both genders, the goals specifically outlined in schoolbooks were very different for young men than for young women. Samuel Worcester's *Fourth Reader,* for use by students of around sixteen years of age, presents moral lessons for young women in a play entitled "The Happiness of Usefulness." Its heroine, Laura Selwyn, is actually allowed to earn money to help her financially strapped family. But this "work" is, paradoxically, suited exclusively to the domestic sphere, and may only be performed within it. Laura gives lessons in music and art, but only as a last resort to avoid the disgrace of poverty: "Our greatest trials always become our greatest blessings, when we permit them to humble and instruct us" (305). In works such as these, the role prescribed for young women is not to strive for success in the world of commercial capitalism, but to provide support and self-sacrifice in an attitude of self-denigration and self-distrust: their only acceptable options are spinsterhood or marriage. If young females chose marriage, they would provide the household support system, maintaining domestic havens for their husbands when they returned at the end of the day from the battlefield of mercantile trade.

Life was never easy for the nineteenth-century woman; we view with dismay her "daily dog-trot of domestic duties" (Garrett 163). A middle-class married woman's lot, even under the best of conditions, may have equaled drudgery, particularly in the infant towns of the frontier. But no matter where she lived, her husband's fortunes, if good enough, would probably provide for some household help. It was therefore in her best interest to find a Good Provider, and if he were lovable—why then, all the better.

Despite the lack of household appliances that we take for granted, nineteenth-century American middle-class women found themselves with more leisure time than at any previous time in history, and with more money to spend on nonessential items. Coupled with the technological advances in printing, paper making, and transportation that took place in the early decades of the century, this fact meant that American's enormous reading public was now deluged by a huge variety of reading materials: newspapers, magazines of all kinds, gift books, how-to manuals, and children's literature. But most important from the point of view of contemporary women authors—who often were writing to supplement household income—what put bread on the table, or supplied the gravy to cover it, were novels. "[This is] an age of novel writing. . . . We of the present generation can hardly estimate our own good fortune. . . . the press daily, nay hourly, teems with works of fiction. . . ." (qtd. in Baym 26).

Though nineteenth-century literary lights such as Nathaniel Hawthorne deplored sentimental domestic novels written by women, his crabby comment about the "damn'd mob of scribbling women" may have indicated more sour grapes than spleen, for these novels sold in staggering numbers. The need for escape from that daily dog-trot, for vicarious fulfillment of needs, and for reinforcement of the values that defined them, went far to drive the burgeoning market for such reading material, for the middle class not only read widely, but also set the moral codes which ostensibly percolated through all of society.

The first bestseller in the earliest years of the young nation was Susanna Rowson's *Charlotte Temple* (1794), a cautionary tale in which seduction and betrayal serve as the foil to the middle-class reader's apprehension of traditional courtship and marriage. The home—and its extension, the well-chaperoned school—is the nest from which Charlotte falls; pregnant and abandoned, she staggers through a snowstorm into a servant's hovel to die in childbirth. She may well be the prototypical victim of antiromance: her slightly befuddled lover Montraville, himself led astray by the falsehoods of a bounder friend and the enticements of marriage to a rich woman, is certainly a Bad Provider as he leaves the hapless Charlotte broke, homeless, and finally dead.[1]

But more in the direct ancestral line of the modern romance was the first literary sensation of the middle years of the 1800s: Susan Warner's *The Wide, Wide World* (1850), a domestic novel which Jane Tompkins characterizes as "the Ur-text of the nineteenth century United States" (585). Appearing two years before Harriet Beecher Stowe's blockbuster *Uncle Tom's Cabin*, and read by men and women alike, it chronicled the domestic and spiritual education of the orphaned Ellen Montgomery as she struggles to survive the tangible and intangible road-blocks flung in her path by an assortment of hateful characters: a nasty aunt, snobbish traveling companions, sadistic clerks, and roughhousing neighbors.[2] Ellen longs simultaneously for independence and for male protection, which could lead to a freedom from "burdens that young women [of the middle class] were neither expected nor prepared to shoulder" (601). At the end of this domestic *bildungsroman* Ellen achieves marriage to a man who provides her with "relief from house-hold cares. . . . Best of all, there is money to burn" (601). Ellen has married the consummate Good Provider, a man who has in fact raised her to become his wife. Her copious flow of tears—245 occurrences by actual count—are stifled.[3] She need not even be a crackerjack housekeeper, for "there is no kindling to gather . . . no tables to set or dishes to wash" (601). There is even a drawer full of ready cash, the ultimate gift of her rather overpowering, religiously correct husband (582). Her financial woes are over, as are her depressive episodes: an orphan once bounced from household to household, she now *belongs*. Her Good Provider has relieved all of the stresses that made her life a soggy morass.

In our own time, Ellen Montgomery's literary great-granddaughters share her tensions, if not her constant tears, and are knowingly or unknowingly on the lookout for virile and spiritually magnanimous men.

Back to the Future

Here at the bitter end of the twentieth century, the domestic novel's lineal descendant portrays its heroines in situations that are clearly analogous to those of its ancestry. Jenny Teale, of Lyn Ellis's *Dear John*, is the nineteenth-century orphan's 1990s equivalent. A woman who has been divorced by her ne'er-do-well husband after severe injuries have left her crippled, she has been flung from the shelter of domesticity. Encouraged by her sister to write to a Desert Storm Army captain, she creates in her letters a fantasy world of married life. The officer, a bache-lor who has been around the block not only in combat but also in sexual experience, yearns to meet her after his return, but Jenny does not want his pity. He does meet her, against her wishes, love prevails, her moribund sex life is revived, and at the romance's conclusion the two are married and expecting a child—something the heroine had been told she could never accomplish.

The classic romance plot. I can hear my colleagues' voices dripping with scorn. But there is an important difference in the fictive reality that exists in this particular romance, as well as in many others: Jenny Teale is presumably capable, once her injuries are healed, of again making a good living in her previous career as a regional sales representative; more to the point, she is a millionaire by virtue of an enormous insurance settlement. She does not need Captain John's money (and in any case, a junior officer doesn't make much). What she wants, and what she gets, is a man who: "loved her before he knew she wasn't perfect. He wasn't worried about endings or luck . . . He wanted to love her now" (215).

In Heather McCann's *The Master Detective,* the heroine, Margaret Webster, reports that she actually is an orphan. But she also has "common-sense independence. I like standing on my own two feet. It's something I've been doing for a long time" (57). She and the hero, Jake McCall, discover that Margaret's new brother-in-law, Robert, previously murdered Jake's sister; concurrently, Jake and Margaret fall in love. Jake may not be super-rich, but we do know that he has "a place in New Haven" as well as "a cabin in Maine" (249). He functions as a Good Provider in the sense that he rescues Margaret's sister from the coils of the evil Robert, who plans to do her in on their honeymoon. Margaret's peace of mind is restored, and at the novel's end Jake gives her a "warm, crushing embrace" which "[surrounds] them both like a golden halo" (251).

The true Good Provider doesn't mind if the heroine is physically flawed: Jenny's injuries do not put off her handsome captain. In Sandra Canfield's *Star Song,* the actor-hero Nash Prather, "royal by Hollywood's standards," decides that he needs "silence in his life" (50). He finds it with the heroine, Claire Rushing, a successful artist who, coincidentally, is deaf. She is also a Big Sister[4] to a teenage girl who has just lost her hearing to meningitis. Nash, a leading man whose tight jeans nearly cause Claire to swoon, puts the teenager in a play that he has written and is directing. The girl, in a secondary plot, succeeds brilliantly in her part in the play and finds romance with a teenage actor after having been dumped by a high school football star. Both women have found men who provide emotional stability, but more to the point, both women, despite their handicaps, are capable—or have the implicit potential—of providing for themselves.

In Sally Bradford's *Out on a Limb,* the heroine, Suzanne Peterson, is a veterinarian whose only family is her dog. She is engaged to the scion of a family that has made its millions in the pharmaceutical business: "With Marty she could do so much. He had money, sophistication, everything a woman could want. She would have a lifestyle that had always been beyond even her dreams" (20). But she soon finds out that he is physically abusive to her; worse still, he hates dogs. She ends up falling in love with a widowed cartoonist, Jed, who is the father of her Little Sister; he can provide her with a ready-made family. Wealth is not attractive to her, but family and stability—and the trappings of domesticity and all that they symbolize—are. Fearful of commitment to the widower who she is afraid might only feel responsibility rather than love for her, she finds herself redeemed by a primal urge:

[Suzanne] had wondered . . . not only why she was baking [chocolate chip] cookies but why she was enjoying the process so much. She hadn't come up with any satisfactory answers except that she knew Jed and Kacie would like them and it made her happy to do things they liked. (267)

The spurned and threatening pill prince later wounds Suzanne in her own clinic, but a dog she once saved leaps onto him and causes his gun to discharge, shooting him dead. It all ends with a wedding, the vet done up in "tea-length, antique satin," wedding guests who are expecting their first babies, and—an echo of Ellen Montgomery—a flood of tears as Jed slips "the plain gold band on her finger" (297). The lesson learned is not lost on the gimlet-eyed researcher of romance, nor on the reader of the same: all that glitters may not be a Good Provider.

Good Providers may provide more than relief from stresses attendant upon engagement to the wrong man. In Dawn Carroll's *Beguiled,* the heroine, Liana, returns from a fourteen-year exile to try to save her father's ranch; the neighboring vineyard is also home to its inheritor and her presumed enemy, Max Valentin. Despite the feud between their families entailed by an old scandal, Liana and Max fall in love, and by the novel's end Liana is twittering "Yes! Yes! Yes!" to his proposal of marriage (220). But before this, Max reveals himself to be a Good Provider in a truly modern sense: the morning after their first (unmarried) night together, he nods "toward the little pile of discarded wrappers on the floor. 'We used the last of those in the early hours of the morning'" (165). The 1990s Good Provider practices safe sex, thus ensuring the heroine's peace of mind in an era of sexually transmitted diseases or unwelcome pregnancies; he's come a long way from the wide world of the nineteenth century.

A glance into magazines that review new romances provides a window into the world of Good Providers and the women who love them. Heroines are not clinging vines: they may be "a straight-laced vocal music teacher" (*Rhinestone Cowboy*), "a caring doctor" (*The Return of Caine O'Halloran*), "a gamin computer expert" (*Give a Man a Bad Name*), "an expert in rare prints" (*The Bruges Engagement*); they are secretaries, schoolteachers, psychic researchers, anchorwomen, biographers, graduate students, riding instructors, talk show hosts, photographers, Hollywood directors, TV newswomen, or even widows who are "job hunting." In these cases, women are not asking to be rescued from financial disaster; even if their economic fortunes are at a low, their abilities and talents will see them through. What they need are men who will relieve the stress in their lives: the vocal music teacher must face down the townsfolk who disapprove of the young man she once "loved and lost"; the caring doctor must "share the healing powers of grief with her ex-husband"; the rare prints expert "can't help but compare her fiancé" to "a real man with personality." In a review of *The Persistent Lady*, we see that the Good Provider "must convince his independent-minded partner that both her company and her heart are safe in his hands" (Helfer 99). The operative word in all of the reviews is *independent;* these romantic heroines can take material care of themselves.

"Romances bolster patriarchal ideology, continuing to reaffirm the centrality of men in women's lives. . . . And, romances help to reconcile women to their domestic role of houseworkers," states Jeanne Dubino (109). But what is plain is that the heroine of the modern romance, far from needing a man to keep the wolf from the door, is looking for a man who will hold her in his arms forever and give her his undivided attention, his heart, and his children. Her need for him has far less to do with his economic success than with psychological and emotional nurturance, and with freedom from the stresses of the outside world rather than with patriarchal reward for services performed. It is this fact that negates the scornful claim that romantic heroines are looking solely for material providers. Readers of romance, like the heroines they encounter, have entered a new world: they can provide materially for themselves. What they are searching for is a man to vicariously shoulder part of the psychological burdens which accompany that economic provision.

Dubino states that "[in] romances heroines don't have to *do* anything to be loved; they just have to *be*" (111). I would take issue with this statement; the reader of romance knows that these fictional women are able to face the wide world prepared to make a living. And yet—and this *is* a paradox—the homes that they will create for their Good Providers in the unwritten pages after the wedding will be exactly the same as those which graced the nineteenth-century's domestic novel: they are havens from the turbulence of everyday life, providing shelter for the heroines as well as their husbands.

So What Does It All Mean?

If I read my own text correctly, I seem to be speaking now of romantic heroines doing some Good Providing of their own. And this may be exactly what I have had to say all along, after all of the rumination that I promised at the beginning. The central idea of any romance novel is less that of reinterpretation of patriarchy than of *human connection:* of the search by honest women and men for a lifelong partner with whom to share the joys and sorrows, the work and leisure, the bitter and sweet of life. And to find that partner, a lover with whom one can also share the most exalting act of our physical lives, is an idea as timeless as the moon.[5]

At the end of the twentieth century, this enduring concept seems to be under attack in some quarters of American culture, and the proponents of the assault on romance novels are often among its most vociferous enemies. This is a sad turn of events for readers and writers of romance as well as for its critics; the romance, albeit vicariously, fulfills needs that go beyond the simple yearning for an emotional Good Provider. The give-and-take that occurs in human relationships, particularly in courtship and marriage, defines the kinds of families that will ultimately arise from those institutions. The providing that is done by men and women alike, within the parameters of their relationship to one another, guarantees that human society will continue in its most basic unit.

Finally, then, the Good Provider's female counterpart is the Heroine, whose function is to provide him with the comfort and support that makes his life not only bearable but complete. The Eastern notion of *yang* and *yin,* of male and female enigmatically separate yet contained within one another and forming a perfect whole, has more relevance in romance than one would expect. Our true loves enter us in all ways, even as we become part of them. And that is not patriarchal domination. It is, rather, an affirmation of life: the halves of the intertwined symbol are identical, symmetrical, and *equal,* one must remember; neither can exist without the other.

Romances end with weddings, just as they always have; and if readers could see beyond the final pages, they would see the daily dogtrot of domestic and workaday duties overtake Claire and Jenny and Margaret. But we know, with hope born of fictional experience, that their lives will continue as fulfilled as when their Good Providers first fell under their gaze.

Notes

1. *Charlotte Temple* remained a best seller for generations, continuing to sell "into the twentieth century, going through at least two hundred editions," according to Ann Douglas. This is despite the opinions of Carl van Doren, who noted in 1917 that Rowson had "'imposed' on a 'naive underworld of fiction readers,'" and, later in the century, Leslie Fiedler, who sniffed that Rowson's work was a "subliterate myth, . . . hardly written at all." Yet, Douglas goes on to declare, "If *Charlotte Temple* did not meet the taste of the few, it answered the needs of many" in America as well as in England, where it was originally published in 1791 (viii-ix).

2. It is probably worthwhile here to say a few words about the unparalleled popular literary hit of the 1850s and beyond: *Uncle Tom's Cabin*—a work awash with Good Providers as well as with genuine villains. A story of love and betrayal, hate and redemption, *UTC* is full of admirable and resourceful heroines—the beautiful Eliza is the most famous—all in need of the helping hands of their Good Providers. The story of George and Eliza Harris's flight to freedom from slavery and enforced prostitution arguably represents the high-water mark of the romance novel: translated into scores of languages, it was read by millions around the planet. Upon meeting its author, Abraham Lincoln is supposed to have remarked, "So this is the little woman who started this big war." In a time unencumbered by stringently enforced copyright laws, the work was rapidly turned into dreadful stage plays and later into equally awful early films; as this century progressed, it was tarred and feathered by such eminent critics as James Baldwin and Hugh Kenner. Stowe's novel of love, courage, and spiritual healing found itself at the bottom of the literary heap, castigated and rejected by the public and academics alike, until a resurgence in works written by women brought it to light once more.

3. F. L. Mott, quoting a contemporary reviewer, lists a few of them:

Her tears almost choked her, began to drop again, brought no relief, came faster than her words, dropped into the water, fell faster, fell from the eyes, . . . flowed, flowed faster than ever, followed in a flood, gushed forth, had to be wiped away, mingled, poured, ran down into her lap, ran down her face and frock, streamed from her eyes. . .

"Worst of all," Mott observes, "they would drop down on her Bible. Poor Ellen!" (*Golden Multitudes: The Story of Best Sellers in the United States* [New York: Bowker, 1947]).

4. Harlequin began sponsoring Big Brothers/Big Sisters in the United States and Canada in April 1988, and has published a line of novels that feature Big Sister-Little Sister relationships. According to Brian Hickey, Harlequin's

President and CEO, "This fitting association between the world's largest publisher of romance fiction and a volunteer organization that assists children and youth in achieving their highest potential is a different kind of love story. . . . We are committed to assisting our young people to grow to become responsible men and women."

5. An idea borrowed from John Cheever in "A Miscellany of Characters That Will Not Appear": "Out with all . . . explicit descriptions of sexual commerce, for how can we describe the most exalted experience of our physical lives as if—jack, wrench, hubcap and nuts—we were describing the changing of a flat tire?" To me, Cheever seems here to be beating a drum for romance, although some would argue this point.

Works Cited

Baym, Nina. *Woman's Fiction: A Guide to Novels by and about Women in America, 1820-1870*. Ithaca, NY: Cornell UP, 1978.

Douglas, Anne. Introduction. *Charlotte Temple and Lucy Temple*. By Susanna Rowson. New York: Penguin, 1991. viii-ix.

Dubino, Jeanne. "The Cinderella Complex: Romance Fiction, Patriarchy and Capitalism." *Journal of Popular Culture* 27.3 (Winter 1993): 117.

Fuller, Margaret. "The Great Debate." *Norton Anthology of American Literature*. Ed. Nina Baym, et al. 3rd ed. 2 vols. New York: Norton, 1989.

Garrett, Elisabeth D. *At Home: The American Family 1750-1870*. New York: Abrams, 1990.

Helfer, Melinda, et al. "May Reviews." *Romantic Times* May 1994.

Mann, Peter H. "Romantic Fiction and Its Readership." *Poetics* 14 (1985): 103.

Radway, Janice A. *Reading the Romance: Women, Patriarchy, and Popular Literature*. Chapel Hill: U of North Carolina P, 1984.

Rowson, Susanna. *Charlotte Temple and Lucy Temple*. New York: Penguin, 1991.

Tompkins, Jane. Afterword. *The Wide, Wide World*. By Susan Warner. New York: Feminist P, 1987.

Warner, Susan. *The Wide, Wide World*. New York: Feminist P, 1987.

Worcester, Samuel. *Fourth Book of Lessons for Reading*. Boston: Hendee, Jenks and Palmer, 1840.

Romances

Bradford, Sally. *Out on a Limb*. Toronto: Harlequin, 1992.

Canfield, Sandra. *Star Song*. Toronto: Harlequin, 1992.

Carroll, Dawn. *Beguiled*. Toronto: Harlequin, 1992.

Ellis, Lyn. *Dear John*. Toronto: Harlequin, 1994.

McCann, Heather. *The Master Detective*. Toronto: Harlequin, 1992.

Wentworth, Sally. *Driving Force*. Toronto: Harlequin, 1989.

From Bodice-Ripper to Baby-Sitter: The New Hero in Mass-Market Romance

Abby Zidle

Amber swooned as Carlo's manly hands spanned her waist. Her heart pounded as he whispered, "Mi amor." As her lashes fluttered closed, she savored the feel of his lips on hers. . . . Jane looks up from her romance at her husband, John, who sits in the La-z-Boy scratching himself. With a wistful sigh, she returns to Amber's adventures . . .

Though the description above has been the typical portrait of the romance reader for many years, how accurate is it? Are women who read romance seeking a vicarious existence to brighten their drab, unromantic lives? Do women really want their husbands to be like "Carlo," eternally passionate and mysterious? On the contrary, most readers recognize the romance hero as a *construction*, one that reflects contemporary ideas of masculinity more than any woman's ideal man. The New Hero draws from ideas of masculinity already available in our culture, but modifies them to make him a woman's fantasy, rather than that of a man.

Over the past 30 years, two different poles of ideal manhood have emerged as white, middle-class fantasies of masculinity: the playboy and the mythopoetic man. Hugh Hefner's playboy of the 1960s has metamorphosed into Robert Bly's 1990s wildman. These two male-constructed roles are widely divergent in many ways, but share one common and disturbing trait, namely, a rejection or devaluation of meaningful male-female relationships. The playboy, characterized by individuals like Donald Trump, certainly desires women ("covets" might be a more accurate term), but his interest is sexual and not particularly individual; glory accrues to him based on the number of his sexual partners, not the depth of his sexual relationships. The mythopoetic man, such as the participants in the recently formed "hairy male" men's groups, is not as openly contemptuous of women as the playboy, but is still totally focused on male-male bonds, particularly with a father figure. Many groups forming under the mythopoetic aegis see their members as *too* close to women, too "soft." In the face of these limited versions of manhood, women have attempted to create their own fantasy man who combines certain elements of both playboy and wildman, but whose central focus is on establishing a committed relationship with a woman. That man is the mass-market romance hero.

Before examining the ways in which the New Hero draws upon and departs from the playboy/wildman roles, let us establish in more detail what those roles entail. As defined by Hugh Hefner in the sixties and criticized by Barbara Ehrenreich in the eighties, the playboy represents a move toward conspicuous consumption and the gratification of desire. As Ehrenreich puts it: "the new male-centered ensemble of commodities presented in *Playboy* meant that a man could display his status or simply flaunt his earnings without possessing either a house or a wife" (*Hearts* 49). The playboy is urbane, sophisticated, well-off (if not downright wealthy), and generally familiar with "the finer things." He always consumes the best in wine, food, and women. He is aggressively heterosexual, but displays his virility by dating a different woman every night rather than starting a family with "Mrs. Right." He considers all women to be gold-diggers, not to be trusted; he does not interact with women on an emotional level. Obviously, this version of masculinity is harmful not only to women but to the men who espouse it. Should their looks or their money not hold out, they would be stripped of their masculinity.

The man of the mythopoetic movement, influenced as he has been by thirty years of therapy, self-discovery, and political upheaval, seems in many ways to be diametrically opposed to the playboy. The mythopoetic man wants to return to his roots, to a primal, natural self. Interestingly, he seems to be at once more sensitive and more chauvinistic than the "typical" modern man. He is usually very concerned with "getting in touch" with his emotions and establishing connections, both admirable traits in themselves—however, the connections he seeks are almost entirely with other men, especially his father. The wildman seeks or possesses animal strengths and instincts, which may foster a renewed communion with nature, but may also encourage a sexism rooted in biological essentialism. Unlike the playboy, the wildman is not particularly concerned with displaying his masculinity to others. Generally, he feels that he has lost his masculinity through extended or overly intense contact with women, and must regain it by fostering a connection to his father or other older men. The mythopoetic movement, in its concern for "lost" or "weakened" masculinity, shares, in a more subtle form, the misogyny of the playboy. In Trip Gabrie's "Call of the Wildmen," he notes that participants in the mythopoetic movement repeatedly invoke the female and declare that they "lack energy, assertiveness and the ability to make commitments" (41). According to Robert Bly, "Soft males could read poetry and talk to their wives and girlfriends" (Gabrie 41). It is disturbing that this sort of interaction has become perceived as emasculating, rather than enlightening, as the feminist movement hoped and expected it would. The mythopoetic movement, on the whole, seems to be a retreat from the peak of Alan Alda-type "sensitive new-age guys" to a more traditionally masculine persona.

Both the playboy and the mythopoetic man are men's inventions. The mass-market romance hero is the invention of women, based on elements of manhood that women find appealing. How much can we expect such a hero to resemble male constructions of masculinity? The romance author creates a hero who draws his external qualities from both the playboy and wildman roles, but whose psychology is significantly different (and much more aligned with a female conception of manhood). The external trappings of masculine roles like these two are important— women as well as men have been convinced that the qualities mentioned above, in various combinations, define manhood. Although the New Hero should "look" like a conventional man, he can't act in either of these roles because he would be forced to reject serious male-female bonds, and the heart of the romance novel is the forging of such a bond between the hero and heroine.[1] Therefore, the New Hero adopts the wealth and the sophistication of the playboy but adds the mythopoetic man's nature-derived strength, power, and ability to express emotion. Fortunately for heroine and readers, he rejects the notion that women are solely gold-digging tramps, sexual objects, or a drain on male energy. The New Hero *wants* commitment and family and finds that the heroine strengthens and replenishes him, rather than sapping his masculine strength.

The romance hero finds his origins in one of two canonical heroes: Charlotte Brontë's Mr. Rochester or Jane Austen's Mr. Knightley. In general, historical romances, perhaps because they can get away with more sexism and use of traditional gender roles, tend to present a Rochester-figure, a Byronic hero. Although the quality of writing in the mass-market romance may not be on a par with that of Austen or Brontë, we can take some lessons from the canonizations of these two romance novelists. Books like *Jane Eyre* and *Emma* are romance novels. They have been canonized not only for the quality of their prose, but because we have accepted the possibility of subtext in their romance plots. I would argue that it is possible to read current romance novels with an eye for similar subtext, to look beyond the constraints of cliché and historical period for a New Heroine and a New Hero.

Romance heroes from the 1970s and earlier were often actors in rape fantasies and other sexual brutalities because the romance industry thought that women would not accept premarital sex unless the heroine was coerced. However, the romance hero has evolved at a pace consistent with feminist thought in the general public. As women became more comfortable with and more vocal about their sexuality, the rape fantasy was rightly rejected[2] and replaced with fantasies in which the heroine can enjoy sex both in and outside of a committed relationship—it is not uncommon to find current romance heroines taking lovers for their own pleasure, without any concern or desire for marriage. No longer the violent sexual predator of novels such as Rosemary Rogers' *The Insiders,* the current hero in historical romance is moving toward a "househusband" role of caretaker (though the dictates of whatever historical period comprises the setting prevents the hero from becoming a truly modern feminist).

The New Hero generally emphasizes the nurturing aspects of the mature man. The hero is older than the heroine and most of the men around him, physically strong, capable, and independent. Often, he has been responsible for his own care since he was very young, and the heroine's desire and ability to care for him frequently surprise him. These characteristics recall the mythopoetic man: he, too, is a strong and independent man, though still in search of emotional maturity. The hero's age and experience dispose him to seek a wife and start a family—he has already sown his wild oats and frequently has made a previous, unsuccessful marriage because he was swayed by externals: beauty, money, or name. His ability to recognize the special nature of the heroine (who, currently, is often described as not conventionally beautiful and rarely has fortune or name) is another sign of his heightened maturity. Readers, in fact, enjoy the New Hero more for his ability to "[recognize] the intrinsic worth of the heroine" (Radway 97) than for any physical or social attribute. His success at this recognition is the romance re-writing of the wildman's journey—instead of finding his "hairy male," the New Hero has found his inner female (by finding the heroine).

As a foil to the New Hero, a weaker hero, modeled on the more charming aspects of the playboy, frequently appears in the epic historical romances that focus on the heroine's growth and adventures over an extended period of time—a romance *bildungsroman,* if you will. This hero is still handsome and successful, but the heroine can be more successful and is generally more practical, effective, and stronger than the hero. The weak hero is charming and fun, but can be unreliable. He makes good lover material, or appears as a husband who dies.[3] Because of the nature of epic historical romance, the heroine needs heroes who won't tie her down for an entire novel—the weak hero's tendency to be cut down in the prime of life makes him a convenient type for the epic romance author.

The romance hero must often take part in a subplot of individual change in which the reader watches him mature. The individual novel can be seen as a microcosm of the development of the New Hero: over the course of the story, the hero (with the heroine's help, of course) shifts from the closed, angry, cynical hero of early romance fiction to the supportive, nurturing, committed hero of Nineties romance. The hero often begins as the playboy (or has played this role in his past), extravagant in his consumption of money, goods, and women. Finding this constant gratification ultimately unsatisfying, upon meeting the heroine, he begins to move through the wildman role. He begins to be more aware of his own feelings, his own need for nurture, and his lack of emotional connection to others. The novel culminates in the hero's departure from both roles, keeping his wealth and his emotional awareness but directing it toward the heroine and *her* needs.

How do we read this change? Most feminist critics have attacked the cliché of being "saved by the love of a good woman" as disempowering, but Mary Jo Putney, a romance author herself, suggests a different, more positive reading: "In reality savior complexes are dangerous because they encourage women to stay with abusive mates, but . . . what matters in a romantic context is that healing the wounded hero is a fantasy of incredible potency. Not only does it appeal to the nurturing instinct, but a woman who can heal an injured man has great power" (Krentz 101). Many romance novelists feel the same way, judging by the number of times the hero, wounded either physically or psychically, is successfully treated by the heroine. The heroine draws power not only from her success in curing the hero, but from her confidence in *knowing* that he needs her. This knowledge is actually what enables Emily to approach Simon in this passage from Amanda Quick's *Scandal*:

[Emily] realized suddenly that she was dealing with a wounded dragon tonight. They were old wounds, true enough, but they had been freshly opened. The pain could cause even a man of Simon's nobility and character to slash at any hand that came within reach.

But she also knew that the dragon needed warmth and love tonight. He needed her. (243-44)

Emily's awareness of Simon's need gives her the strength to challenge him in other facets of their relationship; it also provides some equilibrium in the battle of vulnerability common to many romance plots—the "you say it first" approach to love.

When examining the New Hero, it is impossible not to mention the New Heroine, as the changes in her character directly influenced the growth of his. Carol Thurston explains this relationship quite clearly:

The New Heroine generally is experienced, confident, self-sufficient, assertive and even daring—all traits traditionally assigned to men—which means she no longer needs the male guardian, the rake, or the sugar daddy. What *does* she require in a man? Still a strong-willed character . . . , the New Hero also exhibits many traits traditionally assigned to females—openness, flexibility, sensitivity, softness, and vulnerability—transforming him from invincible superman into fallible human being. (98)

The New Hero and Heroine are marked by a move toward androgyny, toward the exchange and reclassification of sex-type characteristics. Despite their existence in historical periods that were not noted for their advanced gender politics, individual heroes and heroines rise above the limitations of their fellow characters and the time in which they live.

While we have now seen where the New Hero comes from, we still haven't addressed the issue of Jane sitting with her husband and dreaming of "Carlo." Are all women looking for the blend of qualities possessed by the New Hero? Contrary to popular belief and the assumptions many uninformed critics make, the romance hero is *not* the ideal man, nor is he what readers expect to find in real life. In fact, some authors maintain that he is not a man at all. Several writers view the hero as the "shadow self" of the heroine, complementing her characteristics—the union at the end of the book is not a marriage, but a reintegration of the heroine's psyche. This theory is one means of accounting for the androgyny that characterizes the New Hero and Heroine. This integration with the shadow is often discussed in a manner that invokes Lacan's Mirror stage. The Mirror-Stage, analogous to Freud's oral stage, occurs when the infant's "image of its bodily self changes from mere formlessness and fragmentation to a jubilant identification with the unified shape it can see in the mirror" (Richter 646). This stage paves the way for the Imaginary, which represents itself (in both child- and adulthood) as "images and fantasies of the fulfillment of desire" (Richter 646). In the romance novel, the theory seems to apply thusly: the heroine recognizes herself in the hero (as does the reader); this identification of herself as a cohesive psyche (her partnership with the hero) prepares her for maturity and provides her with a glimpse of the Imaginary, the mechanism for wish-fulfillment. Therefore, the marriage union of hero and heroine may *enable* fantasy for the reader, but does not insist that it be the *subject* of that fantasy.[4]

A similar psychological union may occur between reader and hero, in a phenomenon called "placeholding." The heroine is at once replaced and evaluated by the reader, who sees the heroine from the perspective of the hero *and* from the perspective of her own comparison with the heroine. Laura Kinsale sees it as possible for the reader to identify with or "become" both heroine and hero, due to this placeholding effect:

[The romance reader] is experiencing herself as hero, and as heroine, completely within her own personality. . . . But regarding the heroine there is still, and always, that element of not-me, of her, of otherness. There is paradox involved in the placeholding component of the heroine. . . . If one can bring oneself to admit that a female reader might find it more difficult to *be* this fictitious heroine than to *be* this fictitious man—not because she is a pitiful, victimized woman but because within the reader there are masculine elements that can and need to be realized—than reading a romance is . . . integrating." (Krentz 38-39)

Again, the heroine-hero connection is seen as integrating, not degrading; if Kinsale's remarks are regarded in terms of Laura Mulvey's "gaze," the reading of romance becomes empowering. The reader shares the hero's gaze upon the heroine, which provides her with the power to consider, to evaluate the heroine—she avoids the objectification present in Mulvey's gaze, however, because she is also the heroine, and as such cannot objectify herself.

The psychological links between reader, hero, and heroine are made possible in part by the *alteration* of the playboy and wildman stereotypes. The relationship between the New Hero and the New Heroine, while continuing to employ the accouterments of such roles, represents a significant departure from the New Hero's kinship with male media constructs in that the hero seeks a more or less equal partnership with a strong and individual woman—neither the playboy's lust for women as a species or the mythopoetic man's search for his lost father relate to this desire. The hero-heroine relationship, like most romantic/sexual relationships in our everyday lives, is predicated to some extent on power. The romance of the New Hero is a departure from previous erotic novels because power does not lie strictly with the man—the New Heroine establishes herself as a powerful person, both in and out of the bedroom. Many feminists complain about the power dynamics in the romance novel, claiming that the heroine is presented as a naïve, shallow girl who is totally dependent on the hero for economic, emotional, and sexual fulfillment. However, the traditional game-playing of the romance novel can work both ways: the hero leads the heroine to sexual maturity as she, in turn, leads him to emotional fulfillment.

In another rejection of his playboy roots, the New Hero discovers that desire is not enough to satisfy him: he needs the heroine to love him. Furthermore, he usually can't tell that she loves him until she tells him so. In *Ravished,* Gideon makes this clear to Harriet (who seems astonished at his lack of perception): "'It may surprise you to know that I have no real notion of your feelings toward me, Miss Pomeroy. . . . I do not know if you find me amusing or obnoxious or a damned nuisance'" (Quick 224). Gideon clearly wants Harriet to tell him she loves him, without admitting his own feelings for her. Nonetheless, his confession does demonstrate a vulnerability on his part, as well as offering an indication of the importance of emotion to the New Hero. This may seem to be a minor victory for the New Heroine, but remember that the New Hero is still bound by his historical period—to admit that he cares deeply for any woman, even his fiancée, is a major concession.

The major feminist sticking point of most mass-market romance is, unsurprisingly, sex. The question of who does what to whom, how, and why has become the basis of a significant battlefield, largely because the hero is frequently the man who introduces the heroine to sex. In the past, certainly, sex in the romance novel was acceptable only within the confines of a committed (i.e., legally sanctioned) relationship, and was almost unilaterally initiated by the man. Kay Mussell discusses the power relationships inherent in such a sexual relationship in her book, *Fantasy and Reconciliation.* Unfortunately, her sweeping claims are unsubstantiated by current historical romances. For example, Mussell asserts that:

Once heroines have found [sexual] ecstasy, they have no choice but to continue the relationship until death. After Mr. Right, a true woman can be satisfied with nothing less, for sex can never be pleasurable except with the one man the heroine loves. Although she may have other sexual encounters . . . she will never be satisfied by them. (131)

This is blatantly untrue, as a perusal, however brief, of any epic erotic romance will reveal. The epic New Heroine quite clearly knows the difference between love and lust and can experience both. The epic romance is, in fact, characterized by a multiplicity of "Mr. Rights" (as well as a few attractive "Mr. Wrongs") with whom the heroine has relationships of varying length and intensity. Many authors explicitly present their heroines' confrontation with loveless desire, as in this passage from Bertrice Small's *A Love for All Time:*

Aidan was sobbing now with unconcealed pleasure . . . Her body, passionate in its nature . . . could not help but respond to the handsome [Javid Khan], and yet her mind struggled against what she believed was a betrayal of everything her love for Conn O'Malley had been. . . . She had given him [Javid] her body without a struggle because she had believed she could not possibly enjoy the attentions of any man but her husband . . . she had never expected to savor the prince's attentions, and yet she was. (364-65)

Certainly, sex between partners in love is considered preferable to sex without love, but that does not negate the pleasure the New Heroine can find in a physical relationship without commitment. The New Hero, in turn, respects his heroine's decision-making power when it comes to sex—the use of force is reprehensible to him. These attitudes mark another move toward equilibrium between hero and heroine. It is important to acknowledge this successful departure from traditional gender stereotypes; the heroine's reclamation of her own sexual power is a significant step toward true sexual equality in romance fiction, as is the shift in the New Hero from his "manly-man" origins to a more sensitive, woman-centered character.

Just as the playboy is left behind in the sexual arena, we find that his attitudes are no longer a factor on the economic playing field either. The economics of romance are somewhat complicated, largely because they are meant to remain invisible (or at least deeply subtextual). The historical romance rarely, if ever, presents a hero or heroine who is not of the aristocracy or at least country gentry, because life for the lower classes was generally miserable and disgusting. If the New Heroine is not an heiress, she is *never* shown to be interested in her husband/lover's fortune. She observes it to the extent that he and his home are turned out in excellent taste, but she never asks the hero for money or gifts. In fact, she is often unimpressed by expensive jewelry and the like: "[Julian's] smile broadened as he acknowledged ruefully that he could have saved the six thousand pounds he'd spent on the bracelet. Knowing Sophy, she would probably lose it the first time she wore it—if she remembered to wear it" (Quick, *Seduction* 219). The heroine values gifts which demonstrate careful thought on the hero's part. In many novels, two gift-giving scenes are paired: the first involves an expensive gift which the heroine returns or ignores, and the second centers on a present which the hero could not simply purchase. This second scene is another indication of the hero's perception of his heroine's inner worth, so sought by readers.

Current historical romance often inverts the issue of buying power by making the heroine financially independent, often much richer than the hero. In this case, the hero is the one who must not covet the heroine's money (a complicated task, as he has often married her for her inheritance). Romance authors get around this problem by demonstrating that the hero uses his wife's money only to good ends (restoring the family estate and revitalizing the local economy) and by using the gift-giving scenes as an indication of the hero's growth. The question of who plays the breadwinner role (with its male connotations) is defused in historical romance because neither hero nor heroine *have* to work. Amanda Quick's *Surrender* presents a hero who marries the heroine for her money and is thus baffled when he tries to buy his wife a token of his esteem. As Lucas puts it, "Finding just the right gift for a wife who had brought considerably more money than her husband into the marriage was not the easiest task in the world. A man could hardly use the lady's own inheritance to buy her a diamond necklace" (295). Lucas successfully solves the problem by securing Victoria a job as the illustrator of a botanical text; this symbolizes his appreciation of her talents and his privileging of her artistic skills over her external assets of beauty and wealth.

The New Hero, unlike the playboy, is neither acquisitive nor close-fisted; even in situations where the heroine brings no money to the relationship, the hero is fully prepared to be financially generous with her. Tracing the economic patterns in the romance novel reveals the development of the hero as he moves from his initial pre-enlightened state to the New Hero of women's fantasies: the hero is initially quite generous, fiscally, because he has no other means of expressing his (still undiscovered or unexamined) emotion for the heroine. (This starting position reaches back past the playboy figure to the breadwinner who generated him.) As he learns to declare his love in more meaningful and less tangible ways, money becomes less prominent as a theme in the novel.

In general, the New Hero is characterized much more strongly by his distance from his playboy ancestor than from his real-life contemporary, the wildman. In part, this is due to the thirty years of evolution between the two roles—men who participate in the mythopoetic movement are building on the profeminist men's movement of the 1970s, whereas the playboy man is a violently anti-woman response to the economic orientation of men in the 1950s. Many of the qualities Bly and others like him celebrate—"[being] fierce without being violent, [being] strong and powerful without being oppressive" (Blauner 41)—are characteristic of the New Hero. The fundamental difference between the New Hero and either of these role models, however, is that the New Hero's qualities, energies, and emotions are directed toward *women*. This attention to women, lacking in the playboy in the 1960s and lacking in the mythopoetic man in the 1990s, is the most erotic part of the New Hero and seems in many ways to be the answer to the age-old question, "What do women want?"

The New Hero reveals more about his creators and his readership than about men in any historical period. He serves at once as an example of successful communication between men and women, and perhaps as a respite from unsuccessful real-life interaction. He represents a return to the goals of early feminism, which struggled to change men, to "civilize" and "domesticate" them. Whether or not this remains a valid goal, the New Hero is a success story. I would argue, finally, that the mass-market romance gives hope: the picture of a successfully "androgynous" couple, in which gender roles don't limit either partner. Men form emotional connections, women perform acts of bravery—this is fantasy, but it could serve as a model of truly complementary partnerships to come. Jane can use the example of "Amber" and "Carlo" to infuse her own relationship with passion and equality, and John can still keep his La-Z-Boy.

Notes

1. It should be noted that these fantasies of maleness, both male and female constructs, refer to (and for the most part, appeal to) the white middle class. Just as both the playboy and mythopoetic movements are composed largely of white men, the world of the romance novel (containing authors, characters, and a majority of readers) is similarly white, though undergoing change.

2. See, for example, Janice Radway's interviews with readers in *Reading the Romance*, particularly her chapter on failed romances.

3. The men with whom the heroine interacts are not abandoners, even if they are of the "weak hero" type. They are often implicated in their own deaths, however, because of impetuous actions which "get them killed." Their irresponsibility provides an opportunity for the heroine to display her considerable strength and competence, and often adds suspense to a long novel in which the heroine's search for her "true" mate takes her through many men.

4. This reading also counters another frequent criticism leveled at the romance novel, namely, the obsession of the genre with marriage. Not only is marriage frequently *not* the object of the current romance heroine, but this Lacanian reading suggests that marriage is simply a metaphor for the ability to envision the Imaginary.

Works Cited

Critical Works

Barlow, Linda. "The Androgynous Writer: Another View of Point of View." *Dangerous Men and Adventurous Women: Romance Writers on the Appeal of the Romance.* Ed. Jayne Ann Krentz. Philadelphia: U of Pennsylvania P, 1992.

Blauner, Bob, "The Men's Movement and Its Analysis of the Male Malaise, or: Men on the Move? But Why? and Where to?" Reader, Women's Studies 195, UC Davis.

Cohn, Jan. *Romance and the Erotics of Property: Mass-Market Fiction for Women*. Durham: Duke UP, 1988.

Ehrenreich, Barbara. *Hearts of Men: American Dreams and the Flight from Commitment*. New York: Anchor, 1983.

Gabrie, Trip, "Call of the Wildmen." Reader, Women's Studies 195, UC Davis.

Kinsale, Laura. "The Androgynous Reader: Point of View in the Romance." *Dangerous Men and Adventurous Women: Romance Writers on the Appeal of the Romance*. Ed. Jayne Ann Krentz. Philadelphia: U of Pennsylvania P, 1992.

Krentz, Jayne Ann, ed. *Dangerous Men and Adventurous Women: Romance Writers on the Appeal of the Romance*. Philadelphia: U of Pennsylvania P, 1992.

Lowell, Elizabeth. "Love Conquers All: The Warrior Hero and the Affirmation of Love." *Dangerous Men and Adventurous Women: Romance Writers on the Appeal of the Romance*. Ed. Jayne Ann Krentz. Philadelphia: U of Pennsylvania P, 1992.

Mussell, Kay. *Fantasy and Reconciliation: Contemporary Formulas of Women's Romance Fiction*. London: Greenwood, 1984.

Putney, Mary Jo. "Welcome to the Dark Side." *Dangerous Men and Adventurous Women: Romance Writers on the Appeal of the Romance*. Ed. Jayne Ann Krentz. Philadelphia: U of Pennsylvania P, 1992.

Radway, Janice. *Reading the Romance: Women, Patriarchy and Popular Literature*. Chapel Hill: U of North Carolina P, 1984.

Richter, David, ed. *The Critical Tradition: Classic Texts and Contemporary Trends*. New York: St. Martin's, 1989. 645-49.

Thurston, Carol. *The Romance Revolution*. Urbana: U of Illinois P, 1987.

Williamson, Penelope. "By Honor Bound: The Heroine as Hero." *Dangerous Men and Adventurous Women: Romance Writers on the Appeal of the Romance*. Ed. Jayne Ann Krentz. Philadelphia: U of Pennsylvania P, 1992.

Romance Novels

Quick, Amanda. *Ravished*. New York: Bantam, 1992.

——. *Scandal*. New York: Bantam, 1991.

——. *Seduction*. New York: Bantam, 1990.

——. *Surrender*. New York: Bantam, 1990.

Small, Bertrice. *A Love for All Time*. New York: New American Library, 1986.

"I Am Not a Bimbo":
Persona, Promotion, and the Fabulous Fabio

Rosemary E. Johnson-Kurek

I was infatuated with Fabio before I even knew he was real. As a romance cover art aficionado I was incredibly ignorant: I didn't know the art, but I knew what I liked. I had no idea that the heroines, and particularly, the heroes of the covers were so strongly anchored in reality. I assumed that the artists had reasonably attractive models that they greatly improved upon. How was I to know that sweet faced youth on the cover of Johanna Lindsey's *Hearts Aflame* actually existed in the real world?

It was Elaine Duillo's cover illustration for *Hearts Aflame* that provided Fabio with his first big break (Small) and I am convinced that Duillo's renderings of Fabio Lanzoni for Avon were critical to his rise to fame. Duillo, an outstanding success in the profession, executes her realistic style with vibrantly rich colors and a sense of detail. She seems able to draw easily from the human palette of emotions and capture the myriad facial expressions of love, tenderness, vulnerability, and passion.

In the days prior to Fabio's celebrity status, it was Duillo's covers which were most often used to explain or introduce him to unfamiliar audiences. Her covers are still the most commonly alluded to examples of Fabio's work. While the pairing may not be of the same import to the art world as DaVinci and Mona Lisa, it is a combination worth noting.

To become famous under the conditions imposed by an art form whose models had remained essentially anonymous outside the trade, the individual needs to have not only a unique physical presence and appeal but also a very strong and positive persona that transcends the popular art. Fabio somehow achieved this, or rather the artists, Duillo initially and primarily, somehow captured or enhanced this quality. Of all the male models on all the romances why did this particular model succeed beyond the boundaries of this niche? It could be his hair, long and symbolic of Samson-like strength, but he is not the only cover hero depicted with long hair. It could be the esthetics of his body-builder physique, although again he is not alone in this and many a physical attribute can be artistically enhanced. It is most likely some qualitative aspect of his persona, some elusive trait that transcends the art. Whatever it was—his pose, his embrace, his expression, his eyes—he was noticed and emerged as a known entity from a virtually anonymous commodity.

I remember the moment, if not the date, when I assembled my then small collection of Duillo's Lindsey-Fabio covers—*Hearts Aflame, Defy Not the Heart* and *Savage Thunder*—and displayed them for my friends. They were not into the massive amounts of romance reading and buying that I was at the time and I felt it was my duty to keep them informed. "Look at these," I said, "these all look like the same guy. Could he actually be real?" One friend, picking up *Defy Not the Heart,* replied, "I don't know, but if he is I wouldn't mind having my hand on his thigh." Another friend, picking up *Savage Thunder,* said, "Probably, and I wouldn't mind hanging from his vest." Each had insinuated herself into the role of the female model in the picture. I am sure they were not the only women to do so. In fact I know so, they were part of the trend, participants in the Fabio phenomenon.

Certain that I had belatedly discovered something the entire populace already knew, I set out to find the answer to my question—"Who is this guy?" The ivory tower is a good place from which to observe—objectively and from a distance—the shenanigans and play of the popular culture, but there was no readily available information at my disposal. He was in no database. In my quest to find out if such a man existed I showed the Duillo works to several other women. I alerted friends and neighbors to my quest. (I was not yet ready to alert colleagues.) I was confident that an answer was forthcoming as I was already convinced a phenomenon of this magnitude would not go unnoticed. I expanded my database and eventually, at long last, in the summer of 1991, a neighbor informed me that she had a brief glimpse of a brief segment on *A Current Affair* and that indeed the handsome hunk was real and he was called the Fabulous Fabio. Later I would find out that this was indeed when the general media discovered him (Paul). In the developing phenomenon of Fabio Lanzoni, I was near the frontline of the masses of women clamoring to learn his identity.

Earlier that same summer the question of his identity was also raised in *Romantic Times,* the magazine for devotees of the genre. Although he was named as the model for the cover of Kinsale's *Prince of Midnight* in a previous issue, it was not until June that the critical question regarding his actual resemblance to his cover depictions were posed. The letter was written by Zoe Yoon, a student majoring in classical literature who suffered her professors' and peers' disdain for liking romance as well as classic literature. Her question was much like my own: "[D]oes a man with such an incredible face and body truly exist, or is he simply an embellished depiction of an attractive model, made to seem god-like by Elaine Duillo's skillful hand? I'm inclined to believe the latter, but I'll be more than happy to revise my opinion if you tell me otherwise." Ultimately, many fans were more than happy to accept that these Fabio facsimiles were faithful renderings. Yoon's reaction to Fabio's image was similar to those of my friends: "I was love-struck by the first sight of Colt Thunder. . . . my eyes popped out when I . . . saw James Malory's bronze chest leaping from the covers of *Gentle Rogue*."

One summer evening, I was on a neighbor's porch in the company of several other women and one man. I was introducing yet another woman to the visual pleasure of Duillo's renderings of Fabio. By this time I had added *Gentle Rogue* to my collection. The lone male of the group could not understand our interest. "They're drawings. They're cartoons, they're #%!@# cartoons!" he said in disbelief. "But he's real!" we responded as if somehow Fabio's reality validated our response to the fantasy renderings. I finally understood men's fascination with Vargas girls in *Playboy*.

Fabio's type of fame is unprecedented in many areas. He is a famous and financially successful male model who has become a sex symbol because of his modeling career. It is generally women who garner fame and high fortune from modeling. Perhaps even more surprising, his fame came from cover art. Because paperback cover art, as mentioned previously, has historically been an anonymous art form outside the trade, it has never before served as the basis of fame. Garnering fame from such an anonymous fantasy base was unprecedented until Fabio appeared.

As a cultural phenomenon of persona, Fabio is unique despite the fact that parallels can be drawn between his fame and that of other men. He is a sex symbol, but that is true of many other famous men. Famous men have modeled, and models have later become famous men, but prior to Fabio no other man has become famous because of his work as a model. Outside of the romance cover world, Lucky Vanos, the construction worker in the gender groundbreaking turnabout-is-fair-play Coke commercial, briefly achieved male model fame, but not nearly to the extent that Fabio has.

I have often been teased for my interest in Fabio. While usually not denying that I find the man attractive, I do protest that my interest is in the interest of scholarship. I chastise my critics for not recognizing a media and cultural phenomenon when they see one. I found myself defending both my interest and Fabio himself to radical feminists and male chauvinists alike—what strange bedfellows and allies in the fight against Fabio! Do not dismiss him so readily I would tell them. I was convinced that his type of success was so unprecedented it was indicative of something; unfortunately, I didn't know what that something was.

Because I was so curious about Fabio prior to his international celebrity status and household-name days I did not hesitate to ask people if they had ever heard of him or knew anything about him. Much of my early information about him was given to me in a rather casual manner: people who had just happened to run across something about him would forward the information to me. Much of this early information was passed on to me in the oral tradition and I would scribble notes to myself. I would receive phone calls telling me to rush to the television because Fabio was on *Regis and Kathie Lee, Maury Povich, Entertainment Tonight* or *Current Affair* and later, *Roseanne,* and *David Letterman.* I usually only caught the tale end of the appearance. I received copies of tabloid articles with no reference to dates. How is an academic to cite this snowballing mountain of ephemeral evidence?

The first piece of tangible, retrievable information I received was given to me by the same man who couldn't believe women could fawn over a cartoon. It was from *USA Today* (March 30, 1992: 1D). The headline was "Fabio—a novel hunk" and through it I learned that women waited for hours to pose for "10 seconds in his clutch." I'd seen some of these ten second clutches on the television segments, but I had no idea they waited hours. Oh, I could never do that—could I?

I also learned that he had a fan club—no address given—and a 900 number. The article listed the full 900 number and the man who had given me the article had also, as a good humored sign of patronizing jest, included some money to cover the call. My sister fawners and I called— all in the interest of research, of course. The article also stated that he planned to have his own calendar. Later, another man in my extensive database gifted me with Fabio's calendar—he thought it would be a hoot—and through the calendar I learned that he was a Ford model. I had always associated Ford exclusively with fashion modeling—my mistake.

In the *USA Today* article I also learned that he planned on writing his own romances; I looked forward to reading these since I was, and continue to be, very interested in the male voice in the romance genre. Would his book be unique or would he adopt the established conventions? How would his collaboration with Eugenia Riley affect the final product? That in itself would be an interesting gender study. I actually read Fabio's first two works, *Pirate* and *Rogue,* and I can hear the male voice that I've looked for it in other male authored romances.

I treasured the short *USA Today* article, but it didn't provide enough information. I needed to know more. Friends and colleagues who knew of my interest in Fabio began to tell me anecdotes about their encounters with the Fabio phenomenon. I learned via a friend of a friend that a hand drawn posterboard sign was tacked to a tree out on a country road directing sister admirers to a Fabio party. How unusual, I thought. Later I would learn via the television that this was a common practice with women across the country.

Some people, apparently, can't appreciate the Fabio fun factor. One woman friend reported that she had been the only female present at a business dinner that turned into a Fabio bashing session. Is he such a threat to images of masculinity that regular guys feel the overpowering need to denigrate him? Would they have done this to John Wayne? Joe Montana?

Fabio bashing also followed the *People* cover story. In response, Donnamaie E. White, Ph.D., a woman who has met Fabio, came to his defense. She wrote:

[T]he man is more than his pictures. He has manners (how unique these days) and is polite enough to make you cry. He is focused and articulate. He knows what he is selling and delivers it, with enough charm to melt rocks. . . . How refreshing to find a non-threatening man who can look you in the eyes and speak to you as a person . . .

In her letter Dr. White states that her experiences in the field of high tech engineering could make "Tail hook look like a tea-party." She also wrote that she does not dream of the men who have sexually harassed her at work: "These men do not inspire dreams, just disgust. Instead, I dream of Fabio. . . . I have a framed autographed picture of Fabio prominently displayed on my office wall. It keeps me calm" (White). White maintains an impressive and extensive website with essays about her experiences with the Fabio phenomenon as well as Fabio links. She is also the webmaster for the Fabio International Fan Club (IFC) which is maintained with her own homepage.

Granted, Fabio is charming, but he also has an attractive physique as well as a handsome face. He is tall, muscular, and strong—a bodybuilder and a former Mr. Europe. Add the perceived advantage of his romantic image and there looms the threat to the male ego. This is the kind of competition women have had set before them for generations—since the advent of the massive distribution of photo-based advertising and the fashion model of perfection. It is also what *Playboy* dishes out monthly. Such competition has brought out the ire in women; why wouldn't Fabio's image bring out the ire in men?

An example of this ire might be the fact that Fabio has twice won *Esquire* magazine's Dubious Achievement Awards (1993, 1994). Perhaps *Esquire,* a men's magazine, is truly chastising Fabio for breaking unwritten rules of gender bias and double standards, and for being a threat to the male ego, as well as for his most ostensible dubious achievement: writing a romance.

There is a subtle, perhaps unconscious, yet insidious interpretation one could attribute to the *Esquire* stance: It could be viewed as misogynistic, or at the very least a form of masculine elitism. Fabio is, in his public persona at least, not a man's man, but a woman's man and his success depends on it. To ridicule his "dubious achievements" is to say that women are not good judges of masculinity—what women prefer is not of value. From this perspective of masculine elitism, it may be a gender bender to be what women want or even to figure out what women want. After all, why would a man want to cater to the whims of a woman?

Fabio is a man who has achieved fame in a popular genre and art form whose intended and actual audience is women. An initial analysis of the double standards of gender could be, taken to the extreme, that by becoming famous and financially successful almost exclusively because of women, he breaks the taboo that men are not supposed to rely on women for their livelihood.

Another double standard he has broken is the rule stipulating it is all right for women to become famous for looking good, but it is somehow not respectable for a man to become a household name for such work. Men are supposed to accomplish other kinds of tasks: they should create things, build things, design things, sell things—something tangible beside themselves. Fabio is now accomplishing these other kinds of tasks, but it was his romance cover modeling that enabled him to do so.

Romance cover art may be the most popular accepted form of erotic art for women in the post sexual revolution. It is far more successful and widely disseminated than *Playgirl* whose brand of visual erotica is an imitation of men's popular form of erotica. Even its name is an imitation of the men's magazine. The appeal of romance covers in general and Fabio in particular would indicate that women's visual erotica may be of a different form. While the covers are photo based they are nonetheless still artistic renderings. There is no actual nudity and the essential eroticism is derived from the romantic embrace. In early 1992 readers could "feast their eyes on the one, the only, the hot, and the obviously stark-naked body of the fabulous Fabio on the cover of Cassie Edwards' *Savage Promise*" (Lombard). A later 1992 release, Johanna Lindsey's *Man of My Dreams,* featured another buff Fabio in the buff. But it wasn't truly Fabio who was naked—Fabio doesn't pose in the nude; it was his image and likeness. Actually, most of the heroes' bodies are effectively screened by the clothed heroine.

Like many women models and many a *Playboy* Playmate of the month, his physical beauty is an obstacle to his being taken seriously in pursuit of other goals. In a television interview defending himself against detractors who essentially labeled him as just a pretty face who has no business creating his own romance books, Fabio stated "I am not a bimbo." This is not an uncommon defense; what is uncommon, however, is that it was stated by a man. He is also quoted as saying, " I have more to offer than just a body. I'd love to be taken seriously. I have important things to say" (Judell).

The publication of his romances did not endear him to some romance writers; however, one author, Diana Fox, writing in *The Romance Writers' Report,* defends him on this front:

He's brought mega attention to our industry. You never hear him trash RWA the way our members trash him. . . . Sure he got over-exposed. Any star does. Even some writers get over-exposed. But that doesn't make them or Fabio bad. The real bottom line that we, as romance writers, have to consider is this: he brings readers to the romance genre, and we write to sell to romance readers. . . . As to a celebrity writing a romance, when did we become judge and juror as to who can write a romance and on what constitutes a good book? Because we write them? (32-33)

His covers have brought readers not only to the genre, but to individual authors. I confess; I've bought books because Fabio was on the cover and I know I'm not alone. The numbers of romances from which to choose are overwhelming, but I soon realized that Fabio's presence on the cover was one way that publishers drew attention to authors or specific titles. I found it a useful strategy in my romance education. More often than not these covers led me to discover favorite authors previously unknown to me. I shudder to think that I might not have read Laura Kinsale if it weren't for this very shallow reason. Even without Fabio's countenance on the cover, I've bought every new Kinsale release and all her backlist books as well.

Fox does address the matter of Fabio as author as well: "But you say, what about 'his' books? . . . What about them? What difference does it make if he 'penned' them or not. Lots of books are ghost-written. It's done all time. It's business." Actually, Fabio's books are not really ghost-written. They are joint projects and he makes no attempt to hide the fact that his books are joint efforts. He gives full credit, in big type, to his co-authors and thanks them graciously.

Contrary to some of his press, Fabio is not the first male author to use his own name or refrain from using a feminine pen name. Among the male authored books in my own meager collection, those clearly designated as romances include *A Bribe to Love* by William Neubauer (Valentine category romance #4225—1966), *Keepsake* by Sharon and Tom Curtis (Jove 1987), and many Bantam Loveswept titles by Anne and Ed Kolaczyk, and Olivia and Ken Harper. Those clearly designated on the spine as historical romances include: Aaron Fletcher's *Love's Gentle Agony* (Leisure 1978), *Rainbow Saga* by Chet Cunningham (Leisure 1979) and *River of Fortune: The Proud* by Arthur Moore (Zebra 1980). When Fabio moved from Avon to Kensington Publishing, he joined the same house as Leigh Greenwood. While I have most of Fabio's books, I must admit that they are not in my pile of to-be-read books; they are with my collection of Fabio covers. Now that he has retired as a cover model, the only covers he now graces are his own and the Kensington covers are photographs, not artistic renderings.

There would be no interest in Fabio as an author if there had been no demand for his identity. Promotion of the real person of Fabio was necessary to meet demand for identification of the real hunk who was setting hearts aflutter on eventually over a thousand romance covers, if one can believe everything that is written. Once identification of the real model for the fantasy image was made, and widespread personal appearances by Fabio began, a new phenomenon developed. The image of Fabio and the real person of Fabio created a new media star, a combination of fantasy and reality. He now has a secondary following consisting of women who were unaware of his modeling career and/or had never read a romance with his image on the cover. I know I did my part in promoting him among the nonreaders of romance.

While a strong persona mandates promotion, successful promotion, in turn, requires a strong, positive persona. Fabio the real person emerged from the facade of fantasy and not only retained the popularity based on his artistic image but improved upon it. While Fabio has appeared on the covers of contemporary and even some futuristic romances, his primary model image is associated with historical heroes. In this respect his fantasy image is that of a man out of time. Not every model can live up to the standards of fantasy, but the strength of his persona, that which originally transcended the cover art, seems to enable him to do so. This is no small accomplishment.

In order for his persona to transcend a still-life medium, he first of all had to be the real equivalent of his artistic image in physical appearance. However, no amount of physical attractiveness or prowess would be able to compensate if he lacked the quality of a romantic soul. His romantic sensitivity toward women is critical in endearing him to his fans. So, more importantly, the success of Fabio the person required that he actually embody some of the qualities of the fictionalized characters he has portrayed on a multitude of covers. His image is so enmeshed with the romantic fantasy hero, fans would probably invest him with these qualities whether he possessed them or not.

He has been termed "The Sexiest Man Alive" (*Cosmopolitan*), "The Prince of Passion" (*People*), "The World's Sexiest Man" (*National Enquirer*), and "The King of Romance" (*National Examiner*). He is perceived as an expert on romance. His views and philosophies on love and personal values have been sought by the media and dispensed through his 900 number. He, along with Dr. Ruth, judged the most romantic engagement story on the 1993 *Maury Povich* Valentine Day show. His expertise on the subject manifests itself in magazine interviews, television and radio guest spots and personal appearances. He is quoted saying exactly the types of things women would like to hear from men, or at least believe men are capable of thinking. Examples of Fabio's thoughts include:

When a woman has a beautiful soul and a sparkling personality, she will come across as sexy and charming. The physical side of her is secondary and doesn't attract me. (. . . .) a woman need not be physically attractive to turn me on. (Goldfarb 17)

The first thing she (his grandmother) taught me was to respect women. I learned to respect her, so I learned to respect all women. I *adore* women. For me, they are the best thing God ever put on earth. (Judel)

It's much more important to be beautiful inside than outside. (Paul)

I believe in focusing on a woman's needs and desires, and I devote myself to pleasing a woman when I'm with her. (Goldfarb)

All of this information creates and supports fans' perceptions of Fabio. If we can believe his press, in his youth he was an approximation of the nice Italian Catholic boy. He is a former altar boy who placed whoopee cushions on the priest's chair in church (Small). An elementary school teacher thought he was a dreamer and made fun of him for writing that he wanted to "be very successful . . . a movie star . . . and do a lot of good things for the world" (Woods). He drove the priests to distraction; they predicted he'd end up in jail (Small 110). He says he grew up in a family with strong values. Although he rebelled he seems to still cling to some fundamental virtues like faith and humility:

My philosophy for life. People *must* learn to love themselves. . . . First, there's spirituality. Second is power of mind—determine your future. Third is power of body—take care of your body through exercise. And above all, be humble. That's the secret of my success. (Judell 9)

In addition to the virtue of faith he also aspires to charity. "My ultimate goal is to support, financially, as many poor people as I can" (Terrell).

He believes that "Madonna . . .does real damage to society. . . . She's promoting perversion—S and M, raw sex . . . It's one thing to promote eroticism—but even then you should be careful" (Woods). He has confessed to the world that infidelity led to the demise of a serious relationship (Small), but he believes in the "sanctity of a relationship" (Goldfarb). He stated:

When I get married, I don't want to get divorced and leave my kids without a father. I think it's important for kids to have both parents. It keeps the balance. (Judell)

Despite the fact that his father is a wealthy Italian manufacturer, Fabio made his own way to the United States because of parental disapproval of his ambitions (Small). An uncommonly handsome immigrant, he arrived in the United States at the age of 19 and landed a modeling contract within three days time (Woods). Is he proof that the American "Gospel of Success" is still alive? Is the Fabulous Fabio a modern-day Horatio Alger character who succeded with luck and pluck? Perhaps, but he is definitely not *Ragged Dick, Tom the Bootblack* or *Mark the Matchboy.*

In spite of his success he has a self-deprecating humor that is charming; "it's good when you can make fun of yourself. It means you are the most secure person" (Small 110). He personally delivered "The Top 10 list of Fabio's pick-up lines" on *David Letterman.* Among them were "Gee, you're even more beautiful than I am." There is a sense of fun about his pursuits.

Call me a romantic, call me a sucker, call me a wishful thinker, but I think some of the man's thinking, his persona, is what transcended the anonymity of the cover art. There seems to be this rather endearing quality about him that enables him to come across as an affable rather than an aloof Adonis. Was it hype? Was it promotion? Was there any way I'd ever be able to judge for myself?

Jaded person that I am, meeting Fabio became an obsession of sorts. Like many women, I have an almost innate stereotyped belief that exceedingly good looking men are not only untrustworthy, but jerks besides. I liked Fabio better when I thought he was a fantasy enhanced figment of Elaine Duillo's imagination. But I had to see for myself what he was really like. I went so far as to enter a *National Enquirer* contest to win a date with Fabio. (Research had driven me to purchase *National Enquirer* for the first time in my life making me wonder what other out-of-character behavior I would eventually engage in.) I had to write in 50 words or less "What romance means to me." I don't remember what I wrote, I only know that ten minutes after I mailed it I wanted to retrieve it. What if I won? I confessed to my friends what I had done and expressed my fear that if by some bizarre stretch of luck I had the misfortune of winning I wouldn't be able to go through with it. I asked them what they would do if they won such a contest. One friend was adamant: if she won she'd sure as hell want everyone to see her with him. I feared I would not be able to go out in public with him. I would not be able to bear being in the company of someone so high on the hierarchy of physical beauty.

The whole scenario reminded me of a *Sixteen* magazine article from the late fifties or early sixties in which a teen idol such as Fabian would be offered up for a dream date contest or would describe his dream girl-friend. Fabian? Fabio? What's the difference? One difference is that this phenomenon involved grown women not teenaged girls.

And what did Fabio say about this dream date? Well, in the article announcing the contest, he said:

I can hardly wait to meet the winner. . . . I have been working so hard that I need to get out and have some fun. I'm dying to share an evening with the winning woman! (Coz 22)

"Yeh, Right!" I thought, "the guy can't get a date without a national contest?" My negative thoughts didn't prevent me from entering the contest.

As it turned out I had nothing to fear. Mary Kay Lindner, a grandmother from Bigfork, Montana won. I had to give creedence to her assessment of him. "He's gentle, considerate and fun to be with. . . . I was woozy . . . I opened the door and there he was! . . . I felt as if I were floating on air. . . . He's real down to earth" (Susman 16).

After Fabio's date with Ms. Lindner, he commented, "Mary Kay may think she was fortunate to win the date. But I am the real winner because she is gracious, charming and has a wonderful sense of humor" (Sussman).

Although I believed what Ms. Lindner had to say about her date, I still wanted more information about what Fabio was really like. I did manage to find, in an article in *People,* a few more first-person female assessments of Fabio:

His *je ne sais quoi* attracts women; he's one of the few men I've never sued. (feminist lawyer Gloria Allred)

He's handsome, intelligent and nice. (Sally Jesse Raphael)

Fabio has very special magic . . . Just about every woman he meets loses weight. (Tina Jakes coeditor of *The Gentle Conqueror,* a Fabio fanzine)

However, this still wasn't enough. When the opportunity arrived to do my own field research, I had to take advantage of it. In February of 1993, during a travelers advisory storm warning, I drove from Toledo to Detroit to attend an AutoRama show where Fabio was doing a personal appearance. I lost a windshield wiper and slipped and slid all the way, but I would not let danger deter me in my pursuit of academic research. I had to make contact. I had in my possession, on university letterhead, a typed request for information I intended to get to his agent, copies of *Defy Not the Heart* and *Savage Thunder,* and the 1993 calendar. If the opportunity arose I would get his autograph for myself and my friends. I sloshed through mounds of hazardous slush to witness this cultural phenomenon in action.

Fabio and two women I assumed to be his representatives were seated on a small stage. People were in line laughing and talking and admiring. I observed that Fabio's rapport with his audience was positive. He was affable and gracious in his treatment of fans and generous with his time. He did not rush them through. He displayed a sense of humor and fun that appeared to be genuine. Women with toddlers in tow had their pictures taken with him. He would pick up the children and sit them on his shoulder. Husbands and boyfriends good naturedly indulged their wives and girlfriends by acting as photographers. Many women had specific ideas about what kind of pose they wanted. One young African-American woman asked him to pick her up. He obliged her with a smile. She was not a tiny woman with a waspish waist and the audience enjoyed her request. Amidst applause she defended her fantasy to the audience with, "Hey, he can bench press 400 pounds. He can pick me up!" That met with more approving applause.

I stood and watched for a long time. I listened. One man, after watching Fabio interact with his fans, commented aloud, to no one in particular, "That guy has a great personality." Personality is critical to the esthetic of persona. Personality is the outward manifestation of values and values create goals. Fabio has said, "I just LOVE romance, and my goal is to put romance back into the lives of American women. There's not enough of it in the world today" (Goldfarb). Is this not an honorable quest? To accomplish this goal in these jaded, post-sexual revolution times might be better viewed as an "indubious" rather than a dubious achievement.

Eventually, one of the women accompanying him left the stage for a break. I approached her and asked if she was a representative of Fabio's. She said no, but her sister was. I asked if she would forward my proposal to her sister. She agreed. I told her I was working on some academic articles about the romance genre and needed further information about Fabio. We chatted for a while and she asked me if I was going through the line. I told her I hadn't intended to. She advised me to get in line. She would give the letter to her sister and I could get an answer when I came up on stage.

Reluctantly, I got in line, watching his actions more closely as I inched my way up to the stage. I chatted with the women around me and learned many of them were not romance readers; they were not familiar with his work. They were neophyte fans and I was winding up a pilgrimage I had begun years earlier! They were not interested in him as a significant icon of popular culture, as the romance advocate of the nineties. They thought he was one hot hunk.

The woman behind me wanted me to take her picture with him. I was more than willing to oblige. She offered to take mine as well. I told her no. The party atmosphere infringed on me; I was on a sacred mission, a quest for knowledge. I was here to look into the mirrors of Fabio's soul and see what I could discern. I was not nervous. I had met and talked with several famous and talented people in life. Among them were Oscar-winning actors and actresses, men of history, heroes of valor, brilliant scholars whose minds were capable of incredible original thoughts.

Finally, it was my turn. I clutched my books and calendar and set them on the table in front of Fabio. He looked up into my eyes . . . directly into my eyes! His are incredible eyes! His look was open, guileless! I saw no evidence of hype or insincerity, only evidence of a sense of fun. I was appeased. I also went brainless. I could not speak intelligently. I pointed to the books and all I could say was, "This is for Doris. This is for Cindy. This is for Diane." I watched him sign these for my friends and totally forgot about one for myself. I wouldn't feel the loss until much later. I shuffled on. I even think I said something as inane as, "Have a nice day." I somehow spoke with his representative and got a business card. She said to call her. I found a camera in my hand and somehow took a picture of the camera's owner with Fabio.

Fortunately, I changed my mind! What kind of scholar was I? Here I had the perfect opportunity to do primary field research and I was passing it up. I wanted to stand next to him. "Can I have my picture taken, too?"

He complied, graciously I thought, especially since I had already passed by. I went to stand next to him, we were shoulder to shoulder. Well, more like shoulder to ribs, when suddenly he wrapped his brawny, corded muscled arm around me and crushed me to his massive, iconic chest! I didn't know what to do with my right arm! I finally put it around his waist and rested it upon his narrow hips. I was in the ten-second clutch! After he released me from this magnificent embrace I think I said, "Have a nice day" one more time and somehow managed to get my nearly boneless self off the stage. On the way home, just before I reached Monroe, Michigan, I had a flashback of my encounter with the Fabulous Fabio. I shuddered and moaned. *No man had ever affected me like this before!*

I sent a letter—with the list of questions I still had no answers for—to the woman who had been on stage with Fabio. It was returned unopened with a notation that she was no longer at the address. I called the number on the Fabio business card I had been given and was told I would have to fax them before anyone would answer my questions. I faxed and heard nothing. I called again and was asked to write again. I said all I needed was some information, but I was once again put off and told to put it in writing once again. Of course, if Fabio wanted to answer some of my questions I wouldn't have minded, but I wasn't seeking a personal interview. I must admit I was more than a bit miffed and I never wrote or faxed or phoned again. I even threw Fabio's business card away. Maybe I scared them off by using the words "critical analysis." (Perhaps I should have explained I wasn't writing a negative review critical of his work.) They also might have figured that a scholarly treatise wasn't worth the effort. An academic article doesn't pack nearly as much publicity punch as a *National Enquirer* article. Ultimately, I decided I didn't need the facts I was seeking. In fact, who needs, knows, or even cares about the truth when it comes to a phenomenon? I also wrote to the woman who owned the camera and took my picture with the Fabulous Fabio in the ten-second clutch. I didn't hear back from her either. I didn't pursue this because I had pretty much convinced myself that in my state of brainlessness I had put my fingers over the lens and she was probably quite agitated about it. Oh, well . . . what I lack in tangible evidence is well compensated by my memories.

I distributed the Fabio autographs almost immediately upon arriving in Toledo. Cindy took her book into the hospital. Fellow health care workers, serious women dedicated to preserving life and preventing death, begged to run their fingers over his gold inked signature, but Cindy had hermetically sealed it. Diane immediately added her calendar picture to what she calls her Fabio "shrine" which she assembled in retaliation for the cheesecake posters her husband has hanging in his garage.

I no longer have to rush to the television set for a brief glimpse of Fabio. There are videos—he has an exercise video and *A Time for Romance,* a trilogy of romance vignettes—but I don't have them because he shows up frequently enough on televison. He spoofs his own romantic image on I-can't-believe-it's-not-butter commercials. A 1998 CBS program promotion spoofs winning a date with Fabio. The prize team shows up at the winner's house and she declines a date with Fabio in favor of watching CBS. A bemused Fabio is shown saying "That's never happened to me before." There are always the entertainment news magazine formats and the talk show circuits. I've seen him on *The Bold and the Beautiful* and in cameos in films (e.g., as himself in *Spy Hard* and *Eddie*), sitcoms (*Roseanne*) and even Howie Mandel's *Bobbie's World.* It may prove difficult for Fabio to become the actor he wants to become because he is already iconic. His own persona outshone the character he played on *Alcapulco H.E.A.T.,* although this series should by no means be considered the ultimate test. Perhaps his *Thor* cartoon show will appease his acting bug for awhile. He could use the time to tone down the force of his own phenomenon, return to anonymity or perhaps even be forgotten, in order to be accepted by audiences as someone other than Fabio. Nah . . . his image is so heavily imprinted it might be some time before he is forgotten. While Bogie and the Duke derived their personas from their screen performances, Sinatra had difficulties with acting because he had such a strong persona outside the celluloid world. Like these men, Fabio seems to have reached that lofty place of fame—he is a celebrity known by a single name. He is Fabio.

So, is Fabio and all he entails a somewhat naturally occurring cultural phenomenon? I'd have to say yes. Sure, there was and continues to be a certain element of artificial promotion involved, but no one could have orchestrated it to the level of phenomenon, although Rhonda Gainer tried to take credit for it. Fabio fired agent/manager Gainer in 1992 and she sued him for millions. In 1998 they settled for an undisclosed amount in a non-jury trial. Fabio's attorney described the amount as a token sum and Gainer described it as "some of" what she felt she was owed. U.S. District Magistrate Judge Naomi Reice Buchwald stated that Gainer was not entitled to the orchard just because she planted the seed (De La Cruz). I would question whether she can even take responsibility for planting the seed.

No one could have totally fabricated Fabio. As the saying goes, "Who would've thunk it?" Who could have predicted the unprecedented popularity and growth of the romance genre? Who could have predicted the changes in cover art? Who could have predicted that one man could transcend this art and then transcend his own fantasy image to become his own man, a fantasy made flesh, a celebrity?

Eighteen months after my encounter with Fabio, Diane showed up at my front door to apologize for thinking my brainless, speechless behavior upon meeting Fabio was unbelievably absurd. She had met him at an airport and had turned into a chatty, gesticulating idiot. He listened intently, even as she attempted to explain her "shrine" (and frighteningly enough, she did use that word). Never once did he roll his eyes, look askance, tell her she was crazy, or try to convince security to take her away. She said by way of defense, "Those eyes, there's something about his eyes!"

Yes, among other things.

Works Cited

Coz, Steve. "Win a Dream Date with the Sexiest Man in the World." *National Enquirer* Nov. 1992: 22.

De La Cruz, Donna. Associated Press report in Fabio IFC Home Pages: http://www.best.com~dewhite/LINKS2.html

"Dubious Achievement Awards." *Esquire* Jan. 1993 & 1994.

Fox, Diana. "Rabble Rouser." *Romance Writers' Report* Feb. 1998: v 18 n 2: 32.

Goldfarb, Susan. "Fabulous Fabio: The Type of Woman I'd Love to Date." *National Examiner* 25 Aug. 1994: 17.

Hellmich, Nanci. "Fabio—A Novel Hunk." *USA Today* 30 Mar. 1992, sec. D: 1.

Judell, Brandon. "Is This the Sexiest Man in the World?" *For Women First* 22 Feb. 1993: 9.

Lombard, Veronica.. *Romantic Times Magazine* 95 (Feb. 1992): 9.

Paul, Peter. *Fabio.* Livonia, Michigan: Starbur P, 1993.

"Romance Takes Fabio Beyond His Wildest Dreams!" *Romantic Times Magazine* Nov. 1993: 13.

Small, Michael, and Leonora Dodsworth. "Love for Sale." *People* 4 Oct. 1993: 104-10.

Sussman, Ed. "My Fabulous Date with Fabio." *National Enquirer* 16 Mar. 1993: 16.

Terrell, Ellen. "Sweet Gruntings." *US* Aug. 1993: 26.

Thompson, Vicki. "Historical Covers from A to Z: (Avon to Zebra, that is)." *Romance Writers' Report* Mar.-Apr. 1986: 20-24.

A Time for Romance. Dir. Robert Farber. With Fabio. Goodtimes Home Video Corp. 1993.

White, Donnamaie. "Fabio Bashing." http://www.best.com/~dewhite/SHT-STORY/fabbashg.html (June 10, 1998)

Woods, K. W. "Fabio." *Woman's World* 8 Mar. 1994: 38-39.

Yoon, Zoe. "Letters from Readers." *Romantic Times* 87 (June 1991): 26.

This Is Not Your Mother's Cinderella:
The Romance Novel as Feminist Fairy Tale

Jennifer Crusie Smith

Times are grim for the Brothers Grimm: feminist revisionists keep messing with their fairy tales, trying to expunge misogynism while holding on to that elusive something that makes the tales vibrate in the reader's mind, that aspect that makes the fairy tale, in Max Luthi's words, "the universe in miniature" (25). And nowhere is that elusive something more sought after than in romance novels—a genre that relies heavily on the tradition of the tales even while requiring their revision for reader satisfaction. Of course, fairy tales bear a strong similarity to all genre fiction in their certainty about life. As Luthi defines them, fairy tales "aim for clarity, exactness, positiveness, and precision. There is no 'if' and no 'perhaps'" (57). But the similarities between fairy tales and the romance genre in particular are deeper than the tidiness of the universes with which they deal. There is something in the fairy tale that resonates in the romance even though the tales must be extensively revised to satisfy their female audience.

Writers and editors of romance fiction have recognized the close ties of their genre to the tales. Former Harlequin editor Sherie Posesorski has said that all romance novels are "built on" fairy tales, and romance author Tiffany White writes that "fairy tales were the beginning of my love affair with the romance genre" (220). This affinity has not been lost on the publishers' marketing departments. Several houses, such as Harlequin and Bantam, have marketed very successful fairy tale series and others are following suit. But what is it, exactly, that makes this relationship so successful? If the power lies simply in the tale, then the stories would be retold with little or no change in plot or characterization. However, all the authors in the Harlequin series, even those who professed an unambiguous love for the tales, made major revisions in the dynamics of their stories. So what aspects of the fairy tale resonate? Structure? Motif? Theme? A closer look at JoAnn Ross's *The Prince and the Showgirl,* a 1993 Harlequin Temptation romance based on the Cinderella story, sheds some light on the question of just what it was that the Brothers Grimm had going for them, and what it is that romance writers have been tapping into ever since.

The most obvious source of resonance in the translation of Grimm's "Cinderella" to Ross's *Prince* would seem to be the structure of the plot, from "once upon a time" to "happily ever after." Critic Steven Swan Jones argues that "the very great extent to which literature relies upon folk traditions to hook and hold its audience" depends upon "identical narrative patterns and basic sociological premises" (32). If Jones is right, analyzing and comparing the narrative structures of the Grimm's and Ross's Cinderellas should point up the similarities that make the Cinderella plot itself so successful. But the two most common approaches to fairy tale structure—those of V. Propp and Claud Levi-Strauss—both prove barren in this case.

A Proppian analysis is the purest analysis of the structure of the tale because it looks only at the form, not at the specific content. Yet this is the reason that a comparison of Proppian analyses of the Cinderella story and of Ross's book isn't particularly helpful: the comparison reveals generic structure only. There's a protagonist with a lack who decides to do something about it, encounters conflict generated by the antagonist, resolves it, defeats the antagonist, and emerges transformed into a new person. The only specifics at work here are the aspects that tie the tale to family (lack of a father, threat to family, resolution through marriage) and the increase in the status of the hero at the resolution. Although these specifics are certainly romance staples (earlier heroines were often made orphans to increase their plights; every hero is a prince not a frog), they aren't specific enough for readers to recognize the Cinderella plot.

Claud Levi-Strauss's analysis of oppositions and conflict isn't much help either. Levi-Strauss argued that the structure of the fairy tale in its oppositions remains constant even as it crosses cultures, as Cinderella certainly had to do to get to Harlequin. Yet Ross eliminates most of those constants in her retelling. David Pace has pointed out that the oppositions between Cinderella and her step-sisters create tensions because the evil, vain, lazy, dirty sisters are high status while the good, modest, hard-working, clean Cinderella is low status. A reader is invested immediately because the external signs of status have not been assigned properly.

But Ross announces in her author's note that "this is not the fairy tale your mother knew" and recasts the wicked stepmother and step-sisters as hapless victims of the father's trusting nature: he has died, and his manager has embezzled his tax payments, and now the family is poor with a huge tax bill. Not only do the steprelations not vilify the Cinderella figure (here named Sabrina), they turn to her for help, look to her for leadership, and hand over power to her as they travel to a Monacolike country to sing as a sister act at the coronation of the country's prince in order to restore the family's fortunes. Ross's revisions stem from a rejection of the stereotype that casts all women as bitter rivals; she makes it clear in her note that the stepsisters are "worlds different from those original harridans" (220). But the revision also destroys the tension of the opposites that would make the story work across cultures.

Ross's revisions also counter most of the other conclusions that Pace draws from his analysis of the original tale. For example, Pace argues that the opposition of the women in "Cinderella," which shows that there is no familial feeling between Cinderella and her sisters, means that the tale shows that "only blood or marriage ties can hold a family together" (253). Yet Ross's Sabrina feels passionately responsible for her family even though she's acquired it through her father's marriage, not her own. Pace also points out that in the Cinderella myth "unmarried = low status and married = high status" (254). But while this is at work in all traditional romances which demand a marriage or a promise of a marriage at the end, it really doesn't apply to Ross's romance because at the end of the novel, Sabrina and her family have earned the fame they need to establish their careers, pay off their debtors, and return to living well on their own. Sabrina doesn't need the prince to return to living well, although she will certainly rise in status when she marries royalty.

If the structure of the tale isn't what resonates in the romance, is it the motifs that carry the message to the reader? Jane Yolen sums up the Cinderella motifs as "an ill-treated though rich and worthy heroine in Cinders-disguise; the aid of a magical gift or advice by a beast/bird/mother substitute; the dance/festival/church scene where the heroine comes in radiant display; [and] recognition through a token" (298). Ross hits only one of these—Sabrina gets dressed to the teeth and goes to a ball where she dances with a prince—but Ross changes the meaning of the motif significantly because the prince already knows who Sabrina is.

The motifs of the Aarne-Thompson Index reconstruct the archetypes of the tale from variants from cultures all over the world, and Ross hits some of the Index criteria as listed under tale type 510. But once again, the motifs that are peculiar to "Cinderella" are missing. Sabrina is not The Persecuted Heroine, and she has no Magic Help. She does meet the criteria of the next motif—she meets the Prince and dances with him in beautiful clothing—but there is no Proof of Identity scene, no slipper-test, no ring, no golden apple. She achieves motif #5, Marriage with the Prince, but that's the end of every romance novel, not just Ross's Cinderella remake (Ramaujan 266). In fact, meeting with a romantic figure and a happy ending are basic romance genre criteria, so Ross very probably did not choose these elements specifically because they'd resonate with her readers as elements of the Cinderella story.

This rejection of most of the motifs does more than just remove familiarity with the fairy tale from the plot of Ross's book: it also skews the power structure. The power in "Cinderella" comes from two sources: magic and status. By removing the magic elements, Ross has leveled the playing field. As Jack Zipes has noted, fairy tales take place in a "realm without morals" where magic and status determine the winner (8). Cinderella would still be in the ashes if it weren't for the magic of her dead mother, and she'd still be poor if the prince hadn't had the clout to defy her stepmother. But Ross's deletion of the magic elements means that her Sabrina has to use her own talents to rise; her removal of the stepmother as antagonist means that the prince's power is irrelevant to Sabrina's success. In short, by drastically changing motif, Ross undercut whatever resonance the elements of the tale provided.

Although it seems that motifs can easily be shifted, perhaps it is theme that cannot. Theme is the spine of the story; rip that out and the whole plot puddles at your feet. And theme in fairy tales is very consistent. As Luthi has argued, the fairy tale introduction of "once upon a time," or in the Breton, "once there was, one day there will be," means that "what once occurred, had the tendency continually to recur," and that the fairy tale theme is for all time (47). Propp has shown the universal fairy tale theme to be that, if you have a lack in your life and you undertake a quest for an answer, you will be rewarded. And Pace, in his discussion of Levi-Strauss, has noted that behind the idea of Cinderella's social mobility is "the belief that there is an innate justice within the social system and that wrongs will eventually be righted" so that, even though the Grimm's Cinderella is pretty much a passive wimp, she succeeds anyway because good triumphs and the world is a just place (254). These thematic aspects are present in Ross's story because, in romance, there is an underlying certainty that love really does conquer all, and that (to paraphrase Pace) there is a belief in a kind of innate justice within the emotional system of human beings. Still, although this may be an indication of what ties the romance in general to the fairy tale in general, it can hardly be cited as an aspect that demonstrates why the specific story of Cinderella resonates in Ross's novel.

So what does resonate?

In the final analysis, Ross's story is specifically a Cinderella story for two superficial reasons: Sabrina has a stepmother and stepsisters, and she goes to the ball and dances in a beautiful dress. That's enough for readers to identify the story's source as "Cinderella," but not enough for the deep structure of the fairy tale to resonate because the deep structure has been transformed by Ross's revisions.

Which leads us back to the fairy tale in general. Something is at work here; if it's not from the tale type in particular, it must be from the genre in general. And sure enough, if we give up examining the specific tales to concentrate on the general aspects, the resonating elements become clear. Propp's structure of lack/lack liquidated in fairy tales becomes valuable because the generic lack in fairy tales is almost always a double bind of low status and lack of love, both of which translate to a lack of security. And the fairy tale heroine always liquidates the lack; she always rises in status at the end, and she always achieves a marriage that assures her not only of love happily ever after but also of a family structure and protection. The most important aspect of this is the reason that the heroine lives happily ever after: the fairy tale assures the reader that warmth and love are the rewards that a good woman gets naturally. She does not have to earn the reward; in fact, she can sit in the ashes and she'll still get her prince.

This would seem to be skewed in the romance revisions because all the heroines actively pursue their quests, but a closer look shows that the same structure is still at work because the best of these heroines are not pursuing love. The romance heroine pursues a worthy goal and achieves it on her own while the romance plot runs in tandem with her quest; therefore, the romance is something the heroine achieves inadvertently while working to win her external goal. She doesn't have to earn her hero's love; she gets it as a freebie, unconditionally, because she's intrinsically worthy of being loved, and her worth is demonstrated to the reader by the way she conducts her quest. Her hero doesn't love her because she wins; he loves her because of the person she is. As Luthi puts it, the fairy tale hero and heroine "do the right thing, they hit the right key, they are heaven's favorites" (143). Seen in this light, Cinderella, passive in the ashes and Sabrina, spunky in sequins, are sisters under the skin.

In this move from the specific story to the fairy tale in general, even the motifs come into play, especially Meeting the Prince and Marrying the Prince. Every romance hero must be a prince. He can be flawed, but he can't be fatally flawed, and in some way he must offer the heroine something of great value, usually something that will increase her power. So while romance heroes don't have to be handsome, they do usually have to be strong or admired in their communities (status) or wealthy or successful or all of the above so that by offering the heroine marriage, public confirmation of unconditional love within the sanctions of society, they increase her security.

All of these aspects of structure and motif reinforce the most important source of resonance: theme. The generic fairy tale theme is embedded so strongly in the structure and motif of the genre that it has already become obvious in the course of this paper: society is emotionally just and good, and therefore a woman will be rewarded with unconditional love if she remains true to herself (and her culture's concept of a heroine). This becomes evident thorough a cursory survey of the romance genre over the past thirty years. Early heroines were active in their plots but passive in relationships with the heroes. Rape romances were common in the seventies, inspired by the success of Kathleen Woodiwiss's *The Flame and the Flower,* but these romances, as distasteful as they seem today, actually reinforced the romance theme. For although the hero initially rapes the heroine through a misunderstanding, her innate strength and courage force him to love her unconditionally, thereby making the heroine the powerful secure figure at the end of the story. Today, rape romances are anathema at publishing houses because our culture now recognizes that there is no misunderstanding that will excuse rape, but this shift shows only that society's perception of what is acceptable in a hero and heroine have changed, not that the theme of romance has changed. The heroine still achieves security and unconditional love simply because of who she intrinsically is because her society is part of an emotionally just universe. The romance genre has planted its roots firmly in the universe of the fairy tale.

But if the theme alone makes the romance resonate with fairy tale power, then why are the specific fairy tale books so particularly popular? A look at reader response to the individual fairy tales provides a possible answer: the tales don't quite get it right.

Although Steven Swan Jones has argued that the resonance of a tale comes from the text interpreting "the larger drama of life," in fairy tales that larger drama is often of male life, not female, and this has led many women to feel both drawn to the original tales and uncomfortable with them. Luthi states that "the fairy tale is a poetic version of man and his relationship to the world, a vision that for centuries has inspired the tale's hearers with strength and confidence because they sensed the fundamental truth of this vision," but ask even a small sampling of women how they feel about fairy tale heroines, and you'll find a surprisingly consistent lack of confidence in the "fundamental truth" of the genre (144). This unease was captured beautifully by Candace Bergen when she announced at the Academy Awards that her favorite movie as a child was *Snow White* because she learned that someday a prince would come and sweep her away on a white horse, and then added, "It took me years to get over that."

"Getting over that" isn't easy; what we internalize about life as children stays with us at a very deep level. Folklorist Kay Stone interviewed women who reported over and over again internalizing the passive message of the fairy tale. One woman described herself, like Bergen, as putting herself "in the princess's role, waiting for Prince Charming." Another said, "I was homely, and I kept thinking that [what happened to Cinderella] would happen to me, too—I'd bloom one day. But it's never happened. I'm still waiting!" (136). And an eleven-year-old girl, looking back on her earlier interpretation of "Cinderella," said, "I used to like 'Cinderella,' too, like, it should be my story. She starts off very poor and then she gets rich and very successful, and I used to think of myself that way. I thought I'd just sit around and get all this money" (qtd. in Stone 135). Eventually reality sinks in—waiting isn't going to do it—and the real discomfort begins. Here's this delightful fairy tale all about women achieving love and security, and it just doesn't work.

But the fact that it doesn't work doesn't negate the power of the tale. One woman reported to Stone that "I remember a feeling of being left out in the fairy tale stories. Whatever the story was about, it wasn't about me. But this feeling didn't make me not interested in them. I knew there was something I was supposed to do or be to fit in there, but I couldn't do it, and it bothered me" (qtd. in Stone 133). Even the Harlequin authors who embrace the most traditional aspects of the fairy tales put in qualifiers that make the ideas "more about me." Leanne Banks wrote that she had chosen Snow White as her tale because "I fell in love with the brave, handsome prince. I admired Snow White's beautiful complexion and generous nature. I also admired her housekeeping ability . . ." But then Bank follows this traditional list of good girl attributes with a subversive caveat: "When the cameras stopped, did those seven men ever drive Snow White straight up the wall? Did they cramp her love life? Did she dream of opening and managing her own mining company?" (i). Clearly, Banks is like Stone's subject: she has problems identifying with the heroine, but she can't escape the tale, either. As Luthi has pointed out, "Fairy tales are unreal, but they are not untrue: they reflect the essential development and conditions of man's existence" (70).

But what can't be escaped can be revised. The magic of the specific fairy-tale-based romance is that it resolves the problems women have with the specific stories by revising the detail without altering the central truth of emotional justice, thereby coupling the resonance of the story with the satisfaction of getting it told right this time.

The major move in the resolution of the problem is the transformation of the character of the heroine and her movement through the plot to make reader identification more comfortable. As noted earlier, the

Grimm heroines were almost universally passive and static because that kind of woman was a good woman in their culture, but that kind of heroine is frustrating for modern readers. Stone reports that one woman remembered identifying with the Snow Queen, even though she was meant to be a negative figure, because she was so powerful. A twelve-year-old girl told Stone that she identified with the older sisters who kept making stupid mistakes because they were more interesting to her than the heroine figures "who just sit by the fireside and never do anything, and then one day blossom into beautiful girls" (qtd. in Stone 132). The message is clear: female readers need a female heroine who will do something. So JoAnn Ross, while recognizing the inescapable draw of the Cinderella plot, recast the story to make it "more about" the female reader by giving her heroine the capacity for action and power.

Ross's core problem with adapting the fairy tale as a model for her modern romance was that Cinderella is not the hero in her story. In genre fiction or any other form of popular narrative, hero/protagonists must be at the center of the action and must, through their own actions, set and keep the plot in motion by striving for something they need desperately. But the fairy tale heroine is most often a catalyst not an actor. It is her beauty that sets the plot in motion, spurring the hero to pursue and rescue her while she remains passive and pure, patriarchal virtues but protagonist vices. This need for the revision of the passive heroine can be most easily seen by analyzing the Cinderella plot using screenwriting analyst Michael Hauge's character opposition diagram. Hauge argues that in any modern plot, the protagonist must be in direct opposition to the antagonist (Hauge calls these figures "hero" and "nemesis") in order to satisfy the reader's need for catharsis, an opposition that is also prevalent in all fairy tales. For practical purposes, this opposition means that the protagonist's motivation for action must become the source of the antagonist's conflict and vice versa.

Hauge's diagram makes the problem in "Cinderella" evident at once. As shown in the first diagram above, while the stepmother/antagonist's motivation does indeed lead to action that provides Cinderella's conflict, Cinderella's motivation produces no action on her part. Instead, the dead mother and the prince are the characters whose actions haul Cinderella out of the dust and thwart the stepmother. So where is the real conflict in the classic Cinderella? As the second diagram above shows, it's between the prince and the stepmother, making Cinderella a bit player in her own story. And that's not the only problem in the original conflict. Hauge's diagram has two more character slots. One is for the reflection or ficelle character, the sidekick who provides help and understanding for the hero; in "Cinderella," that's the dead mother who works

Figure 1

	Outer Motivation	Outer Conflict		Outer Motivation	Outer Conflict
HERO: Cinderella	Wants to go to the ball, regain her status, marry the prince.	Stepmother won't let her go to the ball.	HERO: Prince	Wants to marry Cinderella.	Stepmother won't let her go to the ball, tries to trick him.
NEMISIS: Stepmother	Wants one of her daughters to marry the prince.	Dead mother provides dress, prince looks for Cinderella, marries her.	NEMISIS: Stepmother	Wants one of her daughters to marry the prince.	Prince looks for Cinderella, marries her.

Figure 2

	Outer Motivation	Outer Conflict		Outer Motivation	Outer Conflict
HERO: Prince	Wants to marry Cinderella	Stepmother won't let her go to the ball, tries to trick him.	HERO: Sabrina	Wants to save family by earning money singing, marry the prince.	Anti-royalists try to disrupt the coronation performance, kill the prince.
NEMISIS: Stepmother	Wants one of her daughters to marry the prince.	Prince looks for Cinderella, marries her.	NEMISIS: Anti-Royalists	Wants to kill the prince.	Sabrina fights back, reveals their plot.
REFLECT: None for Prince; C has dead Mom			REFLECT: Stepmother Stepsisters	Wants Sabrina to marry the prince so she'll be happy.	
ROMANCE: Cinderella	Wants to marry the prince.	Stepmother won't let her go to the ball, lies to him.	ROMANCE: Prince	Wants to marry Sabrina.	

through the magic birds, but she's missing in Ross's version. Hauge's last character slot is for the romance character, the reward the protagonist gets if she completes her quest. In "Cinderella," the reward for the person who completes the quest is—Cinderella. This conflict problem is present in almost every fairy tale with a female protagonist. As Jack Zipes as noted, in female-hero tales, the primary goal is marriage: for Cinderella being a reward is her reward. But in male-hero tales, achievement is more important than winning a wife. As Zipes, puts it, "Women are incidental to the fates of the male characters whereas males endow the lives of the females with purpose" (26). Ross couldn't make her plot work on female hero lines, not in 1993. So she inverted the structure of "Cinderella" to put Cinderella firmly in place as hero; as shown in the second diagram above, Sabrina actively outwits—not the steprelations who have become benevolent reflection figures—but the anti-royalists who intend to bring down her prince and in the process cancel her performance which she must complete to save her family. The double-layered romance plot leaves the prince exactly where he's supposed to be, as the princess-hero's reward.

What Ross has accomplished is to fix the story for the reader by doing what Terry Eagleton has termed "defamiliarizing the systems in the text" (102). Eagleton explains semiotician Yury Lotman's argument that when certain patterns in texts are violated, the violation throws the patterns into relief so that "even the absence of certain devices may produce meaning; if the codes which the work has generated lead us to expect a rhyme or a happy ending which does not materialize, this 'minus device,' as Lotman terms it, may be as effective a unit of meaning as any other" (103). In this case, the changes create a more effective unit of meaning than the original: by "defamiliarizing" the systems in "Cinderella," Ross has created a parallel text with a heroine who shows the reader an acceptable version of "what to do"—not sit in the ashes but be active and aggressive and demand satisfaction in her life.

That is what all the romance revisions of fairy tales accomplish: they take the general elements that resonate from all fairy tales and recast them using just enough concrete detail from the original tales so that the reader can recognize the tale that's being reworked. The reading of the recasting becomes tremendously satisfying because this time, the reader isn't left out of the story anymore; now it's about her.

This combination of resonating theme and liberating recasting is powerful. First, the theme draws the reader in. As Harlequin author Tiffany White wrote, fairy tales "taught me . . . the magic in believing and that there is always a handsome prince" (220), and this is the bottom line that romance has remained steadfast to. No matter how much the genre has evolved over the years, there is always a prince, and the heroine always wins his devotion. But the romance delivers more, promising the modern reader that she will win love only if she remains true to herself—active and passionate. It's a simplistic message but an important one, for in a huge, chaotic world where a woman is sent so many conflicting and impossible signals about who she should be and how she should act, the romance novel offers a precise miniature universe in which, if she follows her instincts and her heart, she'll live happily ever after.

And for women everywhere, that's not a Grimm message at all.

Works Cited

Banks, Leanne. *The Fairest of Them All.* New York: Bantam, 1993.

"Cinderella." *The Complete Fairy Tales of the Brothers Grimm.* Trans. Jack Zipes. New York: Bantam, 1987.

Davis-Todd, Birgit. Telephone interview. 10 Jan. 1994.

Eagleton, Terry. *Literary Theory: An Introduction.* Oxford: Blackwell, 1983.

Hauge, Michael. "Screenwriting for Hollywood from Concept to Sale." Seminar. Cincinnati, Nov. 6-7, 1993.

Jones, Steven Swan. *Folklore and Lit in the United States: An Annotated Bibliography of Studies of Folklore in American Literature.* New York: Garland, 1984.

Luthi, Max. *Once Upon a Time: On the Nature of Fairy Tales.* New York: Indiana UP, 1970.

Pace, David. "Beyond Morphology: Levi-Strauss and the Analysis of Folktales." *Cinderella: A Casebook.* Ed. Alan Dundes. Madison: U of Wisconsin P, 1988.

Posesorski, Sherie. Telephone interview. 23 Nov. 1993.

Propp, V. *Morphology of the Folktale.* Trans. Laurence Scott. Austin: U of Texas P, 1968.

Ramanujan, A. K. "Hanchi: A Kannada Cinderella." *Cinderella: A Casebook.* Ed. Alan Dundes. Madison: U of Wisconsin P, 1988.

Ross, JoAnn. *The Prince and the Showgirl.* Toronto: Harlequin, 1993.

Stone, Kay. "The Misuses of Enchantment: Controversies on the Significance of Fairy Tales." *Women's Folklore, Women's Culture.* Ed. Rosan A. Jordan and Susan J. Kalcik. Philadelphia: U of Penn P, 1985.

White, Tiffany. *Naughty Talk.* Toronto: Harlequin, 1993.

Yolen, Jane. "America's Cinderella." *Cinderella: A Casebook.* Ed. Alan Dundes. Madison: U of Wisconsin P, 1988.

Zipes, Jack. *Fairy Tales and the Art of Subversion.* New York: Wildmore, 1983.

Cavewoman Impulses:
The Jungian Shadow Archetype
in Popular Romantic Fiction

Amber Botts

If a contemporary romance novelist ever wrote a caveman scenario, it might have the cavewoman clubbing the caveman and dragging *him* off to *her* cave. Although so far romances in cave times haven't occurred, the numbers of experimental and other more conventional romance novels keeps expanding. In 1996, sales for romance novels rose to almost 50% of mass-market paperbacks and to a gross of $750 million a year (A. J. 68). In addition, many historical romance publishers have begun issuing their authors in hardcover, which has led authors like Johanna Lindsay, Amanda Quick, and Julie Garwood to the best-seller lists. Explaining increasing sales, recent Harlequin demographic research also contradicts outdated stereotypes of readers by revealing that romance crosses cultural and political boundaries and includes many readers with higher education and jobs outside the home (Linz 12-13). Despite criticism, romance appeals to many women, and many critics and nonreaders ask the questions: why is romance popular and could it be connected to a deeply ingrained psychological urge in women?

Much criticism has been written about contemporary romance to try to answer this question. Much of this criticism has been posited by feminist critics, condemning it as a means of reconciling oneself to society's patriarchal rule. Specifically, those who are critical of romance, like Judith Rabine and researchers Josephine Ruggiero and Louise Weston, claim that women use romance to escape a painful status quo or to mentally reaffirm the patriarchal structure through submission in marriage (Radway 17). Some feminist critics add that since the novels end in marriage, they reinforce patriarchal ideology and offer no challenge to the patriarchal notions of "proper" feminine behavior (Shaffer 21). To these theories, Tania Modleski adds another: "revenge fantasy" against the patriarchy (45). She claims the plots, in which the heroes are humbled and forced to admit their emotions to the heroines, are merely symbolic acts of revenge against the patriarchy. Readers receive the vicarious pleasure of seeing those in power humbled by the socially less powerful.

However, this assessment of romance is still negative since Modleski claims the revenge fantasy is a means for women to deal with their dissatisfaction without making real social change.

On the other side of the debate, the writers and readers of romance take umbrage with the derogatory feminist critics' assessment of the genre, and many feminist critics do not agree that romance novels are merely reinforcers of the patriarchy. Some feminist critics, including authors of romance like Judith Arnold, Jayne Ann Krentz, and Kathleen Seidel, counter that romance is an affirmation of femininity and female empowerment. Critic Suzanne Juhasz offers another alternative: that romances represent the way women are socialized to search for and find self-identity through connections to others in marriage, family, friendship, and love (240-41).

One reason for this diametric opposition could be that, for the most part, feminist critics have focused their study on one line of romance novels, Harlequin, which is the most traditional and conservative. Additionally, and conveniently, the Harlequin novels do generally follow traditional, more conventional plot and character patterns, which easily illustrate the critics' patriarchal theses. For example, the heroes do tend to be tall, dark, handsome, older, cynical men, and the women are young, innocent, naive, and accept the heroes' criticisms and abuses until about page 150 when the heroes confess their love for the heroines. In contrast, most of the contributors to *Dangerous Men and Adventurous Women: Romance Writers on the Appeal of the Romance,* in which romance authors attempt to explain romance's popularity, write books for lines other than Harlequin, and many write best-selling historicals, which are generally overlooked or ignored by feminist critics. However, as regular romance readers know, the romance novels that appear on the best-seller lists are not Harlequins at all, but rather historicals and contemporaries, which vary widely from the Harlequin pattern in style, plot, and character. Furthermore, most of the widely recognized feminist commentary on romance novels was written during the 1980s. While this commentary applies well to early 1980s Harlequin novels, it does not necessarily work when studying historicals, other publishing lines, or novels written since 1990. Therefore, I chose to examine the more recent, widely read romance novels, which may be outside the realm of accepted feminist criticism.

The question then is: what underlies romance conventions and why have they had such increasing popularity? Reinforcing the patriarchy is not the likely answer, since romance writers and readers effectively refute and vehemently reject that theory. Yet, in some ways, the feminists demonstrate their position effectively and clearly, so it can't be entirely dismissed. Therefore, like many other complex issues, a less oppositional position than either patriarchy or female glorification is necessary to explain why romance is widely popular. The deeper answer may lie in the distant human past. Romance author Penelope Williamson offers an interesting alternative for the conventions. She asserts that romance novels reflect a cavewoman impulse deep in the heterosexual female psyche that wants to tie the primary Alpha Male to her, in order to ensure the survival of the woman and her children (131). Williamson argues that romance conventions, in which a heroine attracts the best provider and protector of the "herd" and binds him to her, spring from women's ancient memories, in which the survival of a woman and her offspring were entirely dependent on the family male. Without him, the family fails. Williams then claims that some echo of this memory is still within women, and the romance novels reenact that impulse, fulfilling it (131). While intriguing, this is a difficult theory to prove, especially since feminists usually discount the parallel claim that the reason modern men have trouble with monogamy is due to a cave*man* need to reproduce as frequently as possible. However, Williamson does offer an interesting possibility, and her theory is a compromise between the two extremes. Another critic who offered an even more workable compromise in the early 1980s is Janice Radway, who acknowledges the impact of the patriarchy in "cultural conditioning" and claims that the novels represent a search for personhood which is depicted in the novels and represented by the happily-ever-after ending. She claims women read to evoke the time in which they were nurtured and that the books are therapy (84-85)—a way to meet psychological needs for travel and learning, which are denied by their everyday existence as housewives (113). The problem with this theory is that the demographics have changed since she last did her study. Not every reader is a housewife in search of escape. However, Radway's theories, when connected to her successor's, Williamson's, imply a possible answer to why readers read romance.

An additional layer beyond therapy for denial and cavewoman impulses could be at work. By combining Williamson's connection to the collective unconscious and Radway's theory of novels meeting psychological needs created by patriarchal denial, a true compromise between the extreme ends of the debate can be found. Within the collective unconscious, psychologist Carl Jung identifies certain archetypes as common to all people. He asserts that for self-actualization, a person must integrate several archetypes, including the anima, animus, and shadow (Wehr 55, 60). Of the many archetypes, some are more powerful and difficult to integrate than others. Since the shadow represents denied anger, greed, envy, and sexual desire (60), it is perhaps the most familiar, interesting, and difficult to integrate. Intriguingly, although each of the shadow's impulses are foreign or forbidden in our lives, all are concepts that sound familiar to romance readers since they are regularly addressed through the heroes.

While the concepts of the shadow may sound familiar, using Jung as a guide into the female mind does raise a few issues for women. While Jung has proven quite useful for many scholars, feminists see problems in applying Jung's theories to women. By Jung's own admission, he used his own mind as a research tool and therefore was unable to truly comprehend the archetypes within women's collective unconscious. He wasn't a woman, so he could not have firsthand knowledge of women's psyches (Wehr 104). For example, Jung claims the shadow figure must be a threatening figure of the person's own sex (60); however, in romance novels, the threatening figure is most generally a man and the hero. So do Jung's theories only apply to men or to both genders? Jungian feminists offer an answer. Author and literary critic Annis Pratt advises women to use what they can of Jung's theories and throw out the rest (156). This suggestion helps address the gender difference since, as Pratt posits, "women's trip into the unconscious is much more personal and social. The unconscious *is* society . . . Marital norms and sexual prohibitions mediate full development" (163). As Jung did during his own research, Pratt encourages women to use their own minds to judge the rightness of the archetype. Gender difference may explain the discrepancy in Jung's conception of the shadow. For men, another man would be a greater threat for physical, social, and economic reasons since men hold more power in these areas than women. However, for women, who face greater social, economic, and sexual prohibitions by society and whose psychological development relies on connection to others, particularly in a heterosexual relationship with a man, a man would be a much greater threat than a woman since society gives greater power to the man. For that reason, for women, the shadow figure is male. Romance novels then serve as "psychological maps—insights into the emotional landscape of women," which include "internal archetypes within the female psyche" (Barlow 46). Romance novels are enactments of women's trips into the unconscious.

Taken a step farther, this theory could explain why novels with strong romance themes are so popular. The desire for a "caveman" provider/protector will always be imbedded within the female psyche since, according to Carl Jung, humans carry that prehistoric memory deep in their collective unconscious. Women, then, will always be drawn to the best provider/protector, or, as Krentz has termed him, the Alpha Male: a man dangerous, strong, successful, powerful, a good provider, agile, well-developed, intelligent, ruthless, and possessive, but capable of compassion and love (Donald 82-83). The collective unconscious' urge is to tame the Alpha Male's more dangerous qualities so that he will be an ideal helpmate who retains his caveman qualities, but uses them in service of the woman, not against her, as William suggests. However, as Radway argues, romance also meets psychological needs created by society. So romance is popular since the dangerous Alpha Male represents the shadow forces within the reader, and when he is tamed, it represents the shadow's integration. Thus the reader's sense of satisfaction derives from observing successful personality integration.

This process of integration must be focused on the characters who represent the shadow, the heroes. Every successful novel includes enough description of the hero to invoke women's collective unconscious desire for the Alpha Male, which is subsequently acted out through the hero's interaction with the heroine. The reader then connects to both roles. The hero represents her "other" or her shadow, and the heroine represents the reader's consciousness and its struggle to integrate the shadow. As romance author Linda Barlow asserts, as the heroine learns to love the hero, she learns to love the "angry, aggressive, and sexually charged parts of her personality" (49)—her denied dark side. By extension, the heroine acts out the reader's role, and as the reader observes the heroine taming the shadow male, the reader also learns to accept and integrate her own dark side, which is represented by marriage in the end.

Is personality integration through novels an actual possibility? Critics say yes. Similar to romance writers in *Dangerous Men, Adventurous Women,* Jungian critic Annis Pratt claims that, through novels, women attempt the self-actualization journey during which they encounter shadows (100). Interestingly, Pratt attempts to trace heroines' interactions with shadow men in canon literature by women writers; however, she finds that encounters with "erotic, godlike figures" (103) such as Heathcliff in *Wuthering Heights,* tend to result in the fictional women's destruction, which she claims is the result of women punishing themselves for violating society's gender norms (103). This destruction then prevents the women from completing the journey of self-actualization and shadow integration; however, Pratt never examined romance novels. In romance novels, heroes are commonly associated with "demons, the devil, the dark gods, and vampires" (Barlow and Krentz 24) and are often every bit as aggressive, angry, and strikingly sexual as Heathcliff, yet the heroines always triumph and tame the shadow hero. Thus, her theory is better applied to popular literature than to the canon since, as Northrup Frye points out, "Archetypes are most easily studied in highly conventionalized literature, which means for the most part, naive, primitive, or popular literature" (Frye 28).

Although he wasn't referring to romance novels, Frye's claims can easily be applied to popular women's fiction. The archetypes, especially the shadow, are represented in this form of "conventionalized" literature, and in each of the areas of blatant sexuality, aggression/anger, and danger, the heroes represent the shadow impulses which society frowns upon as inappropriate for women. Therefore, the qualities are projected onto the hero, who represents the shadow in works like Laura Kinsale's *Flowers from the Storm* and *The Shadow and the Star,* Iris Johansen's *The Golden Barbarian,* Susan Krinard's *Prince of Dreams,* Julie Garwood's *Guardian Angel* and *The Gift,* Amanda Quick's *Ravished,* and Anne Stuart's *Moonrise.* Each novel's hero represents the shadow forces in each heroine and reader. The integration of impulses for blatant sexuality, anger/aggression, and danger are represented by the shadow hero's taming.

Individually taken, each quality within the shadow interconnects with one another. Of the many characteristics associated with the shadow, blatant sexuality is the most striking and controversial convention of the shadow heroes. In romance novels, shadow heroes have two socially forbidden parts to their sexuality: extensive sexual experience and clearly demonstrated sexual skill. The second characteristic, anger/aggression, is the characteristic most questioned by feminist critics. They object to the heroes' frequent displays of anger and aggression, which are oftentimes exhibited toward the heroines. The third characteristic of the shadow, danger, builds on anger and aggression. Danger goes beyond mere outbursts of temper to actually threaten the heroine's well-being. Of the characteristics, it is the most extreme and difficult to integrate.

Of these shadow characteristics, the most commonly discussed or commented on is the explicit sexuality. Sexual experience is typical of contemporary heroes and is necessarily part of the shadow since extensive sexual experience in women is still frowned upon by society. In contrast, the romance heroes are nearly always sexually experienced, many to the degree of a near deviant promiscuity. For example, *Flowers from the Storm* opens with an aftermath scene in which the hero, Christian, has seduced a married woman. Later, after his marriage to Maddie, a virginal Quaker, she lovingly refers to him as "her wicked husband, who knew corrupt worldly things" (306), meaning he knows much about sex, most of which was probably learned during adulterous affairs. In Iris Johansen's *The Golden Barbarian,* chieftain Galen is promiscuous from a young age. He describes his past: "I remember on my sixteenth natal day I got drunk and brought several whores and a few friends here for a feast to celebrate . . . Ugly? Oh, yes, but that was what I was. Tamar and I drank and feasted and orgied for three days" (206). In both novels, the emphasis is on Christian's and Galen's active sexual pasts and the way that their near deviancy does not deter the heroines' attraction. Both heroes' experiences—Christian's "corrupt knowledge" and Galen's orgy with "several" whores—indicate the shadow figure has extensive sexual experience, an expertise which is forbidden to both the heroine and to the reader. As Leda of *The Shadow and the Star* exclaims, "I never knew such a thing was even possible!" (Kinsale 301). This response may be similar to the reaction of many a first time reader of romance's explicit sex scenes. Radway claims the heroes' promiscuity stems from the "non-presence of love" (74); however, the reason for this extremity of the hero's sexual experience could be due to the fact that the most extreme sexual behavior is the most forbidden and therefore is the most in need of the reader's integration since society doesn't condone promiscuity, adultery, or prostitution, especially for women.

The second part of shadow sexuality is sexual prowess. The shadow gives access to forbidden sexual experience, but with the added connotation of sexual skill since the collective unconscious believes that if the hero has enough sex, he's bound to learn something useful. This explains why *Flowers* opens with Christian describing his tryst as better than chocolate (1), a woman's "measuring stick" for pleasure, and why Galen's orgy continued for three days. All shadow heroes must have some degree of sexual prowess, even when the degree of sexual experience varies. For example, Julie Garwood's *Guardian Angel* hero, Caine, is a known "womanizer" (46), but Samuel (Sammy) of Kinsale's *The Shadow and the Star,* "kept himself decent" (145), i.e., virginal, and "had never in his adult memory touched a woman so long" (269) until he meets the heroine Leda, who eventually "lay wide-eyed in his shadow" (271). Regardless of the level of experience, the hero always knows how to give pleasure and is sexually adept; even Sammy—"in some deep and corrupt part of him, he understood that this other caressing could assuage the hurt" (277)—ultimately uses his intrinsic knowledge to give Leda pleasure. The skill factor is a requisite for the shadow since it is denied both the heroine and reader. The only women in western culture who are supposed to be skilled lovers are prostitutes. Otherwise, women are supposed to learn from their much more skilled, naturally or by practice, shadow lovers. Integration is achieved with the heroine's sexual fulfillment; the heroine not only accepts her right to societally denied pleasure, but gains skills to equal the hero's. The reader can then also accept her shadow sexuality with the integration of this marriage of the sexually perfectly matched.

One of the most critically commented on characteristics of the shadow hero are anger and aggression. For example, Janice Radway attributes the heroes' anger and aggression to the writer providing a place for women to face and deal with the "consequences of masculinity by evoking male power and aggression" (169). However, these displays serve an even higher purpose; they aren't just a way to illustrate that there is nothing to fear, but also are a way to acknowledge that these unacceptable impulses exist for women—even in a society in which women are expected to be soothers and nurturers—and to integrate them. Thus, as Laura Kinsale points out, the hero provides a means for the reader to "explore anger and ruthlessness" ("The Androgynous Reader" 37), and this exploration can allow the reader to deal with and to resolve those urges through the symbolic interaction of the characters.

Ruthlessness and anger are frequent characteristics describing heroes, especially shadow heroes. For example, during Jade's first meeting with Caine in *Guardian Angel,* she deliberately speaks in circles, confusing him until "For the first time in a good long while, his composure was completely shattered" (11). He becomes angry and expresses it by shouting, a response generally frowned upon by society and one unacceptable for women who must be patient with long-winded and often confusing explanations. As the shadow figure, however, Caine can and does express anger. As the taming begins and Jade breaks Caine's composure, she integrates the shadow of anger by dealing coolly with his displays until they disappear. Garwood illustrates Caine's complete integration as shadow with the ending, in which he is at Jade's side, coaching her through childbirth (373-74). Thus the reader's collective unconscious is satisfied that the shadow Alpha Male has become integrated since he assists her in such a nurturing situation as childbirth and no longer displays signs of either aggression or ruthlessness. This same kind of aggression or ruthlessness appears in and drives other heroes, such as Sammy of *The Shadow and the Star,* who has "a terrible violence inside him" (Kinsale 239), and Galen of *The Golden Barbarian* who feels "Betrayed, angry, the blood lust rising within him" (Johansen182) when he is led to believe his heroine cheated on him. However, in both heroes, this urge is integrated. In the end, Sammy is "awed" (Kinsale 448) and his only remaining ruthlessness is in his kiss (449), and Tess claims Galen as "her own great adventure" since his final expression is "a little impatient, but very loving" (Johansen 316).

The final characteristic, at the extreme end of aggression and anger, is danger. The heroine is, as Bette Roberts indicates, both attracted and repulsed by the hero-villain (50) due to the danger he represents; in the same way, the reader is both attracted and repulsed by the dangerous part of herself. In order to fully integrate this danger, the reader must experience the danger of her shadow side that society deems inappropriate, or, as Krentz claims, "to get the thrill, you have to take a few risks" (109). Danger is even more in opposition to nurturing a family than simple anger and aggression. For the reader to experience completely the forbidden danger, the heroine must feel endangered at some level. Therefore, the hero acts out the reader's dangerous tendencies (Kinsale, "Androgynous Reader" 37) and sometimes directly threatens the heroine. However, as Radway found in her studies of successful novels, there must be some softness in the hero to indicate that he can be tamed (128). Taken a step further, these hints are also necessary to make integration seem not only possible, but plausible. When the heroine successfully tames the dangerous tendencies of the hero, the reader successfully integrates that shadow quality within herself. The collective unconscious cavewoman, who wants the shadow Alpha Male's danger controlled, is satisfied.

Fear-laced attraction is typical of recent romances since women's collective unconscious contains the impulse for attraction and repulsion to the dangerous shadow Alpha Male. In Julie Garwood's historical romance *The Gift,* the heroine, Sara, mentally characterizes the hero, Nathan, as a Viking warlord, after internally debating if he is a villain. Her identification of Nathan as a Viking is significant since it emphasizes the danger he poses to her (Vikings were always plundering). Her fear is so acute that she faints in front of him (46-47). However, Sara's fear dissipates after her single fainting incident, and she discovers his gentler side through his insistence that he doesn't want her to be afraid of him (103). She is drawn to him despite his piratical aura of danger, and begins taming him. He confirms her success in the end by claiming, "Your love has given me such strength" (372). This gentle confession confirms the integration of danger since she no longer feels a threat; the danger that was once a necessity is now integrated.

Other recent romance fiction, similarly to Garwood's novel, often portrays the hero as a demon-lover, since attraction for the powerful, dangerous, but tamable hero represents integration of a highly resisted personality part. In fact, Jayne Ann Krentz insists that the hero must be part villain, or he won't be enough of a challenge for a strong woman ("Trying to Tame" 109); however, the degree of danger varies due to the differences in the amount of danger readers need integrated. For example, Krentz's heroes often have a bit of the villain in them, but it is not long before their loyalty belongs exclusively to the heroine. A typical example appears in her novel *Ravished* (written under the pen name Amanda Quick). The townsfolk believe hero-villain Gideon is a rapist and possibly his brother's killer, which is fairly dangerous, yet by chapter three, Harriet is willingly kissing him and calling him "magnificent" (57); by chapter five, he pledges to marry her and she agrees (111). In a more extreme example—Susan Krinard's *Prince of Dreams*—Nicholas is a vampire who lives off the life force skimmed from human dreamers. In this case, having sex with heroine Diana could kill her, as Nicholas illustrates in a dream (349); however, despite the extreme life and death danger of making love with him, Diana does so anyway and the danger is eradicated; she even makes him mortal; she is his "perfect match in life force, but something more powerful" (423). Here, the shadow is so perfectly integrated that the danger completely disappears since Nicholas is now human.

In its most extreme instance, which seldom occurs in most popular authors' work, the danger is barely contained by the hero and even erupts against the heroine. In Anne Stuart's *Moonrise,* James is an assassin who attacked the heroine and knocked her unconscious (125), considered killing her several times, and killed her father. For a moment, after finding out, she genuinely believes he is going to kill her, too (350). However, in the end, they are together, so even in the shadow's darkest corners, integration occurs as the dealer in death finds salvation and peace in love (403). In each instance, although the hero initially poses an emotional and perceived physical threat to the heroine, ultimately he becomes reliable and loyal, only dangerous to attackers. With the contemporary hero-villain, readers receive the vicarious thrill of watching the heroine take on a hard-to-tame Alpha Male, who is at times an extreme danger, while at the same time, integrating the shadow's darkest side into their own identities.

So why do women read romance? Put simply, romance fulfills a deep-seated psychological urge, the urge of the collective unconscious to seek a man capable of acting out the shadow's darkest impulses: sexuality, anger, and danger. By combining Radway and Williamson's theories, we can see the concept of ancient memory in the collective unconscious extended to include archetypes that fulfill those needs that society denies expression. Women can read romances and satisfy their own desire when the heroine not only attracts, but tames, the Alpha Male hero. Vicariously experiencing this type of man is reassuring to contemporary readers since, as Laura Kinsale points out, the happy ending is a "dramatization of the integration of the inner self" ("The Androgynous Reader" 39). The reader can both experience forbidden impulses and feel integrated at the end of the novel. Thus, reading romance doesn't reinforce the patriarchy as a social institution as much as it fulfills a desire within a female reader's collective unconscious to observe a strong woman attracting, and more importantly, taming the shadow forces represented by the hero, which exist within the self.

Due to the complexities at work, romance's theme of love as a quest shouldn't be considered any more cliché than the traditionally male quest theme, which appears in fiction like westerns and thrillers. Critical studies claim this kind of literature fulfills men's collective unconscious desire for conquest and success. Thus the psychological purpose, fulfilling the collective unconscious' desires, in both female and male quest theme literature is similar. In fact, text analysis studies have found overlap between women's romance and male-oriented adventure novels (Whissell 1570). People can locate an enactment of shadow integration in male quest themes, and it can be found in women's romance as well, just in a form more suitable to women's search for self. The quest will be different, and so will the archetypes, since as Jung himself acknowledged, women and men have distinct kinds of archetypes due to differing social experiences. The next logical step is to acknowledge that women's representations of shadow will be different than men's, since society forbids many shadow desires in women, while accepting them, at least in some degree, in men. Therefore it makes sense that the women's shadow would be represented by the most "other" imaginable . . . a man.

In romance novels, women give other women a safe place to experience these urges, to deal with them, and to ultimately accept and integrate them. And therein lies the true value of romance novels. They give readers a place for expression. Granted, a place different from the male tradition, but just because the novels follow a formula different from the male quest does not make them an affirmation of the patriarchy. In dismissing romance novels, critics ignore the women's tradition inherent in this genre, which produces psychologically satisfying stories for women by women. Romance fiction is a uniquely female tradition, so as romance author and feminist Judith Arnold states, "To belittle romance fiction is to belittle women. To read romance fiction is to confront the strength of women, the variety of their experience, and the validity of their aspirations and accomplishments" (139). Through romance, we can see how women choose and integrate unacceptable qualities as represented by the shadow Alpha Male, and it is that pattern of taming integration, with its appeal to the cavewoman archetypes buried in the collective unconscious, which speaks powerfully as to why women read romance.

Works Cited

A. J. "Romancing the Tome: Jayne Anne Krentz Wants Respect." *Entertainment Weekly* 19 July 1996: 68.

Arnold, Judith. "Women Do." *Dangerous Men and Adventurous Women: Romance Writers on the Appeal of the Romance.* Ed. Jayne Ann Krentz. Philadelphia: U of Pennsylvania P, 1992. 133-39.

Barlow, Linda. "The Androgynous Writer: Another Point of View." *Dangerous Men and Adventurous Women: Romance Writers on the Appeal of the Romance.* Ed. Jayne Ann Krentz. Philadelphia: U of Pennsylvania P, 1992. 45-52.

Barlow, Linda, and Jayne Ann Krentz. "Beneath the Surface: The Hidden Codes of Romance." *Dangerous Men and Adventurous Women: Romance Writers on the Appeal of the Romance.* Ed. Jayne Ann Krentz. Philadelphia: U of Pennsylvania P, 1992. 15-29.

Donald, Robyn. "Mean, Moody, and Magnificent: The Hero in Romance Literature." *Dangerous Men and Adventurous Women: Romance Writers on the Appeal of the Romance.* Ed. Jayne Ann Krentz. Philadelphia: U of Pennsylvania P, 1992. 81-84.

Frye, Northrup. "The Archetypes of Literature 'Forming Fours' and 'Expanding Eyes.'" *Jungian: Literary Criticism.* Ed. Richard P. Sugg. Evanston: Northwestern UP, 1992. 21-37.

Garwood, Julie. *The Gift.* New York: Pocket, 1991.

——. *Guardian Angel.* New York: Pocket, 1990.

Johansen, Iris. *The Golden Barbarian.* New York: Bantam, 1992.

Juhasz, Suzanne. "Texts to Grow On: Reading Women's Romance Fiction." *Tulsa Studies in Women's Literature* 7.2 (1988): 239-59.

Kinsale, Laura. "The Androgynous Reader: Point of View in the Romance." *Dangerous Men and Adventurous Women: Romance Writers on the Appeal of the Romance.* Ed. Jayne Ann Krentz. Philadelphia: U of Pennsylvania P, 1992. 31-44.

——. *Flowers from the Storm.* New York: Avon, 1992.

——. *The Shadow and the Star.* New York: Avon, 1991.

Krentz, Jayne Ann, ed. "Trying to Tame the Romance: Critics and Correctness." *Dangerous Men and Adventurous Women: Romance Writers on the Appeal of the Romance.* Philadelphia: U of Pennsylvania P, 1992. 107-14.

Krinard, Susan. *Prince of Dreams.* New York: Bantam Fanfare, 1995.

Linz, Cathie. "Setting the Stage: Facts and Figures." *Dangerous Men and Adventurous Women: Romance Writers on the Appeal of the Romance.* Ed. Jayne Ann Krentz. Philadelphia: U of Pennsylvania P, 1992. 11-14.

Modleski, Tania. *Loving with a Vengeance: Mass Produced Fantasies for Women.* Hamden: Archon, 1982.

Pratt, Annis. "Spinning Among Fields: Jung, Frye, Levi-Strauss, and Feminist Archetypal Theory." *C. G. Jung and the Archetypes of the Collective Unconscious.* Ed. Robin Robertson. New York: Lang, 1987. 93-136.

Quick, Amanda. *Ravished.* New York: Bantam, 1992.

Radway, Janice A. *Reading the Romance: Women, Patriarchy and Popular Literature.* Chapel Hill: North Carolina UP, 1984.

Roberts, Bette B. *The Gothic Romance: Its Appeal to Women Writers and Readers in Late Eighteenth Century England.* New York: Arno, 1980.

Shaffer, Julie. "Not Subordinate: Empowering Women in the Marriage Plot." *Reading with a Difference: Gender, Race, and Cultural Identity.* Ed. Arthur F. Marotti, et al. Detroit: Wayne State UP, 1993. 21-43.

Stuart, Anne. *Moonrise.* New York: Penguin, 1996.

Wehr, Demaris S. *Jung and Feminism: Liberating Archetypes.* Boston: Beacon, 1987.

Whissell, Cynthia. "Objective Analysis of Text: I. A Comparison of Adventure and Romance Novels." *Perceptual and Motor Skills* 79.3 (1994): 1567-70.

Williamson, Penelope. "By Honor Bound: The Heroine as Hero." *Dangerous Men and Adventurous Women: Romance Writers on the Appeal of the Romance.* Ed. Jayne Ann Krentz. Philadelphia: U of Pennsylvania P, 1992. 125-32.

Medieval Magic and Witchcraft in the Popular Romance Novel

Carol Ann Breslin

Readers of popular romance novels have no doubt noticed how often the writers of such novels use the word *witch* to refer to the heroines in many of their works. This seems somewhat reckless, since most of their readers are women and might justifiably take offense at such an appellation. Most of the writers are women as well, so how do we explain the repetition of this seemingly pejorative term in an environment that is swarming with women as characters, writers, and readers? I must confess that I have been intrigued and, yes, bothered by the repeated use of the word *witch* to refer to the heroines in many of the popular romance novels that I have read, particularly those set in the Middle Ages. Consequently, I decided to research the meaning and implication of the word. Was the term being used in a superficial sense to refer to the seductive charms of the romance heroines, I wondered, or was it meant to connote more profound connections with medieval attitudes and teachings on witchcraft and magic? Additionally, did the term, in any real sense, connect the heroines of modern popular romances with some rather well-known witches and magicians of medieval romance?

It might be helpful to begin by first clarifying the medieval attitude toward witchcraft and magic. According to Will Durant, author of *The Age of Faith,* "Belief in witchcraft was next to universal" in the Middle Ages (985). He asserts that myth, magic, and sorcery "overwhelmed" the medieval mind. Even great men like Augustine, Alfonso the Wise, and Abelard believed in demons who could work magic through their intimate acquaintance with the secrets of nature (984). A vacuum had been left when the true science of the classical period dropped out of sight, and it was quickly filled with superstitions and black magic, both of which were soundly condemned by the medieval Church.

From its earliest days the Christian Church has preached against all kinds of magic. As Ed Peters reports in *The Magician, The Witch, and The Law,* the learned magic of the ancient world had been lost and would not be recovered until the Renaissance (xii). Medieval culture replaced the ancient *magus,* or wise one, with the magician or necromancer, a far less worthy figure. The magician supposedly practiced *maleficium,* a term used throughout the eighteenth century to describe witchcraft, but that Peters says originally meant an injurious crime, "specifically within that category, magic" (xiii). Thus, Peters concludes, it may be more appropriate to speak of *magici* in the period before 1450 than to use the word *witch* (xvii).

The Church considered such magicians to be akin to heretics, associating them with superstition and forms of idolatry. According to Peters, both magicians and witches were thought to invoke demons to achieve their desires, offering them the veneration due to God alone. Thus magic, the earliest and most illicit form of human commerce with demons according to many medieval thinkers, was the equivalent of a false religion, heresy, forbidden knowledge. It caused injury to humankind and could be punished under criminal law (Peters xv-xvi).

Most often those accused of *malefici* or witchcraft were women. For example, the Penitential Book of the bishop of Exeter "condemned women 'who profess to be able to change men's minds by sorcery and enchantments, as from hate to love or from love to hate, or to bewitch or steal men's goods'" (Durant 985). One Berthold of Regensburg believed that many more women than men would go to hell because so many women practiced witchcraft. "[S]pells for getting a husband, spells for the marriage, spells before the child is born, spells before the christening . . . it is a marvel that men lose not their wits for the monstrous witchcrafts that women practice on them," he complains (Durant 986).

Early on, the Church was tolerant of such beliefs, hoping that they would die out with other forms of paganism. But eventually, as such beliefs intensified, the Church found it necessary to invoke punishments. By 1298, says Durant, the Inquisition had begun, and to suppress witchcraft, women were being burned at the stake (986). This practice was to continue through the middle of the eighteenth century.

Further complicating and enriching the status of the witch in medieval society was the continuing association of the practice of medicine with religious ritual and magic. Good physicians in the Middle Ages are said to have relied as heavily on religious faith, magic, and myth, as on herbs, medicines, and various therapies and surgical procedures (Durant 986), often to their great peril. Durant tells of one Arnold of Villanova (1235-1311), whom he praises as "the most famous Christian physician." Arnold treated the rich and famous of thirteenth-century Italy, including Pope Boniface VIII. Because of his interest in magic, and despite his high connections, he was accused of heresy and condemned to prison by an ecclesiastical court (Durant 1000). He is but one of many sincere students of science who were accused of magic and of having relations with the devil because people could not believe that it was possible to acquire such knowledge by natural means.

This injurious attitude often extended to the female members of households, those usually charged with tending the sick and the dying. Such women were thought to have secret knowledge of which men had no understanding. Popular belief purported that these women could concoct potions and philters capable of stealing a man's strength, healing his wounds, kindling or destroying his desire, and so on. Literature of the day reveals numerous stories of old women passing their secrets to their younger protégés and being soundly attacked for doing so. Stephen of Bourbon, for instance, writing in the thirteenth century, condemned old women who taught magic to young village girls (Duby 80).

It becomes apparent that to talk of witchcraft in the Middle Ages it is necessary to speak of magic, the healing arts, and heresy. Writers of modern popular romance novels have adroitly picked up on this necessity as they set about creating their heroines and the female members of their households, characters often called *witches* by friend and foe alike. But these witches bear little resemblance to the caricatures in black pointy hats and green makeup who fill our streets come Halloween night.

If you pick up a popular romance novel set in the Middle Ages, it is very likely that you will find the word *witch* occurring with frequency and intensity. Within the first few chapters you will probably find expressions like the following:

He looked down at the sobbing woman. A witch! A witch who had called him forth to another time and place. (Deveraux, *A Knight in Shining Armor* 26)

He had no doubt it was the witch-woman. Was she bent over a cauldron of snakes' eyes, stirring and cackling and whispering his name? (Deveraux 47)

"Look at me Glendruid witch," he said roughly. "Know my dying truth. You aren't of my blood. Duncan is." (Lowell, *Untamed* 48)

"Lying witch!" he snarled. "Your brother betrays me." (Mills 122)

"Ah, that explains it," he said. "You're a witch." (Lowell, *Forbidden* 27)

Now you could choose to consider such statements as so much bombast and hyperbole on the part of overwrought gentlemen. However, were you to continue reading, you would find that the term indeed has some substance, and that many of the heroines in these novels, and some of their female companions, reflect several of the medieval notions of what constituted a witch. In medieval times, a witch was a woman of strength and power, given to magic and supernatural happenings. She was often a healer, a possessor of secret knowledge, sometimes a singer of incantations, and was always a breaker of stereotypes, who challenged male pride and demanded to be reckoned with as an equal. Where most of these heroines seem to depart from the medieval notion of witch is in their lack of devotion to evil. The heroines of modern popular romance do not commune with evil spirits to achieve their ends. Nor are they destructive. Through their magic, their potions, and their spells, they seek to restore, heal, and promote peace and love for their own hearths and their nations, falling more into the tradition of Glinda the Good Witch of the North than that of Medea and Hecate.

To be sure, you will meet a few genuinely evil women in these novels, women who are more stereotypically witch-like. Mabille, mother of Robert of Belesme, the villain in Anita Mills's *Lady of Fire,* is openly referred to as a witch by her own people. Everyone knows that she has poisoned her husband and has carried on a very public incestuous affair with her own son. She is unnaturally youthful and beautiful for her advanced age, and when Robert rejects her upon his betrothal to Eleanor of Nantes, she cannot resist lasciviously preying on the young pages who serve his household.

Eadith, lady-in-waiting to Meg, mistress of Blackthorne Keep in Lowell's *Untamed,* emerges as the real witch in this tale of eleventh-century northern England. A seemingly unimportant and innocuous background figure at the novel's beginning, she appears sympathetic to the situation of her mistress. As Dominic le Sabre, the formidable Norman chosen to be Meg's husband approaches, Eadith, widowed and made childless by the Norman invasions, whispers a prayer: "God be with you, m'lady, for 'tis certain the Devil will be!" (3). Ironically, this prayer is destined to become a curse later in the novel when Eadith, bent on revenge against the Normans, throws her future into the hands of the Reevers who wish to take Blackthorne Keep away from Dominic. Betraying Meg and all the kindness shown to her since being rescued, Eadith arranges for Meg to be captured by the renegade Reevers, who plan to gang rape Meg in her husband's presence and then slay the husband. While Eadith is never referred to as a witch, her devotion to evil is obvious.

In contrast to women such as Mabille and Eadith, most of the women who are unkindly called witches in the popular romance novels are instead women of strength and power. Having shed the stereotype of inferiority and the status of chattel, they challenge the men in their lives to reckon with them as equals. Hence they are regarded as witches. In *A Knight in Shining Armor* by Jude Deveraux, the twentieth-century heroine, Douglass, draws the fifteenth-century hero, Sir Nicholas Stafford, across hundreds of years with her weeping, pulling him into her time zone. Irritated that someone should so distract him from important letter writing, he calls this strange woman vile-tempered and evil. Since she is apparently a woman with great power, he concludes she must be a witch and thinks of her as such until he understands what has really happened to him.

Likewise, Amber, heroine of *Forbidden* by Elizabeth Lowell, has the power to divine truth through touch. By holding onto a person who is being examined by the lord of the keep, she can tell whether he is telling the truth. This power causes her to live in isolation, both for protection from those who would abuse her and her power, and due to the fear of those who do not completely trust such a woman. Her isolation is exacerbated by the fact that she finds being touched and touching extraordinarily painful, symbolizing rather tragically and graphically the alienation experienced by the woman who does not conform.

Alpin McKay, the voluptuous heroine of *Border Bride,* may be described as "an expert trickster" (Lamb 63), but what she is, in fact, is a lady with brains, an independent spirit, and great managerial skills. Exiled to Barbados at an early age, she has skillfully managed her guardian's plantation there, only to learn upon his death that the estate, which she thought would be hers, has been left to her childhood friend/enemy Malcolm Kerr. In the true spirit of the Middle Ages, Alpin feels controlled by the men in her life, a victim of her own femininity, and she strikes out at this control in a last-ditch effort to capture possession of her future. Employing the only devices at her disposal, feminine wiles, she feigns affection for Malcolm, hoping he will marry her and give her Paradise Plantation as a wedding gift. Yes, she uses Barbados voodoo when she has her servant Elanna whip up some love potions, but her witchcraft consists mainly in her assumption that she has rights, even though she's a woman, and in her pursuit of those rights. In an interesting—if bizarre—touch, Alpin is credited with having made Malcolm sterile as a result of a childhood episode during which she poured bees on his genitalia as an act of revenge for his having killed one of her wild pets. Symbolically, she has stolen from him the power she needs to function as a woman of independence. Once they fall in love, as of course they do, and he recognizes her right to Paradise Plantation and agrees to help her to free the slaves there, she conceives his child and returns to him what the bees had taken.

In Deveraux's *The Maiden,* an imaginative romance set in England in 1299, the author, true to the spirit of medieval romance and travel-

ogues, creates strange lands and peoples as a background against which
to display yet another power struggle.

An English prince, Rowan, inherits the throne to the kingdom of
Lanconia, a seemingly more primitive society where art, music, beauty,
and comfort are valued far below strength, common sense, and prowess
in battle. The women there are Amazon-like, forming a corps of guards
who help men in battle, fight in jousts, and can fight on their own if the
need arises.

Certainly Jura, the Lanconian woman who becomes Rowan's bride
after winning an athletic contest, appears witch-like to her husband. Like
the heroines mentioned above, she threatens her husband's sense of his
masculinity, criticizing him as an Englishman used to soft ways, and as
being unworthy to ascend the Lanconian throne. She scoffs at his
attempts to win over people and to settle disputes peacefully through
negotiation, calling his valor and his virility into question. A witch if
ever there was one! Her ways are rough. (She settles a dispute at a table
by jumping on it, separating the men, and demanding quiet.) She refuses
to act or dress like a proper English wife, saying her battle gear better
suits her work. She rarely, if ever, defers to her husband's wishes. She is
all action; he, all words, using them constructively to win over the rough
tribes he has inherited. The couple remains at odds until she proves her
value to him as a warrior, and he teaches her that real magic is to be
found in the persuasive power of words.

What all of this seems to suggest is that if there is witchcraft in
these novels, it is rooted in the struggle of strong female figures to
achieve equality with men. Doing so makes them appear perverse,
witch-like, and it makes their men feel emasculated. As Rowan says to
Jura: "There is only one thing I want you to beg me for. Other than that,
you are my wife. You are to comfort me when I return from battle, to see
that I have hot food and perhaps someday to bear my children. I do not
plan to run my country according to a woman's counsel" (144).

Although this power struggle and the demand for equality may be
the chief kind of witchcraft practiced in these novels, there are the more
overt, expected bits of witch business and magic as well—potions and
brews, herbs and sacred stones, even a cauldron or two. Dougless, the
heroine of *A Knight in Shining Armor,* for example, has the power to get
whatever she wishes for. When she finds herself abandoned by her
fiancé and his horrid daughter while in London on a vacation, she breaks
down, weeps, and runs into an old church. She rests on a monument and
wishes for someone to help her: a knight in shining armor. Her wish is
granted. She wishes for money (because all of hers has been lost with
her luggage), and discovers that her knight has old coins worth hundreds

of thousands of pounds. In need of a place to stay, she discovers that a very exclusive hotel just happens to have a vacancy when she needs one. She is a time-traveler as well, moving easily between the sixteenth and twentieth centuries, and an artful storyteller, making Nicholas's mother believe that she is a Lanconian princess and winning a place in her household.

Amber, in Lowell's *Forbidden*, uses the powers of the sacred amber stones to restore life and to conjure up images of the unknown. Thus, when she is presented with the lifeless body of an unknown warrior, she massages the sacred, rune-inscribed pendant that she wears about her neck, "murmuring ancient words," hoping to find in it some clue to his identity and the meaning of his appearance. She is guided in her work by Cassandra, a prophetess and healer who is skilled in potions and herbs. Potions appear also in *The Border Bride* and poisonous brews in *Untamed*. But the truth is that much of the magic is of the white, not the black, variety. Amber, for example, has the magical power to divine truth through touch. Meg, the Glendruid witch of *Untamed* practices the magic of love, winning not only the heart of her husband Dominic le Sabre, but also the affection and loyalty of all who dwell in Blackthorne Keep. Jura learns the magic of words that persuade and negotiate to attain peace.

Most often, these heroines practice a magic that heals. When Amber, in *Forbidden,* explains that she is not a fairy but a student of Cassandra the Wise, Duncan of Maxwell responds, "Ah, that explains it, . . . You're a witch" (Lowell 27). Amber quickly replies, "Not at all! I'm simply one of the Learned." He counters, "I meant no insult. I have a fondness for witches who can heal" (Lowell 27), and explains that he has known one, possibly two, such creatures.

Witches who can heal occur frequently in popular romance novels. A fine example appears in Deveraux's *A Knight in Shining Armor.* When Dougless enters the sixteenth century in search of Sir Nicholas, she arrives in the countryside near his castle where local women mistake her for a witch because of her strange clothes and hair. Frightening them off with lighted matches retrieved from her bag, she calls for Nicholas, who has her taken to his mother and there he introduces her as a witch. Observing that Lady Margaret is ill with a cold, Dougless decides to ingratiate herself with the woman by treating her with some common cold tablets which she finds in her tote bag. So successful is the cure that Dougless secures a place in the household as physician and storyteller. Her most spectacular cure occurs when she applies the modern techniques of CPR to Nicholas's older brother Kit, thus saving him from death by drowning and changing the course of history for the better.

Equally successful as a healer is Amber of *Forbidden,* who applies the power of massage to heal and awaken Duncan. But the most impressive of the witch\healers is Meg, the heroine of *Untamed.* The author, Elizabeth Lowell, carefully crafts the portrait of Meg as a Glendruid witch, assigning her a Glendruid witch mother Anna and leaving her paternity uncertain at the beginning of the novel, to allow the presumption of a demonic father. Physically beautiful, she possesses green eyes that burn with a "primal" flame and with the mesmerizing power of the succubus. Her silver wedding dress "smolders," swirls "in silver stirrings," flows into place, fooling "the eye like moonlight on a river" (72-73). She is a sorceress, who, if forced into the marriage bed, can punish her lord with failed crops and livestock and sick vassals (98). She is a witch, and is, in the words of her stepfather John, "cold as a mountain grave," and incapable of love (99). She is a temptress who, Simon says, has bewitched his brother Dominic. She is a maker of potions distilled from herbs gathered at the "haunted place." She is the alleged poisoner of Dominic whom Simon calls "vile witch," and "Hell witch" (224).

But her most impressive role is that of herbalist, healer, mid-wife, and pharmacist. Heir to her mother's profession, she presides over a sophisticated *herbal* where she prepares remedies for the inhabitants of Blackthorne Keep, nobles and commoners alike. For her many ministrations, she has won the fierce love and loyalty of her stepfather's vassals, so much so that he can't disinherit her without risking their revenge. She is clearly a white witch who heeds her dead mother's counsel to "Do that which you can, daughter. Leave the rest to God" (55).

Several key scenes depict Meg's singular devotion to the healer's craft. Aware that a powerful pain reliever has been stolen from the herbal, she risks Dominic's wrath when she escapes his enforced captivity to gather tender shoots that grow near the "haunted place." When he discovers her hard at work preparing an antidote for the stolen potion, he tries to force her back to her chamber. A mighty struggle ensues, during which Meg is dragged from her table, thrashed, pushed against the wall, and thrown over Dominic's shoulder. Knowing that she is no match for his strength, she manages to persuade him to allow her to finish the project by stressing its importance to the well-being of the keep.

Not long after, Meg once again secretly abandons her chambers, escaping through the castle bolt hole to tend to Adela, wife of the gate-keeper. Adela has been confined for weeks with a difficult pregnancy and has been laboring for two days to deliver her child. When Meg enters the dark, dirty cottage, she orders the midwife in attendance to rake the floor and lay down clean rushes. She herself goes outside to bathe her hands and arms in a basin of herbs, water, and soap. After removing her tunic, she pulls on a clean smock made for this occasion and intones a long chant that is part incantation and part prayer. Her healing arts are confined to the laying on of hands and the application of an anesthetic salve, but she delivers a healthy child and leaves the mother to rest.

Her most dramatic cure is worked on Dominic himself. After an afternoon spent at war games, Dominic and his knights relax over some ale, which he finds strangely bitter. Learning of Meg's escape to Adela's and suspecting that she has gone to meet her alleged lover Duncan, Dominic rushes after her. When he discovers her just after she has delivered the child, he feels foolish and bolts from the cottage, cursing the brightness of the sun as he does so. Simon, Dominic's brother, notices that Dominic's speech is slurred and watches Dominic stumble around the yard. Realizing that something is dreadfully wrong, and suspecting Meg of doing his brother harm, Simon puts Dominic on his own horse and hurries home.

Meg's attempts to see Dominic are rebuffed by Simon, who believes that she has poisoned his brother. She is admitted to the sickroom only after she swears that if Dominic dies under her care, she will forfeit her own life. From then on, Meg labors to save Dominic, hurriedly performing the water ritual and administering the antidote for the poison from her own lips, which puts her life at risk, for the potion is powerful. She gives him a form of CPR, ordering as she does that he "take back the breath of life" (233). Later Meg's power to heal Dominic takes a specifically sexual form when they consummate their marriage in the chapel of the ancient druid mound that lies within the sacred stones.

The most touching evidence of Meg's role as healer comes after she has been captured by the Reevers and a huge ransom has been demanded. In great anguish, Dominic learns from old Gwyn that the vassals of the keep have gathered. One by one they approach Dominic, each with a small offering toward Meg's ransom and each with a touching story of how she helped them when they were sick. Quite overcome, Dominic realizes that he loves Meg, and that whether or not she supplies him with an heir—a matter that was previously of great concern—is unimportant: "She was peace and hope in a world of war and famine. She was sunlight and laughter and healing when everything else was pain" (391). Dominic resolves to bring her back no matter what the cost. She has proved, by laying her life on the line and not asking for rescue, that she is no witch, poisoner, or prostitute, but a healer, willing to sacrifice everything for her people's peace.

That heroines like Meg, Dougless, Amber, and others share common ground with their sisters in medieval romances becomes clear as the reader recalls Isolde (of *Tristan and Isolde*), the Three Fair Queens (from the "Death of Arthur"), Lady Bercilak (from *Gawain and the Green Knight*), and Morgan le Fay in her many roles in Arthurian stories. All are healers—even Morgan le Fay who in some versions of the Arthurian stories tends to Arthur on his way to Avalon. All dabble in magic. Consider Lady Bercilak's magic green sash which she promises will protect Gawain against the Green Knight's blows and Isolde's potions that miraculously heal the wounds of Tristan. And all exercise power in a world dominated and controlled by men. Morgan le Fay is Arthur's arch enemy and delights in outwitting him. At his death she remains one of the few enemies he has failed to conquer. Isolde defies King Mark. Lady Bercilak unmans the exalted Gawain, convincing him to accept and hide the protective green sash. Also, along with her husband and Morgan le Fay, she cooperates in a plan to embarrass King Arthur.

One question remains, however, in this consideration of witchcraft, magic, and healing in popular romance novels. Where is the Church in the midst of all this? One would expect the Church to be at the center, pursuing and condemning the practitioners of witchcraft and magic. After all, the Church regarded magic and witchcraft as the work of the devil. In the novels I have read, the Church is represented on only a few occasions. The Church's most significant appearance is in Mills's *Lady of Fire*. When Eleanor of Nantes defies Robert of Belesme and marries Roger de Brione, Robert seeks the help of the Church to have the marriage declared invalid and to force Eleanor to honor her promise of betrothal to him. She appears in ecclesiastical court before the Archbishop of Canterbury, the Bishop of Durham, and the papal legate. Unable to decide her fate because of sharply conflicting testimony, they send her case to Rome and send her to a convent in Fontainebleau to await the decision.

Aside from this instance, there are a few clergymen who appear to conduct marriages and to serve as confessors to those going into battle, but for all the cries of witch and witchery there are no interventions by Church officials. Perhaps they are missing because these are, after all, modern, not medieval, novels and their writers have chosen to reflect the modern de-emphasis on religion and church. Perhaps their absence is meant to serve as a commentary on the rather benign nature of the witches depicted here. Or perhaps it is meant to create a landscape where women of special gifts and powers can work out their destinies unencumbered by the structures of patriarchy. In any event, it is a strange recreated medieval landscape we meet here, at once authentic yet sanitized, a place where any self-respecting witch would not be afraid to walk the streets alone. I started this essay by speaking of witches and magic, but what these novels may well be about is the triumph of the feminine principle and its support of life, healing, love, and compassion.

Works Cited

Deveraux, Jude. *A Knight in Shining Armor*. New York: Pocket, 1989.

——. *The Maiden*. London: Arrow, 1988.

Duby, Georges, ed. "Revelations of the Medieval World." *A History of Private Life*. vol. 2. Cambridge, MA: Belknap P of Harvard UP, 1988.

Durant, Will. "The Age of Faith." *The Story of Civilization*. vol. 4. New York: Simon and Shuster, 1950.

Lamb, Arnette. *Border Bride*. New York: Pocket Star, 1993.

Lowell, Elizabeth. *Forbidden*. New York: Avon, 1993.

——. *Untamed*. New York: Avon, 1993.

Mills, Anita. *Lady of Fire*. New York: Onyx, 1987.

Peters, Edward. *The Magician, the Witch, and the Law*. Philadelphia: U of Pennsylvania P, 1978.

Conventions of Captivity in Romance Novels

Anne K. Kaler

It happens all the time. A girl, wandering into the desert, is swept up by a marauding sheik to his tents, where she is kept captive until she falls in love with him; she is then captured by his villainous enemy and rescued by her sheik, who swears eternal love as they ride off into the desert sunset. Thus goes the plot of E. M. Hull's *The Sheik.*

As ageless as the desert sands and as slick as the latest cover, conventions of the adult fairy tales which hint at a deeper sexual fantasy make captivity romance novels ever-old/ever-new.[1] Like a good chemical mixture, volatile themes and inflammatory conventions of genre fiction can be isolated and analyzed. The skill of the author in selecting just the right conventions, and combining them in the correct proportion, results in a satisfying read. Any work of romantic art, with its larger-than-life characters, can deal with conventions such as captivity-freedom, willfulness-obedience, or master-slave, all of which hint strongly at a type of bondage/discipline more akin to pornography than to the fantasy of romance.[2] Within the romance, however, the interaction of these paired opposites mellows to a middle ground with the reconciliation shown in the compromise and final union of the lovers.

Although captivity is a prime plot device in romance, the specific captivity conventions can best be seen through the lens of the complementary mythological theories—the masculine monomyth of the journey of the hero and its feminine corollary of the awakening of the heroine to creativity. The ambivalent push-pull effect of these two quests working on and against each other causes a natural tension which provides the conflict in a romance. However, in romances, the seeker of each quest switches: in this strange inversion, the female undertakes the journey of the hero and the male undertakes the spiritual awakening. The conventions of the hero's (now heroine's) journey can be divided into the psychological tensions and physical particulars of captivity: the dislocation of the heroine from her familiar environs, the deprivation of her sense knowledge leading to disorientation, her "humiliation," and the culture or customs which contribute to these conventions.

Since the isolation of an escape experience always suggests a spiritual cleansing, the captivity is not limited to one area; therefore, South

Sea islands, Rocky Mountain cabins, South American plantations, lonely Australian ranches, or Arabian deserts are all kingdoms mired in enough ethnic traditions and cultural customs to satisfy captivity's conventions. Often the heroine's situation places her in a rigid city atmosphere or an unyielding job so that she must journey to a distant land or at least a different scene to begin her transformation. Whereas the picaresque and Gothic novels had always lauded the advantage of travel, following the Second World War, the romance also became a glorified travelogue in which an adventuress could explore strange new lands as a way of escaping the harsh British post-war restrictions. The journey motif itself with its separation of the heroine from her home and family helps her to discover her true identity, much as a young hero does.

To dislocate the heroine from her secure environs, authors use conventions such as Shakespeare's "greenwood" tradition, which suggests that the benign atmosphere of the country or nature provides healing while the city promotes confusion and distress. Being abducted and imprisoned, the heroine is forced into an isolation so bleak that she must learn new ways to adapt. Like a crustacean shedding its shell, the heroine's new environment must encourage her to slough off her protective armor of fear and distrust. In a strange way, her captivity does that, by assuring the heroine that she is so lovable that the hero would dedicate all his efforts to making her captive and would pay her the ultimate tribute of making her the center of his universe, however restrictive that universe might be at first.

Her imprisonment itself may take many conventional forms: the interior of a car, a mountain cabin, an isolated ranch, a country house in a snow storm, the hero's arms. By imprisoning her, the hero removes her from a stagnant world to a neutral world where the heroine can metamorphosis into a loving and lovable human. The best example of this occurs in Shakespeare's *The Taming of the Shrew* where Kate is physically removed from the stagnant city of Padua to the captivity of Petruchio's house, then to the neutral ground of the road back to Padua. This movement to neutral ground coincides with the hero's sloughing off the emotions, or lack thereof, which have held him captive. Just as the heroine imitates the mythic masculine hero's journey toward identity, so the hero retraces the mythic feminine hero's inward spiral toward spirituality and compassion. This double action is typical of romance where reconciliation is the goal.

The convention of disorientation occurs when the heroine's senses are purposely confused by the capture process: she is blindfolded or her head is somehow muffled. Hull's Diana is "stifled in the thick folds of the Arab's robes, against which her face was crushed" (*Sheik* 52); a heroine in Johanna Lindsey's novel is smuggled out of her room in a sack (*Captive Bride* 40) and kept blindfolded for several days. When the heroine is displaced into unfamiliar surroundings and the covering is removed from her face, she is "dazed, hopeless, like a fugitive who has turned into a cul-de-sac, hemmed in on every side; there seemed no way out, no loophole of escape" (Hull, *Sheik* 75).

Just removing the heroine from the dangers of the city into the imprisonment of the hero's tent or house is not sufficient to change her. She must be taken beyond the semi-isolated desert camp or harem into total isolation, the ultimate exotic land where the combatants are alone to resolve their problems, rather like hermits who retire from the world to scour their souls. As a reluctant captive, she bides her time until she can escape. However, on her way from this cleansing hell, the heroine stumbles onto an oasis—either real or a literal one—which provides breathing space for her to sort out her emotions; its cool greenness after the blazing sun, its cool water after her raging thirst grant her a reprieve from the loss of control of her own passions.

This hiatus in a greenwood also encourages a major characteristic of the romance genre—the introspective interior monologue which sifts the events through the emotional sieve of the heroine's emotions. Alone for the first time and exhausted by physical exertion, the heroine has time to think clearly away from the commanding presence of her captor. Thus, when Hull's Diana replays her story in her mind, it is a capsulized form of the actual events. In other romances, this interior monologue allows the heroine to reassess her priorities. If the hero takes her to the oasis when he recaptures her (and he always recaptures her), an emotional climax to their physical love often follows, sometimes as punishment or anger, sometimes as relief that she has been recaptured. Since the hero is also moved into the neutral space of the actual desert oasis, the act of love allows him to begin to acknowledge that more than passion may be involved in the relationship. In early romances, this signifying fact is kept from the reader, but later romances stress the split focus which allows the reader to experience both sides of mutual passion. Katherine, in Barbara Faith's *Bedouin Bride,* is both raped and brought to passion in one love-making session as the reader experiences her pain and her growing love as well as the hero's passion and subsequent regret at his rape. The height of passion achieved during this oasis scene represents the death of the heroine's resistance because the intensity of the lovemaking is akin to a mystic's final union with the Godhead. It serves as her catharsis.

To the hero, however, the oasis scene is only one part of his transformation. His catharsis comes later when he realizes he cannot live without her. Even though such heroes may question their morality in keeping the heroine captive, each resolves to keep her "until I tire of you,—and I have not tired of you yet" (Hull, *Sheik* 141). Faith's hero cries that he is "Rashid Ben Hari and you belong to me" (132). Carol Mortimer's *Merlyn's Magic* places her oasis in a movie trailer where the hero insists that "you'll find me a demanding lover . . . I want to be the one who claims your body every night and any other time of the day I want you" (103). The oasis as respite for the heroine is also a turning point for the hero who begins to soften toward her.

Even the method of her escape becomes a dislocating or disorienting convention. Despite skilled horsemanship, the girl often uses a horse who either shies away or runs off when she dismounts. It is expected that the heroine will be able to ride a horse, but not a camel; to drive a car but not pilot a helicopter. If she uses a car, she leaves it, despite all warnings against it; if she goes on foot, she walks in the wrong direction because she has been so disoriented that the sun itself is no guide. The ubiquitous sandstorm can also provide a dislocation device which blinds her sense of direction as well as obliterating any landmarks she might have remembered. Although the hero may be similarly dislocated, he always provides the means to survive in the harsh landscape by shielding her with his body in a mock-love union. The ride home to the hero's domain is usually a peaceful one, the reverse of the heroine's capture. In a mythic sense, if the oasis provides a death of resistance experience for the heroine, the journey home is her return to earth, her resurrection as a person made whole by love. She has found her identity as part of the hero and, while she may deny it to the world, she never questions her love beyond this point. However, this does not mean she acts on the love since, even as she becomes more and more sure of her love, she is still not confident that the hero returns this love. As she becomes more sure of the hero, she begins the healing journey toward trust. The hero's insecurity, which first plagued him into demanding possession, forces the heroine to deny that she loves him and to withhold her love from him. He refuses to admit his love for her until some later event triggers a release of his emotions—a brush with death, an illness, or a compromise.

In some stories, cultural customs are transformed into romantic conventions. When the plot is set in the Middle East, polygamy, purdah, veiling, and the harem threaten the heroine's happiness and sense of privacy. Hull has the Sheik mock Diana's innocent disbelief that he might have a harem or other women with the taunt: "you didn't suppose you were the first, did you?" (107). Linda Lael Miller's *Escape from Cabriz* has the villain possessing several wives yet wanting the heroine as still another. In Mary Lyons' *Escape from the Harem,* the hero's jealous relatives inform her of the existence of the hero's other wife, although his motives for marrying are justified in the end. These multiple wives and concubines, counterparts to the mistresses of western society, demonstrate the hero's continued virility and stamina.

We find another convention of dislocation occurring in the western misconception of a harem. In a primitive society, the harem is a protective device that assures privacy and care for the women and children. However, to a western reader, the harem has become a romanticized fantasy of polygamous pleasure used as a teasing point. Often used as compulsory rites of passage in the adventurous "bodice-rippers," harems serve as coded warnings of the male's exclusive possession of the female. In Barbara Faith's *Lord of the Desert,* Ali Ben Hari's country of Kashkiri is backward enough to enforce purdah and the harem, restrictions which the heroine, New York business woman Genny, cannot tolerate until the threat of political kidnapping makes them a practical solution for her safety. Even though it puts her physically closer to Ali, Genny considers the harem a culturally approved prison of his making. The heroine automatically objects to the hedonistic and wasted lives of the harem women; often she is rescued by the hero who is never a full-blooded native but a fellow Englishman or American.

Another cultural convention arises in purdah, the general name for restricting the sight of a woman outside the home; the woman's wearing of a veil becomes the ultimate expression of a man's possessiveness. However, the veil can also become a device to disguise and protect the heroine during an escape attempt or to help her avoid detection by political enemies. In Faith's *Lord of the Desert,* when she is abducted as a slave, Genny has to wear a black veil that covers her entire face and she wonders "how the women of those countries could bear to be imprisoned by the clothes they wore" (197). In *The Sheik,* there is no question of Diana's wearing a veil, since the only person she sees is the Sheik or his cohorts. Her actions are restricted, however; when a traveler visits the Sheik's camp, he pretends not to hear the woman's voice behind the curtain for fear of what the girl "would have to pay for her own indiscretion in allowing her voice to be heard" (144). Often the need to bedeck the heroines with jewels serves as a veiling effect similar to the signs of sexual bondage—bracelets suggest handcuffs, necklaces replace collars, and ankle bracelets represent shackles.

In tribal societies where large groups of people live under one roof, the sense of privacy differs from its western counterpart where a room of one's own is almost a given. In romance novels, however, the lack of privacy and the continual presence of the captor are irritating because they reflect the heroine's inferior position and how her enforced captivity ultimately suggests her role as possession. Hull's Diana complains that she has "no respite. Day and night she must endure his presence without any hope of escape" (*Sheik* 104) and objects to his familiarity, shown by his "picking up a razor and lounging into the bathroom . . . His manner could not have been more casual if she had been his wife of a dozen years" (83). Likewise, Hull's Isma says that she is "not a guest any more . . . her rooms were no longer a sanctuary" (*Captive* 209-10).

Another disorienting device is the western preoccupation with cleanliness. Hull stresses repeatedly the clean hands and clothes of the Sheik. Violet Winspear, in *Blue Jasmine,* which follows Hull's script closely, has Lorna first kidnapped by an Arab whose dirty clothes offend her, only to be rescued by a second Arab whose clothes are spotless and whose "lean hands were as clean as his robes" (34). Miller's *Escape from Cabriz* parodies the wedding bath ritual by having her condemned hero, Zachary, request a bath and clean clothes, despite the fact that he is surrounded by three armed soldiers instead of bathing attendants (144). It is not just the hero who is concerned with cleanliness. The heroine's short therapeutic showers or lingering bubble baths are used to contrast the frenetic cleanliness of the West against the elaborate bathing, perfuming, painting, and oiling rituals of the East. Such decadence encourages the reader to dwell on texture and color, and stresses the senses of smell, taste, and touch that are so beloved in the romance genre. The heroine's bathing also works as another convention in romances. As critic Emily Toth once noted, "the most dangerous occupation a heroine can have is taking a bath" because every reader knows that, just when the heroine is at her most vulnerable, the hero is going to show up.

All this emphasis on bathing suggests that a romance cannot function without the conventions of servants because part of the fantasy element is the escape from mundane chores. One of the most common types of servants used in fiction is the wicked serving maid, who dates back to Penelope's disloyal maidservants in *The Odyssey*. In the romance genre, these evil women lurk in the tents of villainous captors, just waiting to prepare the heroine for her rape. Hull uses one in *The Sheik* while Faith uses an evil woman as one of the truck drivers who kidnap Genny and two other women who prepare her for the slave market by bathing her in water buffalo milk (194).

The convention of the good maidservant is often used as well. Usually young, she is more knowledgeable than her mistress about emotions and marriage. She acts as a soubrette, providing a lower-class confidante for the heroine's plight, or as an "ear" in the palace, funneling information to her mistress. Although she is unfailingly loyal to her master, she automatically supports the heroine in everything except rebellion. Sometimes she acts to reinforce cultural differences by instructing the heroine on how to behave. Although in the novel *The Sheik,* the servant Zilah offers no advice beyond dressing Diana, in the movie version she sleeps by Diana's bed to protect her virtue, an action which, while it emasculates the novel's impact, may have been necessary in the moral climate of the twenties. Acting as a bridesmaid, the maid prepares the "bride" for her bridal night; specifically, preparing the bedding of the bride which allows the author to increase the sexual tension with detailed setting and costume (or the lack thereof).

The older maidservant occasionally chides the hero for his immoderate acts, sometimes acting as a nanny-cum-chaperone. The maid-servant in Miller's novel interrupts the rape scene and though her eyes were "downcast, as became the lowly servant in the presence of her prince, she obviously knew what was going on. And she wasn't about to leave" (*Escape* 16). In Barbara Faith's *Flower,* Zorah prevents the villain's rape of the heroine because she is the widow of the former tribal chief. Sometimes the older woman will serve as a matchmaker, such as when an aunt in Sara Craven's *Fugitive Wife* provides her deserted cabin as a place for the lovers' honeymoon, subsequent captivity, and eventual reconciliation. The male counterpart is the faithful friend, family retainer, or servant whose loyalty extends beyond the call of duty. Valets, butlers, mentors, teachers, and tribesmen are unswervingly loyal to the hero, although they grow to admire the heroine so much that they risk (and often lose) their lives for her. Some friends, such as Raoul in *The Sheik,* even sacrifice their love for the heroine so that the hero may have her.

To justify the hero's reprehensible abduction of the heroine, authors resort to the use of obscure local customs like ritual elopement, stealing of the bride, *droit de seigneur,* or, in more modern romances, financial or political reasons, or the threat of a scandal which might occur if the girl were released. The most dominant convention used to explain the hero's action is revenge. In Hull's *The Sheik,* the hero is so motivated by his hatred of all things English that he captures and rapes Diana Mayo merely because she is English, and so to "make her suffer as I swore any of that damned race should if they fell into my hands" (178). In Sara Craven's *Alien Vengeance,* Andreas kidnaps Gemma to punish her for her brother's alleged seduction of a local girl. Revenge, these heroes reason, overrides any autonomy the heroine might have.

Revenge for past insults occurs when the couple has been married and, often, when the woman has denied the hero knowledge of their child. In Iris Johansen's *Strong, Hot Winds,* Damon kidnaps his son to have revenge on his former wife Cory. He seeks this revenge both because she has denied him knowledge of the boy's birth but also because he wants his wife back. Mary Lyons's hero in *Escape from the Harem* does not abduct his wife but lures her into captivity by threatening to take away their child. If the hero's revenge is motivated by a desire to pay back a wife who has withheld knowledge of his child from him, their marriage and reconciliation is still foremost in his mind, although never in his conversation to the heroine. Often he reasons that he wants to reestablish the marriage on a sounder footing or to woo the heroine as a mature adult rather than as the child she was when he married her. In addition, the convention of lovers meeting again after separation—like Beatrice and Benedict—has a special poignancy to it. Since their marriage is not yet dissolved, their earlier vows make the subsequent sexual encounters legal and moral. This marriage-on-hold convention also provides a reason for flashback retellings of the lovers' first encounters and of their adventures during separation. Often their mutual captivity is lengthened by natural occurrences—sandstorms, typhoons, flooded bridges, or snowstorms—which isolate them, allowing them to settle their differences undisturbed. An example of this occurs in Sara Craven's *Fugitive Wife,* which has Logan taking advantage of an isolating snowstorm to convince Briony to restart their unconsummated marriage.

If the marriage vows include the word obedience, the bride was not listening. To the hero's demand for complete obedience, the heroine responds by continual resistance. She is never keen on obeying, and when she is forced to it, she rebels. When she realizes that she has become obedient, she makes her final attempt to escape or is abducted by the villain. And the hero is usually willing to disorient the heroine further by convincing her that she somehow caused his passion and that it is she who must make retribution. Hull's hero, Said, in *Captive,* insists that "it is my pleasure you will consider now, my will you will obey in the future. And obeying, you can remember that you brought this on yourself" (203). To further weaken the heroine's self-identity, she is informed that no one will miss her, that no one loves her.

This is the crux of the novel. The readers know that someone—the hero—loves her enough to devote his entire energy to using her captivity to keep her from others. He is willing to "train" her how to be a woman, to "break" her into docility, by reducing her to the *humus* of humility without breaking her spirit. As the language indicates, the woman is reduced to animal status; she must be brought to submission. As Johanna Lindsey's Christina complains, it was "doubly painful to be brought so low. It was degrading to be just a toy for this hateful man" (*Captive Bride* 57). However, while the heroine does feel somewhat degraded, this is certainly not all that she feels. While the Stockholm syndrome usually refers to terrorist-hostage situations—the woman falls in love with her captor—the adaptation of its principles in romance novels works as the major convention of captivity. The heroine must fall in love with her captor early on because to do otherwise would smack of bondage and discipline and might border on pornography. An interesting switch occurs with the heroine's falling in love—obedience is no longer a question of being made to do the will of her captor; rather her obedience stems from her love of him. Romance writers take this language in the same spirit as Kate in *Shrew* delivers her last speech, declaring her obedience—dosed with a large grain of salt. When Carol Mortimer's hero in *Captive Loving* commands the heroine to come, she admits that "he had a perfect right to order her around . . . she was the slave . . . and he was the master. . . . He would have complete authority over her life" (112, 120).

What prevents the romance from lapsing into pornography is what Jayne Ann Krentz, in *Dangerous Men and Adventurous Women,* identifies as simultaneous seduction of consenting adults—that split viewpoint which allows the reader to partake of both perspectives of an act (109). For example, in Miller's novel, when the whipping post is put where both Kristin and Zachary can see it from their prison windows, Kristin knows it was set up to torment her because "knowing the fate that waited them was a form of torture in its own right" (140) and Zachary also knows that its being there "awaiting him, was part of Jascha's vengeance" (*Escape* 141). Split focus allows both to suffer from the same stimulus but the close description of the whipping post leads the reader to the edge of danger and adventure. As Modleski notes, "the reader then achieves a very close emotional identification with the heroine, partly because she is intellectually distanced from her and does not have to suffer the heroine's confusion" (41).

To maintain fantasy, the authors must protect the reader from identifying with any realistic aspects of the capture—trauma, stress, or terror. In novels, when the heroine is traumatized into inertia, she may legitimately give in to the feminine side of emotions because dislocation and deprivation of her senses cause a form of paralysis. Hull's Diana, in *The Sheik,* feels as if a net is "wrapped round her now, inextricably drawing tighter and tighter, smothering her" (78) while Isma complains that piano playing "gets on my nerves" (*Captive* 1) and that her platonic marriage with Said forces "her strained nerves to tatters" (*Captive* 210). Because such dislocation is physically and psychologically disruptive, the shock prevents the heroine from acting in a normal manner. Just as the physical deprivation removes her confidence, so the confusion of emotions bombarding her defenses through sense deprivation takes its toll. When she is blindfolded, stolen away on a horse, plunked down in a strange tent, and raped, her normal defense mechanisms are shaken and her autonomy shattered. Only her valiant attempt to save her virtue interrupts her inertia.

Captivity nearly always means a rape situation—the ultimate blend of physical and psychological tensions. The distasteful topic is made tolerable by the romance readers' coded knowledge that such "male brutality [can] be seen as a manifestation not of contempt but love" (Modleski 41). The mixture here is a highly volatile one of rape, abduction, torture, bondage, and discipline. Yet the sting in each of these is ameliorated by the reader's consciousness that she is reading fiction, and the author's skill in mixing the elements in a potent but non-explosive mix. "Because the novels perpetuate ideological confusion about male sexuality and male violence" (Modleski 42-43), romance makes the abusive behavior, which would be intolerable in real life, tolerable.

To do so, the author gives the heroine a bravery befitting a young hero confronting a more powerful enemy, so that the loss of blood at her deflowering is a form of the "blooding" of a young man after his first successful kill on the battlefield or in hunting. Most heroines bravely plot physical revenge on their captor: both Yasmin in Hull's *Sons of the Sheik* and Carol Mortimer's heroine in *Alien Vengeance* try to stab their captors in retaliation for the shedding of blood at their rapes. The heroine in Violet Winspear's *The Burning Sands* is explicit in wishing that she "had a knife—I promise you that it would be in your back right now" (113). An interesting form of this occurs in Iris Johansen's *Strong, Hot Winds,* when the heroine empathizes with the hero's suffering when he ironically asks, "Do you want me to bleed for you?" She experiences a "knifelike pain" (112). This minor wounding of the hero foreshadows the more serious wound he sustains during the rescue attempt, when he must be nursed back to health and their roles of captor-captive are reversed.

As a carry-over from the convention that fallen women in the Victorian age must die, the early romance heroines seek solace in conventional suicide when they cannot escape their fate. Hull's Isma considers throwing herself from the tower when the City of Stones becomes a "veritable city of stones, a prison from which there was no possibility of escape" (205). Diana tries suicide but is stopped by the Sheik's quick action. Her reason is that of all spurned lovers: "What was life without him? . . . She was necessary to no one" (293). Modern heroines, however, never contemplate suicide.

In earlier novels, the initial kiss is an euphemism for the impending violation of the innocent heroine, shown by her overreaction to the single kiss, which she views as a psychological rape. Thus, in Hull's early novels, the initial kiss represented rape, but later writers, who have more freedom to express passion, use the kiss as a healing device; in Faith's *Bedouin Bride,* the hero tries to "kiss away the hurt he'd inflicted before" (132) after her rapes her. Of course, in a romance, "rape" rarely takes place because the heroine's own physical reactions and psychological emotions overcome any reluctance she might have toward the hero. Thus, at their second union, the heroine finds that "deep within her something stirred . . . the insidious warmth that grew and spread" (130). By having her fall in love immediately, subsequent sexual encounters can be justified.

Delayed rape has also become a convention. This is the best of two worlds that romance authors seek—the threat of rape is always present but is controlled by the instinctive honor of the hero, a far cry from Modleski's definition of "the rapist mentality—the intention to dominate, 'humiliate and degrade' [which] is often disguised as sexual desire—is turned into its opposite—sexual desire disguised as the intention to dominate and hurt" (43). Thus, because it seems strange to think of a rapist as a gentleman, the authors must continually emphasize a well-known convention: their heroes' finer virtues. The Sheik is courteous and solicitous of Diana's welfare; Hull's Said is a gentleman and an aristocrat, placing the heroine's care above that of his father and his country. Like courtly lovers, the heroes are cosmopolitan and experienced; they have seen all of life and have chosen to reject some of it. When confronted with western women, they admire their spunkiness and bravery even as they try to break them down through psychological warfare used to increase their stress level.

Another convention occurs when the hero's apparently "gentlemanly" way delays the rape. Lindsey's *Captive Bride* has Phillip, half-Arab and half-English, arrange Christina's capture because she has refused his honorable offer of marriage in England. Although he insists she can call herself his "slave but not [his] wife," he does not force her to have sex, but waits until she begs him for love. Again, the use of the Stockholm syndrome becomes an expected convention and a neat way to delay the actual "rape." A third convention of delayed rape occurs when the hero wants to bring her to passion on her own rather than by force. Carol Mortimer's *Fugitive Wife* has Logan bring Briony to the edge of passion only to thwart her, just to show her that her body can respond to his. Finally, the heroine's inexperience occasionally causes the hero to postpone the rape.

One psychological ploy used to convince the heroine to give herself to the hero, concerns the hero's threat to turn the heroine over to his men to be gang-raped. The reader knows that his jealousy, or inherent kindness, will prevent this, but the heroine does not. Angela Wells in *Fortune's Fool* has her heroine remark that she has two choices: "rape by the masses—or rape by you" (28), while Hull's Sheik is equally explicit: "Better me than my men" (90). Kidnapping by someone other than the hero is also a distinct possibility in the captivity narratives. This contrast between two captors often strengthens the heroine's feelings toward the hero. In Hull's story, the villain Ibraheim Omair represents everything Diana hates—he is obese, dirty, lascivious, murderous—which contrasts with the cleanliness of the Sheik and his tribe. Genny's villains include a political rival and a slave trader, "a short, bearded man with four chins and a belly that bounced when he walked" (195), who carries a whip and is accompanied by a huge male slave who threatens to rape Genny.

The convention of happily-ever-after proves that comedy is only a hairsbreath (or a chapter's length) away from tragedy. Seldom does a good writer use the *deus ex machina* ending of sudden good luck or the fortuitous death of a villain. Rather, the resolution of the modern romance depends on mutual sacrifice and compromise. In *The Sheik,* the hero is willing to sacrifice his own desires to insure that Diana has a good life; he insists that she go back to her society. This action pushes her toward two conventional ploys: she can commit suicide and be relieved of the problem of loving him and being deprived of his love, or she can hope for a child who will look just like him. (This familiar theme was set down by Robert Hutchins' early novel *The Garden of Allah* where the heroine is left to raise her son while her lover returns to his monastery.) Sometimes the birth of a child will actually provoke the heroine's captivity: Lyons's *Escape from the Harem* and Johansen's *Strong, Hot Winds* both have men who discover that their wives have kept the birth of a child from them. More often, romances resolve their conflicts concerning cultures, jobs, careers, or marriage by showing that compromise is the only way for the lovers to be together.

One romance convention that does not appear in captivity novels is that of "safe sex." Whereas modern romances stress the use of condoms or some other form of birth control to prevent a pregnancy that would complicate the plot, the captivity novels ignore precautions. Several reasons for this exist. The kidnapping of the heroine may have been a spontaneous act, leaving the hero unprepared. The second reason may be that the hero does not want to prevent pregnancy because he knows that a child will bind the heroine to him forever. A corollary to this appears in the captivity novels when the man imprisons the woman just so that he can impregnate her to obtain a child he feels she "owes" him; often the child replaces a lost relative (his brother whom she killed by mistake) or a spontaneous abortion which he assumes was an intended abortion. A third reason arises when the hero thinks that a child of his has been withheld from him and he wants to share in the growth and development of another one. A fourth reason may be the hero's need for an heir to continue his line as ruler of his kingdom. But the overriding reason authors avoid this convention of "safe sex" is to maintain the spontaneity and sense of impetuousness that captive rape implies.

Even though themes and conventions in romance novels can be isolated and analyzed, the effect that they have on the reader is a synergistic one in which the whole is greater than the parts. Taken individually, each convention has a literary history of its own, but taken together, each convention becomes part of a greater whole—the romance novel. To recognize these conventions or patterns should enable readers to decode the message and to acknowledge the skill of the author in her or his refurbishing of new structures with old furniture. Old furniture remains familiar and comfortable, even if decked out in new tapestry. If the convention of the quest of the heroine and the awakening of the hero can create a new world, their final reconciliation and union also help to create the satisfying end. This helps to achieve the purpose of all romantic comedy—the reconciliation of lovers and the communal celebration of a new world order—not a bad goal for a popular genre.

Notes

1. Loosely defined, a theme represents the larger message which a novelist wants to convey to her readers—for example, the theme of love pervades all the novels—while the smaller unit of the convention—such as that of initial hostility—demonstrates how a particular hero and heroine show their love. Often conventions are symbols or patterns which we recognize immediately without words, rather like advertising logos; a symbol rises above mere information-bearing to suggest something else above itself. In literature, a convention can be anything which has happened before—a repeated recognizable pattern or sign or symbol which triggers a sympathetic reaction in the reader's mind. To insure that her readers recognize the fantasy message, the novelist codes her communication in familiar themes and conventions that critics, in essays like this, decode. Jayne Ann Krentz's *Dangerous Men and Adventurous Women,* the best single book of essays on the conventions of the romance genre, reiterates this concept of encoding.

2. Although the reality of capture and rape are distasteful subjects, they are suggested by many romance novels. What makes the subject acceptable is that the entire romance genre, and the larger category of "romance" in general, is not based on reality but on fantasy, escape, and entertainment.

Works Cited

Bianchin, Helen. *Stormy Possession.* Toronto: Harlequin Presents #289, 1977.
Craven, Sara. *Alien Vengeance.* Toronto: Harlequin Presents #815, 1985.
——. *Fugitive Wife.* Toronto: Harlequin Presents #368, 1980.
Edwards, Sarah. *Fire and Sand.* New York: St. Martin's, 1989.
Faith, Barbara. *Flower of the Desert.* New York: Silhouette Intimate Moments, 1992.
——. *Lord of the Desert.* New York: Silhouette Intimate Moments, 1990.
Hull, E[dith] M[aude]. *The Captive of the Sahara.* New York: Dodd, Mead, 1931.
——. *The Sheik.* Boston: Small, Maynard, 1921.
——. *The Sons of the Sheik.* New York: Burt, 1925.
James, Vanessa. *Prisoner.* Toronto: Harlequin Presents #937, 1986.
Johansen, Iris. *Strong, Hot Winds.* New York: Silhouette Intimate Moments, 1987.
Krentz, Jayne Ann. *Dangerous Men and Adventurous Women.* Philadelphia: U of Pennsylvania P, 1993.
Lamb, Charlotte. *Scandalous.* Toronto: Harlequin Presents #731, 1984.
Lindsey, Johanna. *Captive Bride.* New York: Avon, 1977.
——. *Silver Angel.* New York: Avon, 1988.
Lyons, Mary. *Escape from the Harem.* Toronto: Harlequin Presents, 1986.
Mather, Anne. *Sandstorm.* Toronto: Harlequin Presents #382, 1980.
Miller, Linda Lael. *Escape from Cabriz.* New York: Silhouette Desire #589, 1990.
Modleski, Tania. *Loving with a Vengeance: Mass-Produced Fantasies for Women.* 1982. New York: Routledge, 1990.
Mortimer, Carol. *Captive Loving.* Toronto: Harlequin Presents, 1983.
——. *Merlyn's Magic.* Toronto: Harlequin Presents, 1985.
North, Miranda. *Desert Slave.* New York: Zebra Heartfire, 1989.
Small, Bertrice. *The Kadin.* New York: Avon, 1978.
Wells, Angela. *Fortune's Fool.* Toronto: Harlequin Romance #2921, 1987.
Winspear, Violet. *Blue Jasmine,* Toronto: Harlequin Romance, 1970.
——. *Burning Sands, The.* Toronto: Harlequin Presents #174, 1977.
——. *Tawny Sands.* Toronto: Harlequin Presents #39, 1974.
Wood, Sara. *Perfumes of Arabia.* Toronto: Harlequin Romance #2814, 1988.

Time-Travel and Related Phenomena
in Contemporary Popular Romance Fiction

Diane M. Calhoun-French

Until the last decade and a half, collective wisdom, and even the scant existing criticism, treated contemporary popular romance fiction as monolithic—the same story being told over and over again with endless changes of incidentals like names, costumes, and locales. Fortunately, the increase of scholarship in both popular culture and women's studies resulted in a number of major volumes in the 1980s which gave this literary phenomenon the in-depth attention that it merits. Foremost among these works are Tania Modleski's *Loving with a Vengeance* (1982), Carol Thurston's *The Romance Revolution* (1987), Mariam Darce Frenier's *Good-bye Heathcliff* (1988), and, of course, Janice Radway's groundbreaking *Reading the Romance* (1984). And, as critical interest blossomed, so did the genre itself. Never as of-a-piece as their detractors liked to complain, romance novels were now clearly striking out into new territory. As romance author Cathie Linz writes in "Setting the Stage: Facts and Figures": "With the increasing presence of American writers on the scene . . . the marketplace has opened up to all kinds of romance novel hybrids: time-travel love stories, science fiction/fantasy romances, romantic suspense, western romances" (12).[1]

It is not surprising that time-travel fiction should appear first on Linz's list; indeed, it has proved exceedingly popular with readers, especially since Constance O'Day-Flannery began publishing her time-travel stories in 1986. Such novels were not new—Jacqueline Marten (1981), Jo Ann Simon (1981 and 1982), and June Lund Shiplett (1979 and 1983) had all previously found success with similar tales. However, a review of such reference works as Kay Mussell's *Women's Gothic and Romantic Fiction* (1981) and Eileen Fallon's *Words of Love: A Complete Guide to Romance Fiction* (1984) yields no reference to time-travel stories or the variations on them that I will describe below. In fact, the editors of Rita Clay Estrada's 1987 Harlequin Temptation, *The Ivory Key* (written in this vein), question whether their readers will accept its "one extraordinary element . . . never seen in a romance" (i). As late as 1989, responding to a reader inquiry about time-travel titles, *Romantic Times* editors can only list eleven in "this sub-genre which is attracting more readers (and writers)" (57), and four of those are O'Day-Flannery's.

However, by 1992, Harlequin itself refers to the "time-travel genre" in its biographical note to Rebecca Flanders' *Yesterday Comes Tomorrow*, and companies such as Dorchester Publishing are announcing that "every month, beginning in August 1993, Love Spell will publish one book" under the "Timeswept Romance" category, in which "modern-day heroines travel to the past to find the men who fulfill their hearts' desires" (*A Time-Travel Christmas* 444).

Time-travel stories are configured in many ways. Sometimes, in titles such as Dawn Stewardson's *Moon Shadow*, we find the hero traveling back into the past. Occasionally, the hero will travel from the past to the present, as happens in Jo Ann Simon's *Love Once in Passing*. In Eugenia Riley's *Tempest in Time*, two heroines (one a 1990s business woman, the other a Victorian maiden) trade places on their wedding days. By far, however, time-travel and related phenomena most frequently take one of two forms: stories in which contemporary heroines find themselves transported back in time, and stories in which a contemporary couple discovers themselves to be reincarnations of past lovers, whose own story forms a parallel text to the primary narrative.[2]

It is not surprising that romance writers should find time-travel an appealing narrative device. What could be more compelling than "love so special . . . even time itself can't stop it" (Roberts, *Time Was* ii) or "loves so rapturous, passions so strong, they transcend the boundaries of the ages"? (*Timeless Love* i). Pamela Simpson even goes so far as to quote Erica Jong as an epigraph to her mystery-romance *Partners in Time:* "All love is a species of time travel. In order to love we transcend the boundaries of sex, of selfishness, of ego, so why not the boundary of time?" (v). In addition to its philosophical appropriateness, a time-travel theme, on a more practical level, allows the writer to capture both main categories of romance readers with the same novel: those who favor realistic, contemporary stories and those who prefer historical or gothic fiction. In addition, as Janice Radway points out, romances traditionally insist on "temporal specificity" (204); readers expect their novels to "teach them about faraway places and times and instruct them in the customs of other cultures" (107). Clearly, time-travel's juxtaposition of ordinary/present and exotic/past culture fulfills this educational imperative in an especially significant way. Moreover, we might consider that time-travel novels actually solve one historical romance dilemma that Carol Thurston posits in *The Romance Revolution*. Speaking of the erotic historical romances of the 1970s, Thurston writes: "Heroines were becoming more and more overtly rebellious as the decade progressed . . .

which often created an authenticity problem in the historical context." In fact, she characterizes the heroine as "very much like the kind of woman Betty Friedan (1981) described as the natural end product of changes wrought by the 'first stage' of the women's movement" (87). If this is so, then clearly any plot device which permits a legitimate contemporary heroine to confront various ages and past cultures would be a welcome one. Finally, if Susan Elizabeth Phillips is correct when she says that female empowerment is at the heart of the romance and that "the domineering male becomes the catalyst that makes the empowerment fantasy work" (56), then where better to seek him out than the past?

So we might characterize the dynamic underlying time-travel as a conflict generated by the clash of opposing cultures and epochs, usually involving a contemporary heroine and a hero who is definitely not contemporary. Similarly, in novels where reincarnation (or something approximating it) are involved, we witness the flawed, destructive, or incomplete past being reworked, redeemed, or resolved by the protagonists' actions in the present. The effects of these juxtapositions could be profound, especially in highlighting the gains in status that modern women have achieved. Recent feminist scholarship has clearly demonstrated the importance of women examining their collective past for its lessons and its buried truths. But is that what emerges from this genre? Unfortunately, usually not. For it seems to me that these novels generally do not celebrate the fought-for autonomy of the contemporary woman, nor do they actually condemn the subordination of women which characterized the earlier eras being portrayed. Rather, their overwhelming nostalgia for the past, their tacit acceptance of its liberties against women, and/or their manipulation of events in the contemporary narrative all create a subtext which argues not for the primacy of woman's present but, ultimately, for the primacy of her past. This valorization of the past, or of prefeminist male/female relationships, is at the heart of many of the time-travel and related category romances I have read, although this implicit message is not always delivered the same way. Some novels, while paying lip service to the strides women have made toward equality and autonomy, insist that the modern woman will in fact find greater satisfaction in the past, or with a man who is a product of it. Others seem to shift the action of the novel to the past primarily to permit the inclusion of certain kinds of relationships or actions which would be intolerable to contemporary women. Still others might be said to counterpoint the historical past with the present in an attempt to make the very unliberated attitudes and beliefs they embody seem progressive by comparison. Let me illustrate my concerns by examining four novels, two of which involve time-travel and two reincarnation.

Constance O'Day Flannery's *Timeless Passion* and Jo Ann Simon's *Love Once in Passing* exemplify the first type of novel to which I've objected. Both works feature independent career women heroines and both involve actual time-travel. In *Timeless Passion*, the heroine finds herself transported back to pre-civil war days in the Old South; in *Love Once in Passing*, the heroine finds the ninth Earl of Westerham, straight from Regency England, suddenly sitting on the passenger side of her automobile as she's driving home from work. In both novels, the female protagonists insist on the differences between themselves as 1980s women and their nineteenth-century lovers, but in both cases—their supposedly modern sensibilities notwithstanding—the America and England of more than a century ago with their dashing heroes have greater appeal than either the culture or the men of the present.

In *Timeless Passion,* Brianne Quinlan awakens after an automobile accident to find herself at the antebellum plantation home of Ryan Barrington. Although she prides herself on her twentieth-century freedom from outmoded attitudes about women and their roles, she soon discovers that she enjoys being part of a culture she has often read about. Indeed, her own taste runs to traditional furniture and antiques, and her greatest family treasures are "her mother's silver tea service" and "her grandmother's hand-crocheted lace canopy atop her poster bed" (11). In her new environment, Brianne also relishes the "gorgeous" clothes she is expected to wear, especially since they suit a voluptuous body "more fashionable" (9) then than now. In fact, Brianne not only takes readily to the domestication which is her lot in mid-nineteenth century America, but she comes to admit to herself that she is "living out a fantasy" in a world where "she felt wanted, and possibly even needed" (250). Most significantly, she finds in the nineteenth century the sexual fulfillment she has ironically been denied in the sexually permissive culture of her own day. Angry because he believes she is playing a prank on him by claiming to be from the future, a drunken Ryan rapes her the night of her arrival. Despite herself, she is aroused by the phantom lover in her dreams—and surprised, since a single disastrous experience with sex has left her disillusioned and believing herself frigid. Needless to say, learning of this drunken rape, Ryan's family demands that he do the honorable thing and marry Brianne. Once she admits—tipsy herself—to her own lack of sexual confidence, Ryan determines to forego his conjugal rights until she is ready and willing for his tender sexual tutelage—which proves, of course, to be a splendid success. And, in a final act, which truly validates the superiority of the nineteenth-century male, Ryan manages to deliver his and Brianne's baby when the midwife has failed and his wife's life hangs in the balance.

Simon's *Love Once in Passing* also valorizes the nineteenth-century male and his expectations of women. Although Earl Christopher Dunlap insists to his modern hostess, Jessica Lund, that Regency England is not as glamorous as the books she has read would suggest, and although she protests loudly when he fails to agree that women are equal to men, everything about the development of this plot and Jessica's attitude argue for his world instead of hers. Like Brianne Quinlan, Jessica admits to a fondness for things old, like her "Victorian dressing table" (102) and her house, "a small colonial built in the early 1800s. . . . where the feel of old New England remained" (21). Liberation notwithstanding, there are references to smoking and other "bad habits" modern women have adopted. Indeed, Jessica admits her dissatisfaction with women's status in the world of work where men get all the credit and pointedly contrasts today's "rushing life-style" with the "dignity and grace of [Christopher's] era" (40). She even admits her ultimate desire that he "follow [her] into [her] room and tear the gown off [her] back" (79) in proper Regency romance fashion! We are hardly surprised at the novel's denouement which finds Jessica living out a "fairy-tale" (246)—married to Christopher and staying at home on the old Colonial farm they have purchased, rearing their son.

Heather Graham's *Every Time I Love You* illustrates how the introduction of the past can "justify" writers' inclusion of certain behaviors which we would otherwise find it intolerable for the contemporary woman to accept. In this, as in many other books, what seems tolerated is rape. *Every Time I Love You* finds artist Brent McCauley and art dealer Gayle Norman passionately involved after only three meetings and married after a whirlwind courtship of scarcely a month. Soon thereafter, Gayle begins having nightmares in which she fears her husband; similarly, Brent starts experiencing blackouts during which he berates and abuses his wife. Working first with a psychiatrist and later with a parapsychologist, the newlyweds discover that they have already met, married, and died estranged from one another—during the Revolutionary War. It comes out that, as Percy and Katrina—their past selves—they had died violently at the very site of their contemporary counterparts' home. Their parting had been bitter, with Percy believing that Katrina slept with, and later betrayed him to, the enemy.

Only when the current lovers reveal the truth of their earlier incarnations is peace restored—both in the past and the present. What occurs throughout the course of this novel until this painful resolution is reached, however, is a lot of violent sex, both in the past-life flashbacks and in the present past-life regressions, and all of it somehow excusable because of the true passion of the "real" lovers, Brent and Gayle.

In fact, rape appears in many—if not most—of the time-travel type books I have read, although through many different plot machinations. I have already mentioned the scene in *Timeless Passion* during which an innately tender Ryan believes Brianne deserves punishment. In *Love Once in Passing,* a narratively fortuitous case of amnesia on Jessica's part likewise forces her husband into what begins as forcible intercourse. Clearly this is the "fantasy rape" and, as Carol Thurston points out, readers recognize that rape "in the books [is] not the same as in real life!" (78). Indeed, such "bodice-ripping" episodes are a staple of historical romance fiction, and Kathleen Gilles Seidel justifies their inclusion this way: "Historical romances are more likely to depict poverty, violence, and rape than are romances set in the present. The reason is simple. The historical setting makes the dramatization of such perils more remote and therefore less threatening" (166). This rationale aside, I believe that readers more willingly accept the persistence of violent sex in historical romances because such things, though deplorable, used to be—in actual fact—culturally tolerated and are therefore historically accurate. In contemporary settings, on the other hand, in an age where women have struggled to separate sex and violence in the popular imagination, I find it especially distressing to see such activity consistently tolerated in the lives of allegedly autonomous and assertive contemporary women characters.

One key to Jayne Ann Krentz's choice of a reincarnation-style plot for her Harlequin Temptation titles *Dreams, Part I* and *Dreams, Part II* can be found in her persuasive introduction to *Dangerous Men and Adventurous Women: Romance Writers on the Appeal of the Romance.* "Some writers," she says, "myself included, believe that a sense of danger, of risk, is created in the books by the fact that the hero plays two roles: he is both hero and villain. The challenge the heroine faces is unique to romance fiction. She must find a way to conquer the villain without destroying the hero" (8). The duality which Krentz speaks about here finds its perfect expression in a reincarnation story, which allows hero and/or heroine to be multiple characters in fully realized narrative terms. The hero-cum-villain can be both cruel without losing our—and the heroine's—sympathies, and kind without having yet been redeemed by her good auspices. There can, however, be a danger in such telescoping of characters, especially if, as in *Dreams,* the reader may find it hard to keep them separate.

Dreams, Parts I and II are, without question, the most interesting and disturbing romance novels I have ever read, and they illustrate the final use of time-travel/reincarnation I discussed above. That is, they contrast a flawed and tragic past love relationship with its subsequent successful re-enactment in two modern-day protagonists. However, I would contend that—the eventual consummation of the mythic lovers' union notwithstanding—the contemporary love relationship Krentz depicts ultimately fails to redress the male/female power imbalance at the heart of both couples' conflicts.

Successful horror writer Colby Savager (and one must read "savage her" in his name!) has returned at age forty to the small town he left twenty years ago. Career woman Diana Prentice has also come to Fulbrook Corners; she needs a vacation after having been denied promotion at the manufacturing firm where she is the controller's second-in-command. Neither understands why he or she has been "drawn" to this place, but both are undeniably drawn, sexually, to each other as well. At age nineteen, Colby had impregnated and then married the town "princess." After a mercifully brief period of marriage and motherhood, Cynthia packed up and left—only to be killed in an accident, leaving Colby to raise their son alone, estranged from her embittered family. Diana, we learn, has dedicated herself to her career. She has been disappointed in romance and wants neither marriage to an undependable male nor motherhood. However, their irresistible sexual chemistry being what it is, Diana and Colby begin a torrid affair.

Responsibly, Colby is always careful to provide protection out of a little foil wrapper he carries optimistically in his wallet—until, that is, a passionate, dreamlike encounter which Diana initiates at Chained Lady Falls. Chained Lady Falls is not only a local natural phenomenon—with its water appearing to turn blood red at sundown—but the subject of local lore. Legend recounts that the area was once inhabited by a tribe of male and female warriors; the women of the tribe had the added power of controlling their own reproduction. As the story goes, one particularly truculent female warrior, resistant when her mate demanded sexual attentions she would have given willingly were he loving and gentle, refused to produce a child. In anger the lover chained her in the grotto of the cave behind the falls, vowing to rape her each day until she gave him a son. Determined to escape, one day she stabbed him while he was forcing himself on her. Both subsequently died—he from his wound and she from lack of food and water. But, according to myth, the male warrior uttered this curse before his death: that his mate's soul will remain in Chained Lady Cave until a child is conceived and born in the grotto. One incident of unprotected intercourse by Diana and Colby has—in fine romance and soap opera tradition—resulted in her pregnancy. Strange contortions of plot also result, of course, in their child being born in the grotto—Colby delivering the baby of a terrified Diana, just as Ryan had in *Timeless Passion*. Krentz makes it quite clear through her characters' trance-like lapses that Colby and Diana are righting the past lovers' star-crossed relationship, although just whether they are contemporary reincarnations of the warrior and his chained lady is unclear.

If, however, this is the author's intention, one must question the nature of the lovers' twentieth-century revamped relationship and whether it is all the contemporary heroine could (or should) hope for. Consider first the overt male chauvinism of the hero, who explicitly refers to the heroine in her work attire as "a twentieth-century amazon warrior" (*Part II*, 111) and complains that "the amazon bit wears after a while" (*Part II*, 65). "Women like Diana need marriage to settle 'em down" (*Part II*, 31), he tells an old friend. Diana needs "a strong man to take [her] in hand and show [her] what it [means] to be a truly well-rounded woman" (*Part II*, 77). Lest we believe this merely represents an outdated attitude that Diana will teach Colby to abandon, the author has Diana's own mother echo his sentiments: "She can be a real stick-in-the-mud. Spent too many years being a hot-shot lady executive, if you ask me. Look at the result. Thirty-four years old, and never been married. It's a wonder you weren't put off by all those chilly corporate manners of hers. Most men are scared to death of her" (*Part II*, 39). It seems clear that Krentz intends this "patriarchal machismo" (*Part II*, 154) to be the modern equivalent of the dead male warrior's subjugation of the chained lady.

Indeed, we can anticipate that the narrative's ultimate goal would be to redress this past wrong in its present incarnation. However, both the overall tenor of *Dreams* and its unfolding of events not only fail to condemn such male domination, they seem to endorse it. While Colby mellows to some extent by the novel's end, there is scant evidence of any change in his fundamental attitudes. If he has agreed to Diana's opening a small business as the story concludes, it is only because she can be near her new Victorian home, which means she will be available to her family at lunch time and able to get home early in the evenings. In every way, Diana is presented as inferior to Colby—naive, unself-aware, and in need of his tutelage. He has all the parenting skills, having reared a son alone. He can cook and shop for food; she cannot. Despite being an adult who has had some sexual experience, albeit limited, Diana seems totally oblivious to birth control, leaving this responsibility completely up to Colby. He consistently demonstrates more sensitivity to her sexual responses than she possesses, and he is also much more cognizant of what is happening to her body during her pregnancy than she is. In fact, when they discover that she is pregnant, Diana never considers any alternative but the one Colby insists on—marriage—and this despite her loathing and fear of pregnancy and a conviction that he doesn't love her.

I find the depiction of this contemporary couple and the denouement of their story problematic. Not *because* of the encoded fantasy elements, but rather *in spite of* them. Krentz and her sister authors argue eloquently in *Dangerous Men and Adventurous Women* for the fantasy function of the romance; indeed the passionate intensity of the couplings of the past and present lovers in *Dreams* makes for escape literature of the first order. And Krentz is correct to object to the fact that "when it comes to romance novels, critics worry about whether the women who read them can tell the difference between what is real and what is not" (2). Nevertheless, their specificity of settings and their insistence that they explore the real dilemmas of recognizable contemporary women give these novels an inescapable political significance, all legitimate escapist intentions aside. I believe I know the lesson the warrior and his chained lady are meant to learn through the experiences of Colby and Diana: he, that what he could not take by force she is willing to give in a mutually loving relationship; she, that her independence need not be compromised by sharing herself as a loving mate and mother. As the author says, "He had vowed to teach her that she could not escape her destiny as a woman, but it was he who had learned the most important lesson. She had taught him how to love" (*Part II,* 218). And so we, as readers, are asked in the end to applaud the triumph of the present over the past. On closer examination, however, we must ask if the relationship of the contemporary lovers is actually worthy of celebration. I think not. In truth, I find it a retrograde male-female relationship which has only been made palatable by pointed contrast with a violent mythic past over which it cannot help but be an improvement. Everything about Diana and Colby's life together perpetuates the destructive assumption of male superiority at the heart of the primitive conflict. In fact, if we acknowledge that the female warrior's power is best symbolized by the ability to control her own reproduction, we must conclude that Diana is even less powerful than her counterpart. From its opening pages to its conclusion, *Dreams* depicts a Diana powerless in the grip of her own body and sexuality. All this I find at odds with the Harlequin Temptation guidelines which specify a "mature" heroine, "doing work she cares about" with "a strong sense of her own individuality" (1). More important, in our present context, *Dreams* provides yet another example of fiction which manipulates the present to valorize the past, which seems to celebrate the "new" woman when, in fact, it undermines her. Certainly, in these novels, Krentz's explicit comparison of the grotto of the Chained Lady Cave and the "grotto" between Diana's legs (*Part II,* 27) suggests that woman's sexuality—in this novel appropriated by the hero—constitutes her destiny, a relic of past cultural ideology that must be discarded rather than repeated.

In the end, it cannot be acceptable for writers to reinforce negative behaviors toward and destructive stereotypes about women, even with the legitimate ends of creating compelling popular escapist literature. Despite the perils of the modern landscape for women—in a world where violence and inequality, infidelity, and low social status still exist—the present era has witnessed progress. All women, even wives, now have the right to say "no." They have unprecedented opportunities for meaningful work. They can choose whether and when to be mothers and expect child-rearing to be a shared parental responsibility. And they can anticipate being equal partners in sex and marriage. Or, at the very least, women are well along on the journey to a time and place where we can make these assertions with confidence. As readers, we cannot permit ourselves nostalgia for a non-existent, idealized past which obscures centuries-old injustices to women. Nor can we take for granted the strides contemporary women have made and what it has cost them. The fiction we read and the kinds of worlds in which we envision ourselves must embrace not the past we have outgrown, but the present we must be ever vigilant of, and the future we hope to create.

Notes

1. In the short time since Linz's article was penned, the romance market has experienced an even greater proliferation of subgenres. Most interesting among these subgenres are those which feature mer-people, vampires, and a variety of ghosts and angels as heroes or heroines. Silhouette Shadows is regularly printing two titles a month with a variety of occult-like themes.

2. Among the almost fifty titles I examined for this study, only Constance O'Day-Flannery's *This Time, Forever* was a straightforward time-travel story in which a heroine traveled forward into the present. Interestingly, Love Spell's "Timeswept Romance" series includes only narratives in which modern-day women travel back in time. And, in the 1989 *Romantic Times* editor's note I have cited elsewhere, we find this advice to a prospective writer of a time-travel story: "Don't get overwhelmed planning one. Actually, you would be writing the usual historical novel, with the first (and/or) last chapter in the present day" (57, 59).

3. One feature which is common to many romance novels, especially those which espouse more conservative roles for women, is the heroine's fondness for traditional architecture, furniture, crafts, and the like.

4. Ironically, it is the discovery of this same truth which causes Joan Foster, the heroine of Margaret Atwood's *Lady Oracle*, to reject her career as a closet romance writer. Once she understands that in the costume gothic—as in

life—the heroes are actually the villains, the escapist appeal of romance fiction and her ability to write it are lost to her.

Works Consulted

Primary Sources

Alsobrook, Rosalyn. *Time Storm.* New York: Windsor, Pinnacle, 1993.

Atwood, Margaret. *Lady Oracle.* New York: Avon, 1976.

Bennett, Janice. *A Timely Affair.* New York: Kensington, Zebra, 1990.

Bennett, Laura Gilmour. *By All That Is Sacred.* New York: Avon, 1991.

Bonds, Parris Afton. *For All Time.* New York: Harper, 1992.

Bretton, Barbara. *Somewhere in Time.* Toronto: Harlequin, 1992.

Daniel, Megan. *All the Time We Need.* New York: Love Spell, 1993.

Deveraux, Jude. *A Knight in Shining Armor.* New York: Pocket, 1989.

Erskine, Barbara. *Lady of Hay.* New York: Dell, 1986.

Estrada, Rita Clay. *The Ivory Key.* Toronto: Harlequin Temptation, 1987.

Fetzer, Amy J. *My Timeswept Heart.* New York: Kensington, Zebra, 1993.

Flanders, Rebecca. *Yesterday Comes Tomorrow.* Toronto: Harlequin, 1992.

Forest, Regan. *Bridge across Forever.* Toronto: Silhouette Shadows, 1993.

Gabaldon, Diana. *Outlander.* New York: Dell, 1991.

Graham, Heather. *Every Time I Love You.* New York: Dell, 1988.

Harper, Madeline. *This Time Forever.* Toronto: Harlequin Temptation, 1989.

Knight-Jenkins, Vivian. *Passion's Timeless Hour.* New York: Leisure, 1992.

Krentz, Jayne Ann. *Dreams, Part 1.* Toronto: Harlequin Temptation, 1988.

——. *Dreams, Part 2.* Toronto: Harlequin Temptation, 1988.

Marten, Jacqueline. *Bryarly.* New York: Pocket, 1981.

——. *Dream Walker.* New York: Pocket, 1987.

Michaels, Kasey. *Out of the Blue.* New York: Dell, 1992.

Miller, Linda Lael. *Here and Then.* New York: Silhouette Special Edition, 1992.

——. *There and Now.* New York: Silhouette Special Edition, 1992.

Neri, Penelope. *Forever and Beyond.* New York: Kensington, Zebra, 1990.

O'Day-Flannery, Constance. *This Time, Forever.* New York: Kensington, Zebra, 1990.

——. *A Time for Love.* New York: Kensington, Zebra, 1991.

——. *Time-Kept Promises.* New York: Kensington, Zebra, 1988.

——. *Time-Kissed Destiny.* New York: Kensington, Zebra, 1987.

——. *Timeless Passion.* New York: Kensington, Zebra, 1986.

——. *Timeswept Lovers.* New York: Kensington, Zebra, 1987.

Riley, Eugenia. *Tempest in Time.* New York: Leisure, 1993.

——. *A Tryst in Time.* New York: Leisure, 1992.

Ring, Thomasina. *Time-Spun Rapture*. New York: Leisure, 1990.

———. *Time-Spun Treasures*. New York: Leisure, 1992.

Roberts, Nora. *Time Was*. New York: Silhouette Intimate Moments, 1989.

———. *Times Change*. New York: Silhouette Intimate Moments, 1990.

Shiplett, June Lund. *Journey to Yesterday*. New York: Signet, 1979.

———. *Return to Yesterday*. New York: Signet, 1983.

Simon, Jo Ann. *Hold Fast to Love*. New York: Avon, 1982.

———. *Love Once Again*. New York: Avon, 1982.

———. *Love Once in Passing*. New York: Avon, 1981.

Simpson, Carla. *Always, My Love*. New York: Windsor, Pinnacle, 1990.

———. *Memory and Desire*. New York: Kensington, Zebra, 1988.

Simpson, Pamela. *Partners in Time*. New York: Bantam, 1990.

Small, Bertrice. *A Moment in Time*. New York: Ballantine, 1991.

Speer, Flora. *A Time to Love Again*. New York: Love Spell, 1993.

Stevenson, Robin, and Tom Blade. *Switchback*. New York: Pinnacle, 1988.

Stewardson, Dawn. *Blue Moon*. Toronto: Harlequin Superromance, 1989.

———. *Moon Shadow*. Toronto: Harlequin Superromance, 1991.

———. *Timeless Love*. New York: Avon, 1993.

———. *A Time-Travel Christmas*. New York: Love Spell, 1993.

Weyrich, Becky Lee. *Sweet Forever*. New York: Pinnacle, 1992.

Secondary Sources

"Editorial Guidelines." Harlequin, 1988.

Fallon, Eileen. *Words of Love: A Complete Guide to Romance Fiction*. New York: Garland, 1984.

Frenier, Mariam Darce. *Good-bye Heathcliff*. New York: Greenwood, 1988.

Krentz, Jayne Ann. "Introduction." *Dangerous Men and Adventurous Women: Romance Writers on the Appeal of the Romance*. Philadelphia: U of Pennsylvania P, 1992. 1-8.

Linz, Cathie. "Setting the Stage: Facts and Figures." *Dangerous Men and Adventurous Women: Romance Writers on the Appeal of the Romance*. Philadelphia: U of Pennsylvania P, 1992. 11-13.

Modleski, Tania. *Loving with a Vengeance: Mass Produced Fantasies for Women*. New York: Metheun, 1982.

Mussell, Kay. *Women's Gothic and Romantic Fiction: A Reference Guide*. Westport, CT: Greenwood, 1981.

Phillips, Susan Elizabeth. "The Romance and the Empowerment of Women." *Dangerous Men and Adventurous Women: Romance Writers on the Appeal of the Romance*. Philadelphia: U of Pennsylvania P, 1992. 53-58.

Radway, Janice. *Reading the Romance: Women, Patriarchy, and Popular Literature*. Chapel Hill, NC: U of North Carolina P, 1984.

Romantic Times 64 (June/July 1989): 57, 59.

Seidel, Kathleen Gilles. "Judge Me by the Joy I Bring." *Dangerous Men and Adventurous Women: Romance Writers on the Appeal of the Romance.* Philadelphia: U of Pennsylvania P, 1992. 159-79.

Thurston, Carol. *The Romance Revolution: Erotic Novels for Women and the Quest for a New Sexual Identity.* Urbana, IL: U of Illinois P, 1987.

Leading Us into Temptation:
The Language of Sex and the Power of Love

Rosemary E. Johnson-Kurek

During a workshop for gifted high school students, I brought into the classroom eighty Harlequin novels—spanning three decades—for a unit on cover art. Afterward, I told the students they could have the books. I had not read many Harlequins myself, so I asked the young women, as they sorted through the books, to tell me about them. In the midst of simultaneous answers, I heard a plaintive request: "Don't you have any Temptations?" I had the Romance, Presents, American, and Intrigue lines, but no Temptations. When I inquired about that particular line, I was told "They're the hottest."

"The *hottest*!?!" I mused silently. That meant the others were hot and hotter! Had I pandered to the prurient interests of overactive, albeit gifted, libidos? Were parents going to discover these books and demand to know from whence they came? I figured there would be no repercussions because the young women were not going to flagrantly peruse these books if their parents might object.

As an *avid* reader of romances I was a late bloomer. This is not to say I hadn't read romances; I had. These students merely piqued my interest again, so I followed their advice: I read Temptations. I had read two books without realizing they were originally Temptations: LaVyrle Spencer's *Spring Fancy* (#1) and Judith McNaught's *Double Standards* (#16). While Spencer's and McNaught's Temptation titles were limited to these, bestselling authors Barbara Delinsky and Jayne Ann Krentz were early, prolific, and significant contributors whose single titles and mini-series helped shape the line and stretch the parameters of the genre. The Temptation line, which began in 1984, issues four titles a month; I have read nearly seven hundred.

The Temptation writers represent many voices speaking to women's attitudes toward, and experiences with, men, women's roles, work, values, and sex. The attitudes expressed are myriad, and reflect many gradations of both feminine and feminist thinking. It seems logical that the word feminist would be used in a romance. After all, the heroines, writers, and readers are women.

In *Playboy McCoy,* the heroine is not quite sure how she feels about the hero calling her "sugar." She tells him: "'[S]ome people would consider referring to a woman as a granulated sweetener demeaning. Or . . . demoralizing.'" The hero, a history professor, asks, "'You're not going to turn militant feminist on me are you?'" (Sanders 102).

When the private eye hero of *Passion and Scandal* asks the heroine—a client he mistakenly thinks is the new secretary—to get them both some coffee, she repeats his request as a question. "'You want me . . . to get you coffee?'" He comes back with, "'It's just a lousy cup of coffee, not an attack on modern feminist principles'" (21), and promises to get the coffee the next time (Schuler 22).

When the heroine in *The Stormchaser* corrects the hero when he calls her Mrs. Conrad, he silently muses, "Another feminist," apologizes for his presumption and eventually asks her why she prefers the term Ms. (11). Temptation heroines and heroes often use Ms. as a form of address, but this widowed heroine clearly explains why: "'The Ms. means that whether I have a man in my life or not, I deal with my own problems and make my own solutions'" (Estrada 21).

The heroine of *Private Passions,* a television news reporter and writer of women's erotica, confronts the issues of political incorrectness: "[T]he theme of the tale is the heroine getting a fantasy man to do what she wants, while outwardly seeming to be forced to do what he wants . . . [so she may] remain blameless for her most secret, politically incorrect desires" (Ross 92).

Temptation stories may be serious or madcap, heartwrenching or lighthearted, realistic or pure fantasy; however, there is a common thread. According to an Editor's note in Temptation's earliest books, Harlequin, in response to reader demands, "creat[ed] this new, more sensuous series." Early advertisement inserts promoting the series contain the following copy:

A word of warning to our regular readers:
While Harlequin books are always in good taste, you'll find more sensuous writing in *Harlequin Temptation* than in other Harlequin romance series. (1984)

A literary warning? In 1997, the line created *Blaze*—"bold, provocative, *ultrasexy* books"—a Temptation miniseries with the cover blurb "Red-hot reads . . ." Perhaps the "more sensuous" nature of the first Temptations was deemed too mild, but I cannot discern a real difference between Blaze books and other Temptations.

Since I was late to the gate so to speak, there were substantial numbers of Temptations already published. Because I was able to read many in rapid succession it was easy to notice behavioral patterns of social intercourse and language patterns of sexual intercourse. It wasn't long before I was limited to four Temptations a month like every other reader. Shortly after delving into the earliest books, I started wondering why high school girls could overtly buy these books, but high school boys could only covertly obtain copies of *Playboy*. The first and foremost answer is that no individual has been compromised by posing naked. Our culture does not condone the adolescent consumption of erotic photography. The printed word, however, if not crude or degrading, is more acceptable. Temptations reflect a variety of both complex and simple relationships, but each contains sufficiently explicit descriptions of foreplay and intercourse to make it a how-to book of sorts.

Fantasy games (Danson, *Ranger Man*) and mutually agreed upon bondage (White, *Forbidden Fantasy*) are not outside Temptation's bounds. Rita Clay Estrada's *The Ivory Key* broke new ground for the line in 1987 detailing the love life of a ghost hero. Now, in addition to ghosts, Temptation storylines also include aliens (Delinsky, *The Outsider;* Ross, *Star-Crossed Lovers;* Rush, *Kiss of the Beast*), time travelers (Rolofson, *The Cowboy,* and Cresswell, *Midnight Fantasy*), angels (Ross, *Angel of Desire,* and Ellis, *Michael's Angel*), a vampire (Michaels, *Nightwing*) and even a wood sprite and a wizard (Dean, *Mad about You*).

Ultimately *Love Slave* (Rush) prompted me to consider why some erotica is relegated to adult book stores. One can feel censorious about sensuous romances. Such books have been censured at certain times and in certain places; however, widespread availability is the norm. Second only to a storyline that is pure in motive because of the element of love, it is the code of euphemistic language that enables romances to be readily available in grocery stores, drug stores, and libraries. Conventionally understood euphemisms—neither vulgar or crude, nor clinical—are a definitive aspect of the romance genre and critical in the maintenance of the balance between esthetic and erotic sensitivities.

The entire genre has prospered in—as well as slapped—the face of literary denigration at many levels. While a sweet romance may be dismissively maligned as insipid, a sensuous romance is more apt to be dismissed for catering to concupiscence. The heroine of Lass Small's *Collaboration* is a romance writer who is morally outraged at the morally outraged who dismiss romance as trash: " 'To call a romance a sex book is like calling a body "arms." Arms are a part of the body. Sex is a part of romance' " (25).

Writing about sex requires writing about the body. Writing about the body requires writing about body parts, which requires, if not explicit language, then at least euphemistically explicit language. Breasts, bosoms, and buttocks are widely used and acceptable terms; however, euphemisms prevail in naming genitalia.

Both the words penis and clitoris have been used in Temptations, but their use is comparatively rare. In fact, an angel is one of the few Temptation heroines to literally have a clitoris (Ross, *Angel of Desire*).

In *Kiss of the Beast* (Rush) Urich, the alien beast-man hero, is sent to earth to find a suitable mate for his father, who is also the leader of his race. His mission is imperative: his race is threatened by extinction, and his father, Zar, is one of the last aliens capable of siring offspring. Unfortunately, the sterile Urich falls in love with the pre-selected female earthling and, of course, she with him. Urich is to be executed for this treasonous infraction when the heroine, scientist Eva Campbell, agrees to mate with Zar in order to save Urich's life. Her goading words unman Zar, " 'C'mon, what're you waiting for? Put your penis in my vagina, do what it takes to ejaculate, and we're done. Her deliberately clinical summation got the right reaction. Zar flushed as he covered his straining crotch with folded hands' " (209). The terminology she uses reduces the act to passionless biological procreation. Euphemisms may function as a means of transcending biology, of transforming intercourse: mating becomes making love. A case could also be made that it is a matter of perceived indelicacy to call genitalia by their clinical nomenclature; most slang terms are taboo for this same reason.

Contemporary category romances generally stay away from slang terms. Avoiding these and other clinical or crude language creates an additional literary challenge: euphemisms are needed to provide variety in language. In the context of sensuous historical romance what could be thought crude may seem quaint: manroot and staff, for example. Although a term may be medieval in origin, contemporary perceptions may not be that it is quaint; thus, its use is limited. Patricia Ryan's use of "cock" in the narrative of her 1997 release *Twice the Spice* (165) seems neither shocking nor vulgar, but it remains to be seen whether this was groundbreaking or a singular instance. For the most part, the language in romances in general seems to deny that Erica Jong ever wrote *Fear of Flying* in the early seventies.

Euphemistic terminology which is not perceived as crude—the family jewels, for instance—is reserved for dialogue outside love scenes. One heroine, a bestselling author, in telling her friend about her first meeting with the hero, wonders what she would have done had he turned out to be just like the man he had rescued her from. Her friend replies:

"'You'd have kneed him in the jewels just like Desiree did to that creep in *March in Madrid*'" (Sinclair 26). There is one Temptation hero whose "magic wand stirred to life" (Arnold 90). Another has nicknamed his penis, Charlie (Denison 54). The hero in *A Hard-Hearted Hero,* while contemplating the heroine's form is worried that "pitching a tent" will interfere with the blood flow he needs for the task at hand—lifting weights (Burford 103). These kinds of euphemisms tend toward humor and are usually not used in intimate scenes, most likely because they might change the tone. Both historical and contemporary romances often use, or perhaps misuse, maleness, manhood and masculinity—not to describe the character of the hero, but to euphemize his penis. In *Awake unto Me* the hero's "hard maleness throbbed against" the heroine (Joyce 195). McNaught's hero holds the heroine against his body "making her forcefully aware of his hardened manhood" (141). Is that the same thing as a hardened man?

"Anatomy is destiny" in the evolution of the euphemism. Because women's genitalia are perceived to be hidden and more internal than external, heroines are more often described as *having* a core of femininity and thus are more often portrayed as being in possession of their genitalia: that is, their genitalia are part of them. This seems natural because the heroine's uterus and vagina are inside of her: "Laurel's body responded with a warmth that fanned outward from the innermost female parts of her" (Sanders, *Playboy* 118). This possessiveness of genitalia by women is even culturally demonstrated in the notion that chastity, if not actual virginity, must be protected, or at least not given up too freely. Even post-virgins, and the majority of the Temptation heroines fall into that category, do not readily give up this possession, even though, according to the hero in *Double Standards:* "'Men don't prize virginity anymore. . . . We're liberated too, you know'" (87).

The case that men possess their penises is not as strongly made, but it is not unheard of: "Desire burned deep in his core" (Hoffmann, *Wicked Ways* 69). In many cultures the possessiveness women have of their sexual organs has not traditionally been expected of men. A man's penis is external and apparent when aroused: "She took pleasure in the fact that he couldn't hide his need for her" (Estrada, *Time* 27). In *Gypsy,* Glenda Sanders writes: "By nature's design a man wore his need on the outside, blatant and imposing, while a woman's need was hidden away inside, subtler, deeper, less easily defined" (121).

In *Wedding Song,* the hero tells the heroine: "I love that about women. You can have your private little fireworks and practically nothing shows." He says this to the heroine in the back of a limousine after having "pleasured her with deft fingers." His complaint is that men's state of arousal and their orgasms are more overt than women's. After stating his case he says, "'Women have all the luck'" (Thompson 147). The heroine responds: "'And men have all the monuments. . . . dedicated to that certain male idiosyncrasy. . . . the Washington Monument, the Eiffel Tower, the Leaning Tower of Pisa, the Seattle Space Needle. . . . Why, the Empire State Building is a clear representation of—'" (147-48).

In general, the external genitalia of women are not perceived to be symbolic like men's; there is not even a popular term associated with it. Unlike phallic symbol, the term vulvaic symbol is not part of our popular vernacular; however, labial imagery, a la Georgia O'Keefe, is acknowledged. Two of JoAnn Ross's Temptation heroes use rose petal similes (*Roarke* 162 and *Ambushed* 187). A likely candidate for the feminine counterpart to the Empire State Building might be the Holland Tunnel, a vaginal symbol. It is hidden, dark, cavernous and one could feel lost in it: "He wondered if she was aware of how much he longed to drag her into his arms and lose himself inside her" (James 176). "His overwhelming instinct was . . . to lose himself in her" (McWilliams 138). "He wanted to be a part of her, he wanted to lose himself inside her" (Ryan, *Return* 166). In the above examples the heroes aspire to losing themselves; however, one hero acknowledges possible negative ramifications involved in the same act: "Alec had never been so tempted to lose himself in a woman" (Logan 68). Losing himself might be tantamount to surrendering his emotional being to the heroine and not simply limited to having great sex.

As mentioned earlier, the terms maleness, manhood, and masculinity are frequently substituted for penis. Aren't maleness and masculinity culturally defined concepts of characteristics of behavior and appearance? Doesn't a boy demonstrate that he has grown into manhood—a state of maturity—when he exhibits characteristics of male adulthood?

Positive descriptors of manhood are embedded in the Temptation texts: "The characteristics of his sex—strength, power, solidity, warmth —emanated from him . . ." (Sanders, *Gypsy* 58). Culturally defined aspects of manhood also include:

[H]is pa'd taught him what it took to be a man. A man did his duty, no matter the cost. A man was honest and brave and fair, and he took care of those weaker than himself. (Dale 37)

There was a remote, reserved aura about him. . . . It hinted at strength and willpower. . . . Not bad qualities in a man. (Krentz, *Alliance* 7)

I grew up havin' it drummed into me that a man ought to do some good in the world, make a difference. (Ryan, *Spice* 158)

Virility is a less common euphemism than manhood, but it is used: "Her mind-stealing glimpse of his virility left her in no doubt of his masculine endowments" (James 179). Since virility is a state of masculine potency, its euphemistic application probably doesn't require the additional modifier, hardened. According to the hero in Kaiser's *The Texan:* "[T]here's nothing as pathetic as a man with his pants off. . . . Unless, of course, he has amorous intentions and means to prove his manhood" (156-57). In standard English, virility, manhood, and masculinity are generally used as defined, not concrete concepts: manhood cannot be manhandled or womanhandled.

A brief reflection on the story of the Bobbits can illustrate the differences between defined and concrete concepts and how manhood and masculinity can function as both standard terms and cultural euphemisms. Generally, when a man is emasculated or unmanned, his manhood is called into question. Whether John Wayne Bobbit had/has grown into manhood has been publicly debated, but he had characteristics that attested to his masculinity. Even though Lorena attempted to rob John of his *manhood,* his *masculinity,* she did not kill the man, thus even prior to his reconstructive surgery, he still possessed qualities of masculinity. Lorena did toss some of his virility out the car window; however, while John's procreative powers were definitely resting along the side of the road for a time, was his masculine spirit languishing there as well? Was the search team cautioned to step carefully so as to reduce the risk of delivering a crushing blow to his manhood?

The use of manhood, masculinity, and virility to name the penis rather than to describe states of being or characteristics can be distracting, but the use of the personal pronouns—me, he, him, himself—to signify this body part can be downright confusing. The seemingly unavoidable use of these pronouns is a more curious euphemistic practice because it equates the man's penis with the man himself, and thus may create additional, perhaps unintended, imagery for the reader or perhaps even alter a sentence's meaning. The Bobbit case is applicable here as well. "Himself" in the statement "John Wayne Bobbit was beside himself on the operating table" has both an idiomatic and euphemistic meaning. I imagine he was upset as the surgeons prepared to reattach him to himself. The following passages illustrate both the possessiveness of genitalia/body by women and the substitution of the word "himself" for penis:

He pushed her back against the mound of pillows and in one smooth motion buried himself in her eagerly accepting body. (Alexander 169)

He pushed himself through her fingers, seeking the more satisfying warmth and tightness of her body. Heather gasped as he probed the entrance to her throbbing feminine core. (Krentz, *Destiny* 100)

Himself in the above examples clearly means penis and is such a common euphemism that most readers would probably not conjure any additional imagery; however, isn't it physically impossible for a man to push through a woman's fingers or to become buried inside her?

Another euphemistic term often used is *burying*. The hero's act of burying himself is somewhat akin to the act of losing himself inside the heroine. Sometimes the hero wants to bury himself in the heroine, sometimes he wants to bury himself *into* her: "A few more thrusts and he joined her, burying himself into her over and over again" (Rolofson, *Honeymoon* 167). Where did he join her? "Nick plunged full-length into her, burying himself into her welcoming softness" (McNaught 85). Full-length? A man, generally, doesn't bury into something; however, he might burrow into something with a *tool*.

The use of personal pronouns as euphemisms for the penis can have an odd effect. In *The Last Great Affair,* Kristine Rolofson writes: "She took *him* [emphasis mine] between her hands and stroked *its* [emphasis mine] hard, satin length until *he* groaned with pleasure" (153). Don't we have a problem with agreement between pronouns, possessives, and their antecedents? Is *its* a part of *him*? Is it his or is he it? Again, figurative and/or literal meaning is at issue. A hero who exposes himself may be emotionally open, thus vulnerable to the heroine; or he may be flashing passers-by and vulnerable to arrest.

Another Rolofson title, *The Cowboy,* contains a similar passage. It is a euphemistic companion to the one cited above:

He groaned, threw his head back and swore . . . He felt like hard satin as he swelled in her hand. She wrapped her fingers around him and brought her lips to the tip of his hard flesh. She heard him groan again, and tentatively took him in her mouth. It was an act she had avoided until now, an act she'd found no pleasure in trying, but . . . she wanted to . . . take him into her mouth and feel that soft flesh against her tongue. (174)

Questions: Is the tip of his *hard flesh* the top of his head? Or rather his cranium? If she's not nibbling on the *soft flesh* of his earlobe at passage's end, then what is going on? Finally, does a penis groan?

Sometimes the use of personal pronoun euphemisms might confuse the reader. A passage in *A Wanted Man* illustrates this. First, the hero says to the heroine, "'Touch me'" (Forest 136). The reader might initially thinks he means his person. She touches his abdomen and chest and her hand "travels lower." He says "'Don't stop. . . . Kiss me . . .'" (137). She responds by kissing his eyelids and mouth. He says, "'I meant . . .'" (he does not say what he means) to which she responds "'I know what you meant." He questions her, "'Will you?'" and she responds "'Yes. . . . Close your eyes . . .'" (137). Apparently me = him = it: he wants her to kiss it/him, that is, his penis. That the heroine requests that he close his eyes holds interesting implications: she does not want him to watch her kiss him/it.

The next action to be described is of his fingers tangling in her hair and his thighs trembling. Those actions are followed by this section:

His body fought to release the unbearable tension soaring and diving within him. He fought so, writhed so, tearing at the sheets, that Beth became alarmed.

"No . . . don't stop . . ." he pleaded. "Don't let *me* [emphasis mine] go. . . ."

She stayed with *him* [emphasis mine] until his groan filled the quiet of the room, and even longer, until *he* [emphasis mine] lay still again. (137)

What is going on in the above passage? It depends on what the pronouns *me, him* and *he* mean at any given time.

When he puts his arms around her and holds her, his last words, "'Don't let me go,'" reverberate in her ears. The heroine then muses: "She hadn't [let him go] then; she wouldn't now. Not if she could help it. Unless he chose to leave her or unless forces more powerful than both of them took Kirk away from her, she'd never let *him* go! She loved *him*" (138).

This passage has enough imagery variables to give a reader pause, as does this next example. In *Passion and Scandal,* the heroine "wrapped her fingers around him in blatant demand, leaning backward to pull him down on top of her" (Schuler 174). If you have him by his manhood, his heart and mind will surely follow.

In *An Intimate Oasis,* the fully clothed heroine sinks to her knees in front of the fully clothed hero. "Now that she was on her knees she could touch him in a way she hadn't before; he couldn't stop her. She wrapped her arms around him and pressed her face to the force that announced his own aching need. What you love, you kiss. Holly kissed him" (Victor 99).

Perhaps a passage in *Star Ride* is the best illustration of when "him" truly means penis; then again, perhaps it is merely a matter of style. The heroine and hero are engaged in sexual intercourse . . . that is to say, *he is inside her:* "Only then did he allow the movements of him within her carry her over the edge . . ." (Cameron 169). The sentence could have been written differently, eliminating *him,* so that *he* clearly means the man, not his penis: "Only then did he allow his movements within her to carry her over the edge." *His* in this case is possessive of movements and means the movements of his person and all connected parts, all extensions of him.

Do the personal pronoun euphemisms reflect women's own attitudes toward men, signify acceptance of the male identification of self with penis, or are they simple word replacements? I don't know. I suppose it could be argued that the use of personal pronouns euphemizes the penis to the point of sexual objectification of the man. Does it beg the question whether a man is his genitalia? When a man is called the equivalent of a penis in crude slang it is not a compliment. It could also be argued that equating he/him with penis is a near equivalent of a misandric joke. "What is the definition of a man? A life support system for a penis."

Patricia Ryan addresses this very issue of objectification in *Twice the Spice* from the hero's point of view. The heroine assumes her identical twin's sexier, more worldly persona which leads the hero to believe she is sexually experienced. Twice she fails to inform him of her virginity. Just short of breaching her maidenhead, the hero asks why she would want to be deflowered by a man she hasn't known long. She stumbles through a near explanation with: "'I'm going to be thirty soon and . . . I just . . . I felt like I was missing out on something . . .'" He accuses her of using him "'to get rid of an unwanted hymen'" and unapologetically continues: "'Sorry I didn't finish the job. Maybe you can place an ad in the *Village Voice*—Wanted, one erect penis. Man optional'" (142).

Even when a man is not his penis, his body may be. "This time when his body slipped inside her, it was with great tenderness" (Spencer 193). "Max poised himself above Emma and entered her with his body" (Liholm 131). For some these passages might conjure up a vision of Tom Thumb sheathed in a condom, but for others it is more a matter of a body part signifying the whole man.

The hero in Tori Carrington's *Constant Craving* offers one explanation for the dilemma of this dichotomy of masculinity, or why the hero is sometimes equated with his penis: "[Her] fingers curled around his erection. Holding tight. Making him feel that everything that was him resided there and was hers for the taking" (prepublication manuscript 152). This is not a woman's point of view of what a man's point of view might or even should be. These particular lines were written by the male half of the husband and wife writing team of Lori and Tony Karayianni. The heroine in Susan Liepitz's *That Wilder Man* expresses similar thoughts from the heroine's perspective: "Sheathing him to the full depth of her feminine core, Elizabeth felt as if his entire being had entered her body" (215).

Note that his entire being enters "her body" and not simply "her." Euphemistic pronoun confusion may be somewhat reduced for heroines because English has three masculine, but only two feminine pronouns. *Her* does double duty for objective and possessive case (e.g., She pleased him when he entered her body and made her his). This may account for some of the gender differences apparent in intimate scenes. Use of *her* in the objective case may create a feeling that a sentence is somehow incomplete, as if the word has the will to insist on being used in the possessive. The differences are most apparent when the couple can no longer keep their hands off each other. It is fairly clear what is happening when she cups him with her hand, but the same cannot be said when he cups her. The tendency is to follow up with breasts, mound, or derriere. Even when the meaning is obvious, *her* may still beg for an object. She may use her fingers to encircle him, but he rarely uses his fingers to part her: he parts her feminine folds.

Perhaps it is not the struggle to avoid using certain words, nor the need to vary language, but anatomy itself that directs the evolution and use of euphemisms. The penis is, literally, an extension of man. The uterus and ovaries are not extensions of wom(b)an; breasts are and, as such, it is conventional for breasts to often receive the same pronoun treatment as the penis. For example, "she pulled . . . his briefs down and he sprang free" (Denison, *Pleasure* 155) is similar to "he unhooked her bra, freeing her" (Liholm 128). Of course, a man is not his penis and a woman is not her breasts. While the hero in Ryan's *Twice the Spice* is upset about the possibility that the heroine values him more as a penis than as a man, the situation in Rita Clay Estrada's *Dreams* is more a matter of the heroine's amusement. After the hero bares the heroine's breasts, "he stared with unabashed desire. 'My God, you're beautiful.' The heroine chides him with the rebuff: "'Look at all of me when you say that. . . . Or don't say it at all" (106).

Perhaps using the language in this manner developed because gender extensions *project* the apparent differences independent of cultural practices (e.g., hairstyle, or clothing). These very body parts often strain against clothing, asserting gender identity. Examples of this would include "[T]he fleshy mound straining against the stretchy elastic of her bra" (Verge 162); and "His pale boxers did nothing to hide his fabric straining erection" (Bond 169).

The masculine gender extension, sometimes euphemistically referred to as "his virility," may have a power, a potency, beyond reproductive potency. Julianna Valderian, the Sarnian heroine of the science fiction fantasy *Moonstruck Lovers* is an avowed feminist working in the field of cultural anthropology. She observes:

I'm sick of being a second-class citizen on my own planet. And I'm fed up with males strutting around as if they own the galaxy, simply because they happened to be born with their sex organs on the outside of their bodies, rather than the inside. (Ross 161)

Jennifer Crusie devotes several pages to the issue of gender extensions. The couple meet when Mae hires Mitch, a private investigator, to look into her uncle's death. They have just met with her deceased uncle's mistress when Mae raises the issue of male infidelity. Mitch puts forth his theory that men cheat because of a biological imperative. Mae responds, "'This would be testosterone we're talking about here, right?'" Mitch explains that testosterone is only part of it: the other part is a man's need for adventure, and discovery. He continues his explanation with a hypothetical case: "'[F]or the sake of argument, let's say I'm married.'" His scenario wife is a beautiful, intelligent, exciting woman with perfect breasts, but this biological imperative creates an urge in him to personally see another pair of breasts. Mae's witty commentary and requests for clarification along with Mitch's droll, continuing explication of his theory ultimately lead to the following:

"Men need multiple breasts in their lives and women need to commit to one penis."

"That is garbage," Mae said flatly.

"Then why do women always want to get married? Because they want to commit to a penis."

"Then why do men get married?"

"For backup. That way they always have a set of breasts at home."

Mae picked up her purse, using every ounce of self-control to keep herself from hitting him with it. "Stop the car, I'm getting out."

Mitch blinked at her in alarm. "Why?"

"There's a man on the corner back there, and I think his penis is bigger than yours." (Crusie, *Lady Wants* 69)

Gender extensions, because they are more obvious, also function as arousal meters. In *The Drifter* the naked hero is talking on the phone and the cord is stretched across the heroine's breasts.

With a little smile he eased the cord back and forth across her nipples, which snapped to attention at the casual contact. How easily he demonstrated his power over her. She would have resented that power if she hadn't glanced down and noticed his penis stir and gradually stiffen as he gazed at her breasts. (Thompson 176)

Mac, the time traveling hero from the future in *Midnight Fantasy* arrives in the twentieth century wearing the apparel of his day, permapel, a silver, spray-on body covering, which he realizes is too shocking for the people in the past. Mac, in an attempt to blend in and appear less naked, dons a pink ruffled blouse and some flowered pants he has lifted from a clothesline. After Ariel, the heroine, informs him that, " 'Flowers and frills signal that the person wearing them is a woman,' " Mac replies:

"Are you suggesting that without flowers and ruffles to designate a female wearer, the citizens of your time could not distinguish between a man and a woman? There are surely many visible differences that fabric does not conceal. For example, a man does not have enlarged breasts, suitable for the suckling of infants and a woman does not have a pen—" (Cresswell 53)

Ariel interjects with " 'For heaven's sake! Of course we can tell the difference,' " before the author completely pens penis. It is somewhat interesting that Mac is defining the genders based on the absence of extensions —that which one gender is lacking and the opposite gender possesses.

One cannot put the issue of gender extensions to rest without at least mentioning the issue of size. There is a certain esthetic parameter related to gender extensions that, while not well defined, does suggest that there is a certain preferable size range. Chase, the proud father of an infant son, comments, " 'Pretty impressive equipment, Bart,' " to which the boy's mother responds, " 'As if that's the measure of a man.' " Chase answers her rebuff: " 'Hey, it's a start. . . . Don't let her kid you, Bart old buddy. They all say they don't care about size and pretend it's our hang-up. But I've seen *Playgirl* magazine. They care' " (Thompson, *Drifter* 169). The hero in *Timeless Love,* in contemplating the heroine's gender extensions, muses:

She wasn't even his type. He'd always been partial to . . . macromammaries. . . . How could he be thinking of Hope in sexual terms? Even worse, how could he be finding fault with her physical attributes? He was more despicable than he'd realized. (Arnold 39)

While the heroines in Temptations frequently grapple with the physical standards of sexual appeal, it is not something the heroes usually wrestle with. There is a simple reason for this, I believe: the readers and writers are women. The heroines may be exquisitely beautiful or plain, petite or tall; they may have have tiny or large breasts, thick thighs or skinny legs, a flat abdomen or stretch marks. The body curve is toward the norm, not a fantasy. The actual fantasy is that the hero loves the heroine because of, or perhaps in spite of, the shape she's in. In *The Stormchaser,* the finely built, sexy-as-sin hero, "his expression one of pure lust," gazes upon the naked body of the fortyish heroine, the widowed mother of a grown son. Under his scrutiny, she tries to cover her nakedness, but he objects and says, "'You're so sexy I want to drink it in.'" To this she responds, "'Don't make fun of me. . . . I know what I am.'" Slowly he asks, "'And what is that?'" The heroine proceeds to tell him the "litany of things" wrong with her:

> "I have heavy thighs, and stretch marks. . . . And my breasts are too small—"
>
> "Enough of that. It's a bunch of hogwash. You're beautiful, sensuous and desirable because I can see your body and I know your giving spirit. . . . All I have to do is look at you and I'm on fire."
>
> It was her turn to disagree. "No."
>
> "Yes. All the rest is just plain crap." (Estrada 142)

Stretch marks are obviously not an integral aspect of a heroine's gender identity, but neither is her womb. A woman may be sterile because her uterus and ovaries are missing, but she is still capable of sexual congress and pleasure. The heroine in *Looking Good* has had a hysterectomy, but she is not presented as having been robbed of her femininity, only her ability to reproduce:

> Finally, with a powerful surge, he filled her and Emily gasped, transfixed by his possession. For a brief second her body struggled to accept his maleness . . . . Then her muscles seemed to contract about him, and she was the one holding him captive to her femininity. (McWilliams 157)

In this instance, the heroine's femininity is being defined by sexual performance rather than reproductive potency. Only when the issue of children comes up does it become problematic to the couple's relationship. The absence of the male reproductive organs, however, affects both reproduction and performance. Perhaps this is why the language of sex is so seamless when it comes to the hero.

The testicles are often acknowledged as the seat of bravery and courage and it is an insult to accuse a man of lacking them. It is also suspected that they may be responsible for producing unmitigated gall. Having *balls* is more likely to be used to describe a hero's character than his anatomy. Male identity is so tied to the presence and performance of the genitalia that it is no wonder women writing romance might adapt a similar perspective. This happens each time a personal pronoun euphemizes the penis. Does such thinking lead to a corporal variation on "I think therefore I am: I have a penis therefore I am one?" Or perhaps "I have a penis therefore I think with it?" The heroine in *Holding Out for a Hero* tells the hero: "'Mama always said men think with their . . . male equipment'" (Thompson 53). In *Manhunting in Memphis* the heroine asks the hero to think of a solution to a particular dilemma while he is hugging and kissing her. His initial response is: "'You're asking *me* to think up something now?'" She answers in the affirmative and continues the conversation:

> "Are you thinking?"
> "Hmmm." He pressed close against her.
> "You're thinking with the wrong part of your body."
> "It has a mind of its own." (MacAllister 214)

In his *Esquire* review of "do me feminism," Tad Friend asks whether the language of "giving it to" is "a denial of female sexual authority or a recognition of basic anatomical functions" (52). Some euphemisms describing sexual intercourse may be derived from the act of intercourse and/or anatomy. Others may be derived from the culture's gender norms and may reflect what could ultimately be termed a sexist stance. The phrase Friend questions does reflect a function of anatomy, but consider the following: Can *himself* be substituted for *it* without changing the meaning? Central to this question is the general mistrust heroines seem to have of heroes; they doubt whether a man is giving *himself* to them when he is giving *it* to them. At what point does the euphemistic use of the term "him/he/himself" cease? Furthermore, if one accepts the anatomical function aspect of language then only the woman can take the man; he cannot take her.

The term *taking* is most commonly used not in the sense of anatomical function, but as a central part of the fantasy of sexual power. The hero's desire to take the heroine is often due to an unrelenting and absolute power that the woman has over the hero's mind and body. The conventional line is often literally "No other woman had affected him like this before." Following are further descriptions of the heroine's sexual power:

Why couldn't he stop thinking about her? Why did he desire her so strongly? Other women had never affected him to such an extent. They had attracted him. But they had never distracted him from his work. (Lee 78)

Other women had made him want. Other women had made him ache. But no other woman had ever made him experience this emotional and spiritual need. She was like no woman he'd ever met. (Ross, *Prince & Showgirl* 136)

Generally, the heroine is initially unaware she has this power over him; however, once she encounters his physical response to her, she revels in it. Often the heroine's sense of power is newly found; even if the heroine is not literally a virgin, she is embarking on virgin territory. After discovering she has this power over the hero, her sexual self-confidence increases: "Marvelous, she thought, exulting in a very feminine power she'd never before exercised. Her hand traveled lower, and she was rewarded by his eager reaching for her" (Cameron 140). The heroine in *Beneath a Saffron Sky* reacts similarly: "She loved having this power over Cooper's body. It was awesome in its way, and the awe drove her" (Weger 106). The hero in *Charlie All Night* tells the heroine, "'Don't mind me. . . . This is just ecstasy.'" The heroine realizes he's not kidding:

He was in ecstasy. *And I'm doing this,* she thought. She squeezed him with the muscles inside her and her heart pounded as she watched him suck in his breath. . . . She licked her lips and breathed in and thought, *God, I'm powerful. No wonder men love sex so much.* (Crusie 103)

The power the heroine has over the hero is often present in their initial meeting. Something about her—her presence, her self, her beauty, her sensuality—produces a profound and immediate reaction in *him:* "He was certainly no stranger to desire, but never had he experienced that gut-twisting hunger so instantaneously" (Collins, *Hitch* 21).

The hero often wants to take her right then and there, regardless of when or where then and there is. The heroine's sexual power is such that the hero is nearly reduced to a state of pure organic arousal. His penis takes on a life of its own. *It* becomes *him,* in more ways than one. He becomes uncomfortably hard: "'These tight jeans weren't made for trysts with you. They're killing me'" (Forest, *Lady and Dragon* 125). Conventionally, he then pulls her against his hardened length or the hardened length of him. It is not always clear whether this length is closer to six feet or six inches.

The heroine nearly unmans the hero to the point that he has a base desire—which isn't at all like him—to have sex at a premature point in the relationship. He wants to *take her* immediately and hastily, without romantic overture, in an inappropriate place: "He wanted to stride across the kitchen, push that huge teddy bear cookie jar out of the way and take her right on top of the kitchen counter" (Rafferty 89).

Anatomical function is not the basis of this language: he wants to take what hasn't been offered, often what has not as yet been contemplated by the heroine. There is a difference between wanting something and being given it, and wanting something and taking it. Even though we know the heroine will come around to the hero's way of thinking, he is generally the first to think these thoughts. When she does have the same thoughts they seldom involve inappropriate immediacy or place. But while it is rare, it is not totally unheard of: "A few more minutes alone with the man and she might . . . attack him right where he stood" (Rafferty 97).

Because the hero is a male grown into manhood, he is in control of his behavior and base desires. Because he is a gentle man/gentleman the hero is able to control his masculinity, his manhood—himself. The hero is a man who, if not actually in control of his penis, can at least control what he does with it. In *The Trouble with Tonya,* Kirk and Tonya meet at the inner city youth center where he is the director. She represents her family's philanthropic organization. He grew up on the streets of the city and views his desire to "take" Tonya in socio-economic terms:

If he hadn't used every ounce of control, he'd have . . . taken her right there on the concrete parking lot or dragged her in the building like a caveman.

He snorted. *Caveman.* That's probably what she thought he was. A woman like her was used to finesse . . . men who wore tailored suits . . . had Ivy League educations and Old Money connections, who knew how to court a woman gently. Guys like that made him want to puke. (Michaels 109)

Tonya is particularly concerned about a boy at the center who reminds her of herself when she was younger. Through her intervention, the boy is ultimately diagnosed with Attention Deficit Disorder and helped. Tonya realizes she has ADD as well and vows to get her own life under control. Ultimately, the hero who earlier wanted to take her, succumbs to her: "For the first time in his life, a woman had him completely in her power, reduced to . . . longing. He thought dreamily that there was something to be said for occasionally relinquishing control" (171).

In *This Thing Called Love* the hero, Max, also struggles with self-control. "Dammit! He wasn't an adolescent! But he'd come very close to losing control of his libido. . . . he'd wanted to take her that minute, on the floor if necessary, and hang the consequences. Such a loss of control was completely foreign to him" (Collins 50). Later in the story, when Max and Samantha finally do consummate their relationship, after he "sank at last into the cradle of her womanliness" he says to her, " 'You take me so perfectly, my only love' " (106). The hero's use of "take" in reference to anatomical function is rare.

While "take" is used in the context of the current relationship, "had" is reserved for references to past liaisons. It is not uncommon for the hero to muse that "It had been a long time since he'd had a woman." This rumination is unique to heroes; heroines might bemoan the fact that they have not been with a man for a long time, but not that they haven't had one. Attached to this masculine lament is a subliminal negative weight from the world outside of fiction. It is the kind of language men use in the company of other men. Romances conform to this practice in that the phrase is either thought by the hero, or said only to other men. This euphemism is probably not an abbreviated version of "had sex with," but an expression unto itself. Some alternate definitions for "had" would not be welcome substitutes: It had been a long time since he'd owned, embarrassed, vanquished, procured, exercised, or occupied a woman? These don't exactly imply gender equity. Entertained, held, esteemed, obliged, or regarded are more positive, but are not likely substitutes either. There are slang definitions that are equally unlikely: It had been a long time since he'd duped/conned a woman. The common meaning—possessed—is the most likely meaning. This sublimates the conventional line because possession and passion are positively aligned in romance: It had been a long time since he'd sexually possessed a woman.

The variation "he'd had other women, but none special" is also problematic. That the hero's previous women pale by comparison may seem acceptable because it is not the heroine—thus, vicariously the reader—but another faceless woman he last had. The heroine's specialness is critical in romance (it takes a special heroine to attract a special hero), but who are these faceless women?

Some of these faceless women function as whores to the heroine's madonna. The hero might think of them as recreational interludes; however, the last woman a hero had could just as easily be the brokenhearted heroine of another romance who'd been vanquished by the last man who had duped her into being had as entertainment. This would represent an ironic incorporation of the double standard in women's fiction.

Sometimes, even if only inadvertently, "faceless women" lines reinforce negative stereotypes: "Not one of the women he'd had over the years had ever come close to stimulating him beyond a sexual level" (Denison 46). Regardless of how many women he'd had, apparently they weren't very bright.

It certainly casts aspersions on the female gender when negative stereotypes involve all the women a hero has had because by presenting the heroine in opposition to all these women, she is viewed as an exception to the gender. Even one woman may have the power to destroy the gender's reputation: "Working with a woman to whom honesty and integrity were more precious than slender hips and unblemished skin could serve to renew the faith he'd once had in women—faith Lily had almost destroyed" (Leto 101).

Whenever the women in the hero's past are dull, promiscuous, greedy, vain, weak, prissy, manipulative, demanding, egocentric, vindictive, whiny, predatory, disloyal, etc., it may not be his poor taste, but gender stereotypes that are at issue. At some level, devaluing faceless women in order to elevate the heroine reinforces the mythology of divisiveness among women caused by competition for men; such conditions only feed the ego of the patriarchal macho-beast.

Heroines don't *take* or *have* because this is the language of masculine assertiveness and it is rare for heroines to be sexually assertive. Anthony Gawain, a rare Temptation hero who is literally described as figuratively in possession of *balls*—read that audacity—asks, "'Why aren't women subject to the rule of the loins, like men are?'" (White, *Naughty Talk* 120). He is suggesting that it is biology that drives men to go after women. Madeline Harper's highwayman from the past initially does not even understand the concept of female assertiveness; however, when understanding dawns on him, he welcomes the heroine's assertiveness. In this story female assertiveness is attributed to twentieth century American culture (171).

In *The Private Eye,* when Maggie, the heroine, hesitantly assertive, seeks out the hero he responds, "'[S]weetheart, you really want me, don't you? . . . It took a lot of nerve for you to come here like this'" (Krentz 131). This passage speaks to the common understanding that female assertiveness is atypical. So, is the nerve, or courage, that the heroine musters needed to overcome cultural conditioning, or an innate behavior connected to self-preservation, a sort of variation on fight or flight if you will? Maggie, "transfixed by the evidence of his arousal," realizes that he wants her as well and "The knowledge filled her with sensual assurance and a glorious feeling of her own power as a woman" (134). While Krentz's heroine notices the *evidence* of his arousal, there are other heroines who stroke, rather than stoke, the hero's arousal: arousal is another common euphemism for penis.

Jackie Weger's Temptations' heroines are unique in their assertiveness. Her rural, often backwoods, heroines are forthright and direct. *Eye of the Beholder* is a deviation from the convention of the lady-in-waiting. Phoebe is a thin, unsophisticated, and inexperienced young woman who wants Gage for a husband. Despite these traditional characteristics and her financial vulnerability, Phoebe is a very strong, liberated woman.

Phoebe acknowledges that "smart women used what was available" (63). She knows her brain is her best feature, but she feels that Gage is the type that is uninterested in brains (63). She muses: "[I]t ought to be a sin for a man to judge a woman by what she had or lacked, from nipple to thighbone. Best thing she could do was to convince Gage Morgan just how much of a sinner he was" (63). While she practices her physical wiles on him, she also tries to convince Gage she has other assets: she is smart, caring, hard working, interesting, funny, and a good homemaker who knows the value of a dollar. Although Phoebe is in dire straits, she does not want marriage in order to solve her financial dilemma. She wants Gage because she knows he is a good man; she sets out to convince him that she is a good woman. Despite the fact that he initially tells her she is too skinny for his liking, she is determined to make him hers. She also hopes to appeal to his wallet by making him realize that she is not a costly woman: "Best thing she could do was to attack Gage Morgan at his purse line. Seems like, she thought . . . everything a woman wanted and needed about a man was below his belt" (63).

Despite the fact that she is a virgin, Phoebe musters her courage and, uninvited, climbs naked into his bed. She believes he wants her even though he has not said so. The reader, being privy to Gage's thoughts, knows that he likes having her around, enjoys her company and is surprised at his growing attraction to her.

Phoebe speaks her mind in a colorful way. She is direct, unsophisticated, and unvarnished. When she encounters his erection she is astonished and says, "'Lor! . . . Gage, is that your tallywhacker?'" Weger's unconventional use of the slang euphemism is preceded by the possessive, *your*. Gage is not his penis, and Phoebe is definite about this: "It's a miracle the way the body parts work" (135). Hesitating to follow through with consummation because Phoebe is a virgin, Gage says, "'I'll hurt you.'" She counters his concern and encourages him to proceed "with ferocity against a mounting panic that she had no feminine power with which to hold him to her" (137).

Sexual power is a key factor in romances, as it is in life. A focus on male dominance, oppression and subjugation is tempting, but appropriate to a minority of Temptation texts. (Although one hero's presence in the heroine's bed is humorously referred to as "evidence of her subjugation to irrational lust" [Bond 171]). True, some of the language used to describe intercourse emphasizes aggressive masculine power. Heroes often *impale, pierce,* or *invade,* but not Roy McCoy: "McCoy joined his body with hers and there was no sense of invasion" (Sanders, *Playboy McCoy* 162).

In many Temptations it is the hero who succumbs to the heroine. As mentioned earlier, the heroine's often unknowing, but powerful sexual effect on the hero may prompt him into thinking about taking her. It may also lead him to do something he doesn't plan on, or want to do—like fall in love, commit to a relationship, or emotionally lose himself in her. This power the heroine often unwittingly wields may even cause the hero to initially feel a powerlessness where his feelings are concerned: he doesn't understand himself anymore, so he puts himself on guard against her. In most cases this kind of power is unique to the heroine in that no other woman has had this kind of influence over him. A few heroes, however, feel they are weak, or particularly susceptible when it comes to female sexual power in general: "A woman could use a man's sexual weaknesses to manipulate him, he reminded himself" (Williams 102). Or, as Remi Balfour, a medieval knight propelled into the future, puts it: "Did not Satan always use a man's lust against himself?" (Steen 33).

Temptation romances are primarily about contemporary compromise even when characters are traditional. In situations of compromise (as opposed to compromising situations) sexual power is mutually exchanged: "She pressed her palm against his rigid erection, dizzy with feminine power. Power she understood he'd willingly ceded to her" (Ross, *Prince & Showgirl* 183).

When sexual power is not mutually exchanged or acknowledged then dominance and subjugation can be involved. Some behavior and situations become problematic when one considers the possible ramifications of a romance story's potential in presenting role models of behavior. Two Temptations, *Summer Surrender* (1984), by Abra Taylor, and *The Right Direction* (1993), by Candace Schuler, speak to the issue of the impassioned hero and the reluctant heroine.

Even the title, *Summer Surrender,* implies subjugation. The virgin heroine, twenty-four-year-old Christy Sinclair, is hired for the summer to tutor the daughter of thirty-five-year-old widower, Dr. Joshua Brent. She is in his employ and living in his home while engaged to a medical student she rarely sees. The suggestion of dominance, subjugation, and sexual harassment is apparent: he is eleven years her senior and her employer.

Joshua is upset with Christy because his daughter's nanny and Christy have personal problems. He does not want his daughter upset by their failure to get along and mistakenly suspects Christy is the villainess. While sitting in a parked car, he tells her that if these problems continue he will not hesitate to fire the responsible party. He says, " 'Don't expect me to show you any quarter just because I happened . . . to kiss you . . . in a moment of weakness' " (77).

Christy, not caring for the direction of his conversation, attempts to bolt from the car, but her shoulders are "seized with compelling force" and Joshua snaps "'Don't run away when I'm speaking to you!'" (77). He yanks her backwards across the seat and she is "totally trapped": "Christy knew the situation was fraught with peril. . . . She saw the harsh set of his jaw, the tightened muscles in his throat, but it was not his anger she feared. It was simply *him*'" (78). The emphasis on *him* is not mine here and one can only wonder at its true meaning. If she is not afraid of his anger—a possible precursor to physical violence—but afraid of *him*, is she then afraid of his manhood, his masculinity—his penis?

After some angry, verbal repartee, Joshua pulls her close and stops her verbal outburst with a kiss. The punishing kiss is generally unique to the hero; however, at least one Temptation heroine indulges in the practice. Driven by a furious jealousy, Nikki grabs a handful of Carter's hair and plunges her tongue into his mouth when he gasps at her action. "Reveling in her power she changed the tenor of their kiss, caressing rather than branding. Rewarding instead of punishing" (MacAllister 119).

The nature of the punishing kiss is a phenomenon definitely open to feminist criticism. It is the intent that is important. Some punishing kisses are passionate, lip-bruising consummations: "He took her lips in a powerful, punishing kiss, pushed beyond gentleness by two days of more frustration than a man should ever have to endure" (Schuler, *Passion* 172). Joshua's kiss, however, "started in anger, a seal to stop the provocation of her words" (79). The former is physically punishing in that it is a bruising kiss; the latter is a kiss meant to punish the heroine by intimidating her.

Joshua's anger almost immediately cedes to other "more primitive instincts" and he begins to unbutton Christy's shirt. When his lips descend to her breasts she begins to think of her fiancee and the unresolved issues of her engagement. Her engagement ring serves as a painful reminder of her cognitive and emotional dissonance and she is determined not to give into Joshua. She realizes that she is "too well pinioned to fight free." She is "sandwiched into place . . . effectively trapped . . . a captive of his passion . . . only one of her hands was able to move—a small defense indeed, considering his superior strength" (80).

Before he can kiss her exposed breasts, breasts that give "traitorous evidence of desire" with nipples that "betrayed a state of high arousal" she begs him to stop. His response is "'You tell me no, but your body tells me yes. . . . You're too old to play virginal games like that'" (81).

There are layers of meaning in the above statement. First is the assumption that virginity in the post-sexual revolution era is a state no longer associated with single status: even good girls have premarital sex. Second, implicit in this statement is that virginity can be correlated with an age beyond which it is inappropriate. Third, Joshua's reference to virginal games indicates that once the hymen is broken so is the covenant of respect due a woman's preference to say no. Is virginity, or rather the hymen, a symbolic shield that alone can justify a negative response to a man's overtures?

In the case of Christy and Joshua, the assumption that she is not a virgin because she is engaged is erroneous; however, Christy does not correct him. Instead, she begs him to stop again, "but he merely manacled her wrist" with his hand and says " 'Let's see what your body says' " and begins to assault her with the "weapon of seductive gentleness" (81). He tells her, " 'How can you pretend you don't want this when I can see for myself you do?' " (81).

Christy's body betrays her. There are at least two interpretations of the betraying body. In one instance, the heroine's body is traitorous and responds to the hero's overtures thus betraying her mind and will's opposition to him. In the second instance, the heroine's body betrays her only in that it offers evidence of her arousal. For example, in *A Burning Touch,* the heroine's mind and will are in agreement with her body: "Her body betrayed her with a lightning flash of arousal. She needed him inside her. Now. Nothing else mattered" (Ryan 189). In *Summer Surrender,* Christy's traitorous body fuels Joshua's you-know-you-want-it argument which is really a rather hedonistic justification: just because a woman may be aroused doesn't mean she has to follow through with intercourse.

In the post-sexual revolution era, defining the meaning of certain sexual behaviors is the basis of much misunderstanding between the sexes. Had Christy made a behavioral agreement to proceed to intercourse without knowing it? Is "heavy petting" foreplay? That is to say, is sexual intercourse the foregone conclusion of heavy petting?

Christy rebuts Joshua's argument. She whispers "no" twice, but "her body belied her words" and so his mouth descends to her breasts. She arches toward him even as she faintly begs him to let her go (82). Finally, she tells him that he's so oversexed he's sick. He responds to her accusation by releasing her. She levers herself off his lap using her elbow to "dig into a vital part of his anatomy." Once outside the car, he mutters, " 'I wouldn't have forced you. . . . I promise I won't be so impetuous again. I do know how to be patient with a woman, how to wait' " (84). Although dropping immediate demands, Joshua's contention that intercourse is inevitable is still threatening. (It is interesting to note that, unlike the 1980s Joshua, Mac, the twenty-third-century time traveler, has had years of training in sexual sensitivity [Cresswell 116] and in his time "Custom dictated that when a woman said no, a man backed off right away" [118].)

Joshua bides his time and, later, when his tactics are "erotic in the extreme, no longer passionately predatory," Christy succumbs "unreasonably" to his "male mastery" (104). He carries her up the stairs toward his bedroom, but Christy is "not fully aware of the direction he took" (105). Unthinking unawareness due to arousal is often used as an excuse for behaving in a manner that contradicts the image of the good girl. They are fully clothed, on his bed, when Christy hears his daughter enter the house; he does not hear her. She tells him to stop, but he comes down on top of her, "his face consumed with a dark purgatory of desire" and tells her " 'Oh, God, let me . . . You can't stop me now' " (107). He then "shames himself"—although this particular euphemism is not actually used here—which essentially means he has an uncontrolled, spontaneous orgasm outside of intercourse.

Despite the fact that he loses control of *himself,* he does not have intercourse with Christy; the question is, therefore, did he violate her? This story reckons that he did not. At the same time, Christy cannot be termed a tease because she stops him for a reason outside of her own befuddled thinking: his daughter is coming into the house. Pre-coitus interruptus by an outside agent is not uncommon.

Both men and women can misuse sexual power and frequently the heroines and heroes may, but this must be followed by personal growth on their part. They must be penitent: they must confess and make retribution. Love is redemptive and the flawed characters must realize and apologize for faults lest they be considered unheroic.

In Schuler's *The Right Direction,* the hero, Rafe, suspects that the heroine, Claire, had been raped. Her reaction to his first kiss reinforces this:

She hadn't been merely hesitant . . . or even simply displaying a smart woman's instinctive caution with a new man. And it hadn't been nervous excitement that had caused her mouth to tremble beneath his. It had been fear. Primal, gut-wrenching fear. (111)

Rafe calls a rape hotline for advice and is told "don't make any sexual demands or push her to respond to you. Let her be the one to lead the way" (112). Although he intends to follow the advice, he is also determined to be very present in Claire's life "until she trusted him enough to give in to the passion locked away inside her" (111-12). Rafe denies himself the reins of sexual power. Eventually, Claire tells Rafe about the rape. It was a date rape about which she has told no one. Rafe helps her deal with feelings which involve unwarranted responsibility and guilt.

When Claire asks him to kiss her goodnight he understands it as no more than a kiss. During the kiss Rafe realizes that it "wasn't passion that drove her but a . . . desperate bravado . . . like throwing open the closet door to confront the monsters within" (130). When he presses his palms lightly against the sides of her breasts she stiffens and he breaks off the kiss (132). As he is about to leave she says, "'But you're . . . that is, you've got a . . .' to which he responds: 'Got a hard-on? . . . Yeah, I do. . . . But didn't anybody ever tell you a guy doesn't have to score a home run every time he's up at bat. . . . a hard-on isn't something a woman has to do anything about unless she wants to. Is that clear?'" (133-34). While it is not rare for a hero to have an erection, it is rare for him to have a "hard-on." The hero is clearly in possession of his penis, not vice versa: he is neither hard, nor a hard-on.

It is Claire who initiates the lovemaking (164), but Rafe asks if she is certain (165). As they engage in the foreplay of dance she asks him to kiss her. While kissing her he realizes that he wants to "pick her up . . . lay her down on the bed . . . cover her body with his," etc. (169). Instead he restrains himself.

After a time spent caressing her back, he says, "I want to unbutton your blouse. All right?" (170). Claire hesitates and then nods, but he does not take this for consent. He says, "'The words, Claire. . . . So I can be sure'" and she replies, "'Yes'" (170). Before unbuttoning her blouse he adds, "'You can stop me anytime you want. . . . Just one word, *no,* and I'll stop'" (170). Rafe seeks permission for every action from fore-play through penetration.

When he asks "'Do you want to take this all the way? . . . . Do you want me to make love to you?'" she replies "'yes.'" After he lowers her to the bed, she stiffens. He changes his position and falls onto his back, pulling her on top of him. He then asks, "'Will you take me inside you, Claire?'" (176-77). Note that he is asking her to *take* him. He even goes so far as to halt her "slow descent onto his turgid flesh" and he tells her she can stop anytime.

Taylor's and Schuler's books, written nearly a decade apart, illus-trate changes in the rules of chase and courtship, and acceptable gender behavior, roles, and thinking. While Joshua and Christy are both fully clothed, he tells her that she has, in essence, allowed him to go too far to stop short of intercourse. Rafe, on the other hand, tells Claire that it is perfectly all right to tell him to stop microseconds before penetration.

In *The Six Gun Mystique* John Cawelti writes:

For no matter how many social and psychological functions a formula fulfills, it will probably never survive unless from time to time it attracts the interest of original and imaginative artists who are capable of revitalizing its conventions and stereotypes to express contemporaneous concerns. (113)

Schuler is one author who has revitalized popular romance by dealing with contemporaneous concerns. The genre has a few chapters in its written record wherein rape functions as sexual fantasy, but Schuler takes on the subject with a sensibility that refuses to exploit rape for titillation. Schuler's 1993 release and Lori Foster's 1998 *Fantasy* both address the issue of rape, but the latter involves multiple rape by unknown assailants. There are similarities in the stories; however, in terms of sensuous subtlety, credibility, and consistency in the heroine's behavior, differences are apparent.

The heroes behave similarly: each tries to convince the heroine that her feelings of responsibility are unwarranted—Brandi feels responsible because she forgot to lock her cabin door while on a cruise (111); each states that men should and can respect a woman's wishes and accept no as an answer; and each recognizes the heroine's need to control the pace of intimacy and his need to control his own behavior in pursuing the heroine. Like Rafe, Sebastian wants the heroine to feel comfortable with him: "The more she thought of him as just a man, male to her female, the less she'd think of him as a dominant counterpart to her feminine vulnerability" (129).

Despite a fantasy element in nearly every romance, realism—to a greater or lesser extent—is also required. The context in any fiction determines this level of realism. The title of *Fantasy* does not automatically dismiss the need for realism. Even though *Fantasy* is far removed from using the rape of the heroine by the hero as means of establishing a relationship, the relationship and the attendant fantasy are strongly influenced by the context of rape.

Early in the book Brandi tells her sister: "'[I]t's past time I got on with my life. I'm going to start acting like a normal woman again if it kills me'" (12). The reader is not yet privy to what compels her to make this vow. The serious nature of the varied effects rape can have on its victims plays an important role in determining what kind of willing suspension of disbelief will be required of the reader. Thus, the first disbelief that might have to be willingly suspended depends on how one defines a normal woman. Brandi does not display a smart woman's caution with a new man.

The heroine was raped eight years prior to the story. She received counseling, but has refrained from intimate relationships. Some would disbelieve that a normal woman, particularly one who had been raped, would act as Brandi does. First, she accepts the hero as a birthday gift from her sister who has purchased (procured?) Sebastian, and a getaway vacation, at a bachelor auction to benefit a women's shelter. Second, the couple take off on this dream date almost immediately following the auction. Third, Brandi agrees to stay with him on this unchaperoned getaway not in separate rooms at a hotel, but in a bungalow with one bedroom. Fourth, the chemistry of attraction, as opposed to shared history (beyond Sebastian's acquaintance with Brandi's sister, they are strangers) is primarily what compels the heroine to initially trust the hero. Fifth, she overcomes eight years of trauma-induced relationship dysfunction and becomes intimate with the hero within days of meeting him.

For this reader, these parameters beg to be disbelieved. Her past trauma is used to serve a fantasy of sexual control and dominance, but does not really explain why she behaves the way she does. She is an awkward blend, at times incredibly ignorant for a twenty-six-year-old woman. She behaves as if she had never been in counseling, nor done any relevant reading. She cites her sister as a source of knowledge: "She told me once that a man who's really excited doesn't always know what he's doing" (110). At other times her behavior seems inconsistent with her ignorance and fear. She quickly becomes intimate with Sebastian, which defies her characterization as sexually shy.

It is Sebastian who first brings up the issue of ground rules. He tells Brandi he is attracted to her, but doing anything about it will require a word or move on her part; otherwise, he is content to simply serve as her companion for the next five days. From this point until she tells Sebastian about the rape, Brandi's behavior causes difficulties with disbelief.

Even prior to learning of her rape, he abides by her rule that she can touch him, but he can't touch her. He thinks she is playing games to heighten sexual tension (122). On the verge of orgasm, he calls a halt to the "games" because he does not want to lose control; Brandi believes he is rejecting her. It is only after a flashback nightmare that she tells him about the rape. His response is: "'I thought you were playing a game of dominance, that you didn't want me to move so you could tease me. And I liked it . . . . But then it was just too much. . . . Now I know you weren't playing'" (120). His guilt over failing to intuit Brandi's past abuse seems misplaced because her behavior seems practiced rather than inexperienced or dysfunctional. Given her operational belief that aroused men don't always know what they are doing, she should have considered it risky to toy with Sebastian.

Brandi's proactive vow to get on with her life seems like that of a woman who understands rape as an act of violence, not desire; however, she assigns value to the rapists' opinions about her body. She is vexed because they did not find her attractive. In a "trembling voice" Brandi tells Sebastian: "'They told me I wasn't much to look at, that I was all bones and no meat. They . . . they laughed at me. I know I'm too skinny. . . . (136). You don't think I'm too small?'" He responds:

"[D]on't you dare believe anything those idiots told you. Listen to me. You're small and delicate and feminine. You're also the sexiest woman I've ever met in my life. And . . . I'm not an idiot. I know a beautiful woman when I see one." (137)

Brandi obviously quit counseling prematurely and it is going to take more than Sebastian's weak comparison of himself to these rapists—they are idiots, he is not—to promote further healing. Because the rapists held her emotionally captive for so long, perhaps her reaction could be attributable to a variation on the Stockholm Syndrome. While this may account for her emotional hurt over the rapists' disparaging remarks, it is also problematic: a heroine is expected to have the intestinal fortitude not to entertain such a weakminded notion.

It seems ludicrous to have a heroine express such inane concern about her rapists' opinions. It is also inconsistent with Brandi's vow to start acting like a normal woman again, for it is not normal to value the opinions of one's rapists. While it is conventional for heroines to grapple with standards of appeal, Brandi's concern is not really within the norms of this convention; however, it may be that her self-doubt is so conventionally framed that it seems acceptable.

What exactly is the fantasy being fulfilled in *Fantasy*? It would be incongruous to have Brandi think of herself as Sebastian first does—as a woman playing a game of sexual control. The fantasy of finding a compassionate, understanding, man must also be dismissed because all Temptation heroines find such men and this is a *Blaze*. If Brandi's ultra-sexy fantasy is not about sexual dominance, but control over her fear, then her timidity becomes an obstacle. Unlike Claire, Brandi does not seem to be driven by a "desperate bravado to confront the monsters within." Sometimes she runs from her fear; other times she almost embraces it. One option is that the fantasy of dominance is being explored for its own sake, for the vicarious benefit of the reader, and may not need to be the heroine's fantasy, nor consistent with her character.

It is questionable whether Brandi's rape is integral to the story. It may function more as a contrivance for motivation. This is somewhat subversive because it facilely twists post-traumatic fear into the service of sexual fantasy. The rape allows Brandi to remain innocent and provides the explanation for her fear. Her fear is her defense for controlling the hero, and it is her need for control that is her defense for teasing him. Her defense for not recognizing her behavior as a game of sexual dominance relies on her innocence. Without the rape, the heroine would be responsible for her own sensual, erotic behavior. The rape and the fear serve as a means of denying that "nice girls" are capable of recognizing, and/or can be knowing participants in, erotic play. Thus, she is innocent of engaging in "naughty" sex games and Sebastian cannot hold her responsible for knowingly teasing him to excess. Ultimately, given the obstacles to willing disbelief, the function of the rape seems to be that of absolving Brandi of the "sin" of expressing her own sexuality.

Contemporary romances can serve the affective function of providing improved role models and images of women (I am not certain Brandi is an improvement). The best of them may function as collective consciousness-raising. It is one thing to reflect social change by adjusting the heroine's professional life in the milieu of the contemporary romance— from legal secretary to high-powered attorney, or nurse to doctor; however, it is quite another to reflect the changes in the way men and women relate to each other.

In recent years most contemporary romances have dealt openly with the couple discussing protected sex. One Temptation series, *Lovers Apart,* focused on maintaining relationships over geographic distance because of career choices. Another change in Temptations is an increase in the number of heroines who actively seek a husband, as opposed to a marriage, which is a subtle difference. They are not seeking marriage for the sake of social convention, or financial security; they are seeking a companion, a soulmate. Stephanie Bond, whose heroine finds her grandmother's handwritten version of *The Rules,* offers some insight into this subtle change:

Manhunting is a natural, biological urge, but things get complicated because society has always dictated *men* should be the hunters, and women should just be grateful. *Hmmm.* (Letter to Reader)

Women's expectations of both themselves and men, their understanding and misunderstanding of men, and their potential to deal with men's behavior or misbehavior are revealed in contemporary category romances such as Harlequin Temptations. Some aberrations aside, these books do present criteria for what constitutes a good man. They also define the qualities and behavior of a bad choice.

Although I would never recommend that high school girls read sensuous romances, my initial concerns about this issue changed somewhat after I immersed myself in Temptations. Though reality based, contemporary category romance may be viewed as mythic fantasy written by some very liberated and feminist women. Harlequin openly acknowledged the myth aspect of romance with the 1993 *Lovers and Legends* series which retells fairy tales and legends in the Temptation style. Ultimately, if one defines myth not as the false, but as the most sacredly true, then the romance genre is clearly more than simple fantasy: it is *powerful* myth. While the western embraces the mythic hero and true grit, the romance embodies the mythic emotion of passion and true love.

The sensuous contemporary romance may involve a young, never-married virgin, but it is a guarantee that the story will not end before the couple experiences bedded bliss. Because Temptations deal somewhat candidly with intimate relationships, the authors are able to delve more deeply into the sexual and emotional intricacies in the life of a relationship. They are able to go beyond premarital life and happily ever after conclusions. Some Temptations even revolve around marital reconciliation, a nearly sacred chapter in the myth of true love (e.g., Ellis, *Michael's Angel;* Hoffman, *The Honeymoon Deal;* Logan, *The Last Honest Man;* Morrison, *An Imperfect Hero;* Roszel, *Unwilling Wife;* Schuler, *Designing Woman;* White, *Forbidden Fantasy*).

The women's liberation movement and the sexual revolution left confusion in their wake. Models of gender roles are still evolving and the issues—expectations in employment, relationships, marriage, and reproduction—are being worked out in contemporary romances by authors, some of whom were not yet born and some of whom were teens and young women in the early sixties, when these movements began. It takes a liberated heroine to recognize a man who is deeply flawed by a need to dominate and/or has very little understanding of love and commitment. Heroines who might have made the wrong decision about a previous husband or lover are shown as having the strength to overcome. It takes a liberated heroine to demand a liberated hero and to recognize that not having a man is preferable to having an insensitive, egocentric one: "I decided I was responsible for my own happiness. A woman doesn't have to—to have a man to be whole, to be alive" (Harris 68).

The primary reading gratification, despite the more sensuous nature of Temptations, is the fantasy of satisfying intimacy involving love, romance and commitment. Conventionally, it is the Temptation heroine who wants intimacy; however, Kate Hoffmann's *Struck by Spring Fever!* offers a rare hero in Hawk: "He'd never wanted a woman so badly. But it wasn't just that—a matter of selfish satisfaction. He wanted to share his desire with her, to make her feel this craving for intimacy, to bring her to her peak and then catch her when she fell" (144). Hawk, however, does not deviate too much from the heroic norm because what he craves is primarily sexual intimacy.

Kimberly, the heroine of Krentz's *Witchcraft,* has a different perspective on intimacy. She says that one of her greatest rewards in writing fiction is that she is "free to work out my fantasy of total intimacy with a member of the opposite sex to my own satisfaction" (18). The hero responds:

"You see? There's a good example of why there can't be perfect communication between a man and woman in real life. You say the words 'total intimacy' and the first image that comes into my head is being in bed with you; having you completely nude and lost in passion. But that's not what you meant at all, is it?" (18)

At least initially, the hero's concept of total intimacy may be described by physical intimacy, but for the heroine, physical intimacy is merely a subset of total intimacy. The conflict is that the heroine's belief system dictates that a relationship go beyond good sex or the relationship is over; the hero thinks good sex makes for a pretty solid relationship. Radio producer heroine, Allie, brings up this very issue with all-night deejay hero, Charlie: "[W]omen are stronger because they talk to each other, and men are weaker and concentrate on sex and ignore other more important things like establishing warm human relationships" (Crusie 154). Charlie's comeback is a typical hero's complaint: "women always bring every discussion back to relationships." Allie must then inform him that "relationships are the basis for life." He makes the immediate and perhaps logical leap: "Tell me you're not talking about marriage." She's not. She's talking about warm connections with other people and contends that men just don't make these connections. Of course, this meets with an eyebrow wiggling, "I have a warm connection with another person." And she retorts: "That's sex. . . . That's what men use as a substitute for relationships. But it's not the real thing" (154).

Charlie contends that it "feels real," but Allie is more concerned about whether he can keep the relationship going without sex. He believes that their relationship is more than sex and that she knows it. This, however, is not the point. Allie believes that women do not get all the warmth in their lives from sex and that men do; thus, as long as a woman is getting her emotional needs met, she can survive sexual deprivation. On the other hand, a sexually deprived man would become depressed, irrational, and would finally crack. He accuses her of making a sexist argument; she contends there is only one way to find out who is right. She throws down the gauntlet: A month of celibacy (154-55).

They both become irritable and full of doubt about the relationship, but at the end of the month there is reconciliation and an accepted proposal of marriage. When they put an end to their celibacy, things are different. Charlie tells Allie: "'What we had before was fun, but it wasn't this'" (214).

And then they moved together, breathed together, and the heat rushed through them, and Allie surged and bloomed, feeling Charlie in her fingertips, in her heart, in her brain, as his warmth and light and love moved through her. . . . (218)

The moral motif of the Temptation line is that "you can't have one without the other." Suffice it to say, it would break a major convention if either member of the couple had been involved in a previous relationship that was significantly more satisfying than the current one. Furthermore, there is no such thing as a conventional line even remotely resembling, "You're pretty lousy in bed, darling, but I love you."

The sweet romances can deal with the mental, emotional, and spiritual aspects of love, but only the sensuous, euphemistically explicit romance can explore the melding of these with the physical. While the storyline of *Charlie All Night* deals with the mind-body aspects of a relationship at some length, other novels are more brief. Estrada's *The Ivory Key* simply has the passage: "The message his body sent was clear. His love" (159). In *Mad about You,* the wood sprite restores the wizard's power and saves him by making love with him (Dean 179).

Impetuous treats the issue somewhat unusually in that it begins with the fantasy of anonymous sex—a taboo in reality—in a pool house while a Halloween party is going on at the main house. The experience is anonymous only for the hero because the heroine refuses to unmask. The hero, having had the greatest sexual experience of his life, cannot understand his growing affection for one of his sister's friends—who turns out to be the masked woman with whom he had been intimate (Foster). What is the moral of this story? Great sex causes great love? Great sex cannot be separated from great love? Love and sex are not two separate issues?

In *A Burning Touch,* the telepathic heroine feels what the hero feels and hears his thoughts; when they first attempt to make love she can't handle it (163). Later she manages to control the flow of his thoughts and feelings into her so that she is not so overwhelmed. "Two voices cried out in unison; two bodies quaked with a single, shattering release," and she faints from the power of the mind-body-soul experience (170).

A liberated heroine settles for nothing less than a considerate, satisfying lover: "He was promising sexual fulfillment, assuring heady, climactic orgasms most women only dreamed of" (Roszel, *Devil* 103). Sexual expertise, however, cannot compensate if the hero lacks in other areas. While the hero must be reasonably attractive and sexy, the intimacy fantasy further stipulates that he be kind, solicitous of the heroine's thoughts and feelings, and protective, but not overly so. The romantic hero is virile, exudes masculinity, and has grown into manhood. He is also—if only ultimately—capable of communicating.

The hero must be able to put into words what he is thinking and feeling. In *C. J.'s Defense,* Roarke confronts his feelings prior to speaking about them:

He loved her. It had taken him long enough to put that word to what he was feeling, to what he had been feeling for some time. He knew better than most the power of words. If you didn't say it, it didn't really exist. Now it did, for him at least. The next step would be to see that it existed for C. J., too. (Andrews 166)

It is the hero's promise of love, commitment, and fidelity as well as his utterance of "I love you"—or in the case of *A Burning Touch* his thinking *I love you*—more than the physical consummation of the relationship that is the real climax of these books. The sensuous romance shares this with its sweeter, more innocent sisters. This promise is the one convention of the genre that cannot be broken. Love, not eroticism, is the greatest gratification in Temptations. Romance readers wouldn't have it any other way.

Works Cited

Alexander, Carrie. *Fancy-Free.* Temptation #536. Ontario: Harlequin, 1995.

Andrews, Carolyn. *C. J.'s Defense.* Temptation #498. Ontario: Harlequin, 1994.

Arnold, Judith. *Timeless Love.* Temptation #565. Ontario: Harlequin, 1995.

Bond, Stephanie. *Manhunting in Mississippi.* Temptation #685. Ontario: Harlequin, 1998.

Buford, Pamela. *A Hard-Hearted Hero.* Temptation #644. Ontario: Harlequin, 1997.

Cameron, Barbara. *Star Ride.* Temptation #66. Ontario: Harlequin, 1985.

Carrington, Tori. *Constant Craving.* Temptation #716. Prepublication manuscript. Ontario: Harlequin, 1999.

Cawelti, John. *The Six-Gun Mystique*. 2nd ed. Bowling Green, OH: Bowling Green State University Popular Press, 1984.

Collins, Marion Smith. *This Thing Called Love*. Temptation #35. Ontario: Harlequin, 1984.

——. *Without a Hitch*. Temptation #86. Ontario: Harlequin, 1985.

Cresswell, Jasmine. *Midnight Fantasy*. Temptation #574. Ontario: Harlequin, 1996.

Crusie, Jennifer. *Charlie All Night*. Temptation #570. Ontario: Harlequin, 1996.

——. *What the Lady Wants*. Temptation #544. Ontario: Harlequin, 1995.

Dale, Ruth Jean. *A Million Reasons Why*. Temptation #380. Ontario: Harlequin, 1992.

Danson, Sheryl. *Ranger Man*. Temptation #503. Ontario: Harlequin, 1994.

Dean, Alyssa. *Mad about You*. Temptation #524. Ontario: Harlequin, 1995.

Delinsky, Barbara. *The Outsider*. Temptation #385. Ontario: Harlequin, 1992.

Denison, Janelle. *Private Fantasies*. Temptation #632. Ontario: Harlequin, 1998.

——. *Private Pleasures*. Temptation #679. Ontario: Harlequin, 1998.

Ellis, Lyn. *Michael's Angel*. Temptation #575. Ontario: Harlequin, 1996.

Estrada, Rita Clay. *Dreams*. Temptation #687 Ontario: Harlequin, 1998.

——. *The Ivory Key*. Temptation #166. Ontario: Harlequin, 1987.

——. *One More Time*. Temptation #450. Ontario: Harlequin, 1993.

——. *The Stormchaser*. Temptation #573. Ontario: Harlequin, 1996.

Forest, Regan. *The Lady and the Dragon*. Temptation #355. Ontario: Harlequin, 1991.

——. *A Wanted Man*. Temptation #176. Ontario: Harlequin, 1987.

Foster, Lori. *Fantasy*. Temptation #675. Ontario: Harlequin, 1998.

——. *Impetuous*. Temptation #572. Ontario: Harlequin, 1996.

Friend, Tad. "Yes." *Esquire* Feb. 1994.

Harper, Madeline. *The Highwayman*. Temptation #601. Ontario: Harlequin, 1996.

Harris, Lisa. *Trouble in Paradise*. Temptation #495. Ontario: Harlequin, 1994.

James, Sandra. *Like a Lover*. Temptation #379. Ontario: Harlequin, 1992.

Joyce, Jenna Lee. *Awake unto Me*. Temptation #134. Ontario: Harlequin, 1986.

Kaiser, Janice. *The Texan*. Temptation #556. Ontario: Harlequin, 1995.

Krentz, Jayne Anne. *Call It Destiny*. Temptation #21. Ontario: Harlequin, 1984.

——. *The Private Eye*. Temptation #377. Ontario: Harlequin, 1992.

——. *Uneasy Alliance*. Temptation #11. Ontario: Harlequin, 1984.

——. *Witchcraft*. Temptation #74. Ontario: Harlequin, 1985.

Lee, Sandra. *Love Lessons*. Temptation #387. Ontario: Harlequin, 1992.

Leto, Julie Elizabeth. *Seducing Sullivan*. Temptation #686. Ontario: Harlequin, 1998.

Liepitz, Susan. *That Wilder Man*. Temptation #652. Ontario: Harlequin, 1997.

Liholm, Molly. *The Getaway Groom*. Temptation #672. Ontario: Harlequin, 1998.

Logan, Leandra. *The Last Honest Man*. Temptation #393. Ontario: Harlequin, 1992.

MacAllister, Heather. *Jilt Trip*. Temptation #543. Ontario: Harlequin, 1995.

——. *Manhunting in Memphis*. Temptation #669. Ontario: Harlequin, 1998.

McNaught, Judith. *Double Standards*. Temptation #16. Ontario: Harlequin, 1984.

McWilliams, Judith. *Looking Good*. Temptation #372. Ontario: Harlequin, 1991.

Michaels, Lorna. *The Trouble with Tonya*. Temptation #632. Ontario: Harlequin, 1997.

Michaels, Lynn. *Nightwing*. Temptation #542. Ontario: Harlequin, 1995.

Morrison, Jo. *An Imperfect Hero*. Temptation #370. Ontario: Harlequin, 1991.

Rafferty, Carin. *My Fair Baby*. Temptation #319. Ontario: Harlequin, 1990.

Rolofson, Kristine. *The Cowboy*. Temptation #569. Ontario: Harlequin, 1991.

——. *The Last Great Affair*. Temptation #348. Ontario: Harlequin, 1991.

——. *Make Believe Honeymoon*. Temptation #560. Ontario: Harlequin, 1995.

Ross, JoAnn. *Ambushed*. Temptation #613. Ontario: Harlequin, 1996.

——. *Angel of Desire*. Temptation #482. Ontario: Harlequin, 1994.

——. *Moonstruck*. Temptation #436. Ontario: Harlequin, 1993.

——. *The Prince & the Showgirl*. Temptation #453. Ontario: Harlequin, 1993.

——. *Private Passions*. Temptation #562. Ontario: Harlequin, 1995.

——. *Roarke: The Adventurer.* Temptation #638. Ontario: Harlequin, 1997.

——. *Star-Crossed Lovers*. Temptation #432. Ontario: Harlequin, 1993.

Roszel, Renee. *Devil to Pay*. Temptation #422. Ontario: Harlequin, 1992.

——. *Unwilling Wife*. Temptation #378. Ontario: Harlequin, 1992.

Rush, Mallory. *Kiss of the Beast*. Temptation #558. Ontario: Harlequin, 1995.

——. *Love Slave*. Temptation #448. Ontario: Harlequin, 1993.

Ryan, Patricia. *A Burning Touch*. Temptation #571. Ontario: Harlequin, 1996.

——. *The Return of the Black Sheep*. Temptation #540. Ontario: Harlequin, 1995.

——. *Twice the Spice*. Temptation #631. Ontario: Harlequin, 1997.

Sanders, Glenda. *Gypsy*. Temptation #234. Ontario: Harlequin, 1989.

——. *Playboy McCoy*. Temptation #510. Ontario: Harlequin, 1994.

Schuler, Candace. *Designing Woman*. Temptation #102. Ontario: Harlequin, 1986.

——. *Passion and Scandal*. Temptation #557. Ontario: Harlequin, 1995.

——. *The Right Direction*. Temptation #467. Ontario: Harlequin, 1993.

Sinclair, Selina. *A Diamond in the Rough*. Temptation #688. Ontario: Harlequin, 1998.

Small, Lass. *Collaboration*. Temptation #54. Ontario: Harlequin, 1985.

Spencer, LaVyrle. *Spring Fancy*. Temptation #1. Ontario: Harlequin, 1984.

Steen, Sandy. *The Knight*. Temptation #593. Ontario: Harlequin, 1996.

Taylor, Abra. *Summer Surrender*. Temptation #23. Ontario: Harlequin, 1984.

Thompson, Vicki Lewis. *The Drifter*. Temptation #559. Ontario: Harlequin, 1995.

———. *Holding Out for a Hero*. Temptation #600. Ontario: Harlequin, 1996.

———. *Wedding Song*. Temptation #502. Ontario: Harlequin, 1994.

Verge, Lisa Ann. *Loving Wild*. Temptation #671. Ontario: Harlequin, 1998.

Victor, Cindy. *An Intimate Oasis*. Temptation #60. Ontario: Harlequin, 1985.

Weger, Jackie. *Beneath a Saffron Sky*. Temptation #53. Ontario: Harlequin, 1985.

———. *Eye of the Beholder*. Temptation #181. Ontario: Harlequin, 1987.

White, Tiffany. *Forbidden Fantasy*. Temptation #367. Ontario: Harlequin, 1991.

———. *Naughty Talk*. Temptation #464. Ontario: Harlequin, 1993.

Wilkins, Gina. *A Valentine Wish*. Temptation #576. Ontario: Harlequin, 1996.

———. *A Wish for Love*. Temptation #592. Ontario: Harlequin, 1996.

Williams, Roseanne. *Seeing Red*. Temptation #431. Ontario: Harlequin, 1993.

Changing Ideologies in Romance Fiction

Dawn Heinecken

Introduction

Many critical writings about romances have argued that romances promote the patriarchal oppression of women and have depicted their readers as cultural dupes. However, in the early and mid-eighties, scholars such as Tania Modleski and Janice Radway attempted to account for the appeal that romances have for their readers from a feminist perspective. Both found that the popularity of romances stemmed in large part from the fact that romances expressed something about readers' everyday lives as women.

Modleski's examination of Gothics and Harlequins reveals that romances have a subversive potential because they express women's fears about their powerless role in society. Harlequin heroines, for example, are forced to learn how to read the emotionless hero, while subverting their own identity in order to make "masculine hostility bearable" (Modleski 58). Gothic heroines must deal with the threat of powerlessness and lack of safety within the home, testifying to "women's extreme discontent with the social and psychological processes which transform them into victims" (84).

Janice Radway, in *Reading the Romance,* attends to the critical issue of what *readers* feel is important in the text. In this study, Radway attempts to explain why romance readers enjoy the particular narratives they do. Through interviews with readers, she locates specific texts and sections of the romance that the women feel are most important. Drawing from these moments, she exposes the narrative structure of the romance genre. This structure highlights the "heroine's transformation from an isolated, asexual, insecure adolescent who is unsure of her identity, into a mature, sensual and very married woman who has realized her full potential and identity as the partner of a man and as the implied mother of a child" (134). Despite moments of subversive pleasure like that involved in the escapist act of reading, Radway concludes that the narrative structure of romances ultimately serves to further indoctrinate women into an oppressive patriarchal system. She finally conceives of romance novels as antithetical to feminism.

Radway and Modleski's arguments are convincing and thought-provoking. However, because their conclusions are largely based on their analysis of the meaning of the *narrative structure* of romances, and narrative structures have undergone a change in the decade and a half since *Reading the Romance,* the appeal of romances needs to be reexamined in light of current romances.

In *Mystery, Adventure and Romance,* John Cawelti notes the presence of conventions-inventions in genres. Cawelti asserts that genres evolve over time. Successful texts in the genre replicate the basic rules of the genre while simultaneously adding something new, which may consequently change the nature of the genre (36), which I believe is the case with romances. Further, Radway points out that the institutional nature of romances means that it is difficult to pinpoint precisely which conventions of the genre make it "work" for its readers. Because of the way romances were marketed and sold at the time of Radway's writing in the early eighties, readers often had no way of knowing, prior to reading it, if an individual book would fit their model of the ideal romance (69). They read what was available to them, not necessarily what they would have preferred. Thus readers may have desired romances that were quite different from what they were actually reading. The fact that more and more romance readers have entered the field as writers since the seventies (Krentz 3) is undoubtedly a response to this situation and suggests that it is very likely that the structure of romances will have evolved as a result.

While investigations of romance novels, like those done by Radway and Modleski, have always been able to point to moments of subversiveness in the romance text, I believe that romances of the nineties are markedly influenced by the feminist movement. Ann Rosalind Jones has shown that the presence of feminism in the eighties is evidenced by the genre's specific engagement with feminist themes, an engagement which reveals itself in uncomfortable contradictions throughout the text (195-220). For example, the texts Jones examined were likely to feature dialogue that explicitly criticized the women's movement while at the same time they featured a working heroine.

However, I would argue that since the time that Jones was writing in 1986, feminist values have been incorporated and naturalized in romance texts. Novels since the late eighties have moved away from evidencing moments of "subversiveness"—i.e., implicit or hidden critiques of patriarchy—to revealing more overtly feminist positions which are "feminist" in that they present ways of thinking that run counter to the traditionally "masculine" ideology of competition, hierarchy, and autonomy. Thus, the incorporation of feminist values means that not only is the presence of working women widespread and validated, and female characters have both greater social and personal power, but that romance novels embrace a sense of social justice and the necessity for a cooperative relationship that is in direct opposition to masculine modes of thought. At the same time that women's power is on the rise, descriptions of acceptable male behavior and proper uses of masculine power have been radically altered. No longer content to *imply* gentleness on the part of the male, romance novelists have launched a penetrating investigation into the male psyche and have constructed a new breed of non-violent hero. Furthermore, sex itself has been problematized and consequentially politicized.

These new representations of gender, power, character, and sex found in current romance novels need to be reexamined in order to understand their meaning for readers. For the purpose of this study, I have chosen to examine novels that follow the same general structure of Radway's "ideal romance." These are longer, historical romances that detail the development of a one-man, one-woman relationship. The novels that I will be focusing on include the works of two of the best-selling contemporary romance authors, Amanda Quick and Laura Kinsale. While their work, I feel, is perhaps the most overtly "feminist," of the recent novels I have encountered, their extreme popularity as writers points to their successful manipulation of the genre. Further, both Amanda Quick and Laura Kinsale consider romances to be espousing feminist ideals, in that romances promote female empowerment, the subversion of patriarchal power structures, and female identification with male characteristics like aggression (Kinsale, *Dangerous Men* 40; Krentz 5).

Heroines

Heroines in romances of the seventies and early eighties, exemplified by the works of Kathleen Woodiwiss, are like the heroines of countless fairy tales. They win the hero in the end not because of their actions, but because of their attractive appearance. It is important to note that along with stressing the heroine's beauty, earlier romances focused on the female form in a way that is reminiscent of mainstream cinematic techniques. In her classic article, "Visual Pleasure and Narrative Cinema," Laura Mulvey observes that classic film presents women's bodies as "stylized and fragmented by close-ups . . . [as] the direct recipient of the spectator's look" (120). Mulvey shows that such fragmentation results in film women who are more valuable for their individual body parts than their character, and who are essentially passive objects, existing only for the pleasure they give to the viewer. Further, the power to look is coded as male, while to be female is to be the object of the male gaze.

A typical moment in *Shanna* exemplifies an acceptance of the male gaze and an emphasis on fragmented female beauty that is found in many of the earlier romance novels. At their first meeting, Shanna asks Roark to marry her in order to avoid being forced into marriage by her father. Roark tells her he never "buys a mare with a blanket on" and takes off her cloak to get a closer look:

Her carefully devised attack was spent in an unplanned rush. . . . She was the gem, the jewel of rare beauty. . . . Above the hooped pannier . . . the tightly laced bodice showed the narrowness of her waist while it cupped her bosom to a most daring display . . . her skin gleamed like rich, warm satin . . . her soft, ripe curves made him ache with the want of her. Her breathtaking beauty quickened his very soul, stirring his mind with imaginings of what loveliness lay hidden from view. (Woodiwiss 19)

The primacy of body parts and the importance of the female body as a thing to be looked at and used is apparent in this scene. Although there are repeated assertions that Shanna is unaware of her beauty, such excuses are counterbalanced by phrases that suggest female complicity in the male gaze; for example, Shanna's beauty is a "carefully devised attack," which "tortures" Roark.

Throughout the course of the novel, Shanna's looks never lose importance:

Roark raised his eyes to the window. His breath caught in his throat at the stirring sight there. Shanna . . . her face presented in profile. . . . The diffused light made her seem some classic statue cast in gold . . . her hair appeared almost transparent, tumbling like an amber waterfall of dark rich honey to her waist. The gown clung to her breasts, conforming to the natural swell that dared the touch of a man. As he stared . . . she became a carving in fresh white ivory. . . . The dark clouds sapped the brightness from the sky, and with its fading, her skin became the oiled oak of a ship's bold figurehead. . . . Her face was pensive, her smile sad. Her eyes alone took on a lighter hue, that of a brilliant green sea stirred and swirled by the storm.

"My God," Roark groaned, inwardly frozen at the table by this innocent panorama. "Does she know how beautiful she is? Does she know how she tortures me?" (333)

These scenes not only demonstrate the presence of the male objectifying gaze but also its dangers for the female reader. The heroine's excessive beauty makes her worthy of attention but it also transforms her from a woman to a thing. Shanna is no longer human, but a "carving," a "figurehead" made from wood, or a "gem." The comparison of her eyes to the sea draws on the stereotype of women as a natural, elemental being. Although she is unaware of it, she has power over Roark but it is power based solely on her looks. Further, her pensiveness and her sad smile are not emotions which have any value in and of themselves. Rather, it is the visual effect of her pensive sad smile that appeals to him. In addition to constructing woman as an object of the male gaze, one of the unspoken messages in these passages is also that sorrow in a woman, as long as it is visible but *silent* sorrow, is attractive.

A similar sensibility about the necessity of female beauty and the essential role of woman as an object to be looked upon is transmitted in the other bestselling books of the seventies and early eighties. All of Kathleen Woodiwiss's heroines are remarkably beautiful. In *The Flame and the Flower,* the defining characteristics of the heroine are her timidity and her beauty; her breasts are mentioned so often they become secondary characters. Sabrina, the heroine of Laurie McBain's *Moonstruck Madness,* is so often described as beautiful that it is hard to remember she has any other traits. For example, the hero tells Sabrina "To think I drove my sword through this small, perfect body of yours," and "I can't even look at you without wanting you again" (115-16).

Not all romances feature beautiful heroines, but many current romances still feature attractive heroines. However, it is certainly true that Quick and Kinsale's heroines are less likely to be exceptionally beautiful. More importantly, even when heroines are beautiful, they are attractive because of their personalities and abilities, rather than their appearance. Physical descriptions become much less precise, detailed descriptions giving way to comments on the expressive quality of the woman's face. There is greater emphasis on how the heroine *emotionally* stimulates the hero.

In Kinsale's *The Shadow and the Star,* for instance, there is *no* description of the heroine's appearance, other than the color of her hair and eyes. When the heroine is described, the focus is often confined to the face, individual quirks, or expressions which indicate character. In *Flowers from the Storm,* the hero describes the heroine to her blind father; though the description includes some physical commentary, tellingly, the hero focuses on her gestures and movements. Christian describes "her face is dignified, but not quite stern. Softer than that but she has a way of turning up her chin that might give a man pause. . . . I've never had a spinster look out beneath her lashes at me the way you do" (28-29). This overt male gaze is criticized by the heroine, who tells the hero he describes her "Rather like a good milk cow!" (28).

Quick is also less prone to focus on the heroine's looks. It is her character, rather than her body, that initially fascinates the hero and is the reason he falls in love with her. For example, the hero's first sight of Emily Farringdon in *Scandal* is notable for his awareness of Emily's personality in spite of her lack of beauty.

[T]he woman on the mare's back was riding astride . . . this certainly was no gilt-haired Farringdon [who are known for their good looks]. . . . Emily Farringdon was wearing a pair of silver-framed spectacles. The sight of them held him riveted for a few seconds. No other women of his acquaintance would be caught dead wearing spectacles in public. . . . He saw with amazement that there were a handful of freckles sprinkled across her small nose . . . this particular Farringdon was no statuesque goddess. She was much too short. . . . Sunlight glittered off the lenses of Emily's spectacles as she turned to look down at Simon. He found himself pinned beneath that inquisitive green gaze. It was a gaze that fairly glittered with a curiously refreshing blend of lively intelligence and good-natured innocence.

Simon decided in that moment that Miss Emily Farringdon was going to prove anything but dull. (12-14)

While there are less detailed descriptions of physical beauty, and physical descriptions are used as indicators of a unique character, such as "lively intelligence," it must be noted that even with the lessening focus on the woman's body and a greater focus on her personality, these women nonetheless have their worth as individuals based on the subjective evaluation of men.

Despite this evaluative aspect, this portrayal is nonetheless a radical improvement, from a feminist perspective, because of the growing range of acceptable images of women—not all of which are based on female pulchritude. In addition to representing women as something other than mere physical vessels, these images are empowering because they extend the kinds of physical qualities a woman can have and still be defined as attractive and worthy of love by men. Physical perfection is no longer required to be a heroine. For example, Olympia St. Leger, of Kinsale's *Seize the Fire,* is plump and sees herself as ugly. The hero does not think she is ugly, but is "intrigued by the curve of one plump cheek."

His first impression was of green eyes, wide as a baby owl's and just as solemn. Dumpling cheeks, a straight nose, and firm little mouth—all ordinary . . . there was nothing notably strange about her features—and yet it was an odd face, the kind of face that looked out of burrows and tree-knots and hedgerows, unblinking, innocent and old as time. If she'd had whiskers to twitch it wouldn't have surprised him, so strong was the impression of a small, prudent wild creature with dark brows like furry markings. (21-22)

While the male gaze once more constructs the heroine as a young animal, it is important to note that this animal, like Emily Farringdon, is looking back at the hero, and is looking back with the prudent, wise eyes of an owl. Furthermore, the animal to which Olympia is being compared is far from sexy—yet is nonetheless beautiful in its own way. Different notions of beauty are quite liberatory given the current beauty culture with its rigid definitions of beauty, health, and slenderness.

For example, the presence of fat heroines has been rare in romances. However, Kinsale's Olympia is fat. Although Olympia feels herself to be ugly, it is notable that Olympia's fat body is one of the few bodies in Kinsale's works that receives marked attention and commentary from the hero, with the inclusion of a three-page monologue by the hero prior to his first love-making session with the heroine. In the scene, the hero woos the heroine with a loving, detailed description of her individual body parts and their erotic effect upon him (238-40).

As feminist film critics like Mulvey have shown us, part of the danger of the male gaze is that it works to divide and separate. Not only does the gaze make women into objects, but it makes women into individual pieces, which may be judged positively or negatively. Women are thus denied an essential wholeness or worthiness of self. Many women can only eroticize themselves by looking at their parts, they cannot see themselves as whole, as being erotic, if their individual parts are inferior. In this scene the hero tellingly focuses on a wide range of parts like chin, ankles, and shoulders, in addition to bosom, hips, and stomach, expanding the range of what body parts may be considered erotic. Such scenes create an image of a whole person, whose imperfect parts come together to form a lovable, attractive person. This scene is even more notable because, as mentioned above, it is not at all standard of Kinsale to include such detail. In this construction, the gaze is still paramount, but it is a refined gaze that creates desire for the whole being. The scene's inclusion suggests to me that Kinsale is aware of the inherent discrimination against fat women in a world where power for women is linked to beauty and slenderness. The description of a fat body as erotic is thus a great step forward, showing that even women who are unattractive by society's standards can be found erotic by desirable men.

In addition to de-emphasizing their heroines' looks, Kinsale and Quick create stronger female characters. While Radway has noted that readers tend to believe that the heroine is assertive throughout the novel, she also found that, during the course of the narrative, the independent female identity dissolves. While romance heroines are initially described as spunky and assertive, their later actions are not (Radway 123). For example, in the opening of *Moonstruck Madness*, Sabrina, dressed as a highwayman, duels with the hero. The hero hates her independence. As the story progresses, she becomes less and less physically assertive, even losing her memory. The passive Sabrina, unaware of her true identity, becomes the woman the hero loves, because she is sweet and childlike (McBain 300). Romance heroines are also likely to be orphans, or economically imperiled—situations which emphasize their childlike, helpless nature (Radway 135).

However, Quick and Kinsale's heroines are more likely to be independent and in control. In Quick's novels, the women are always economically independent, often due to their professional abilities. Her women are usually occupied in some career, such as zoology, architecture, classical study, or investment banking. They are often surrounded by large support networks of relatives and female friends. These women are all psychically healthy. While they love their husbands, it is always clear that they do not *need* their husbands to survive. Unlike Sabrina, none of these women give up their interests or careers when they marry. For example, in *Mistress,* Iphiginia Bright is a self-made millionaire and architect. After pulling herself up from poverty by running a girl's school, she makes real estate investments with a pool of widows and spinsters and makes a fortune on her architectural designs.

Recent heroines are also more likely to articulate a need for feminist reform. Augusta in *Rendezvous,* for example, founds a club for women called Pompeia's. Pompeia's is a "room of their own" for women to write in peace, engage in intellectual discussion, or even gamble. The decor of the club is dedicated to illuminating the historical contributions of women from history, like Sappho and Cleopatra. The club is decorated with portraits displaying notable women in action—composing poems, or dedicating monuments to education.

The need to expose women's historical presence is a motif of the novel. For example, reading the historical tracts written by her scholar husband, Augusta says:

I find them quite interesting . . . if one overlooks the obvious flaw in all of them, that is . . . The chief irritation I feel in reading your historical research, sir, is that in every single one of your volumes, you have contrived to ignore the role and contribution of females. . . . I have decided one gains [the impression that women do not make history] chiefly because history is written by males . . . for some reason male writers choose to pay no attention to female accomplishments. (158-59)

Later Augusta notes:

Only consider . . . how many famous heroes of antiquity have been absolutely terrified of female monsters like Medusa and the sirens and such. It certainly leads one to believe women might have had a great deal of power in those days. . . . Fully half of the world's history has never been written because it concerns females. (196)

Augusta is not alone in her enthusiasm; her point of view is shared by several of the other female characters. Sophy Doring, in *Seduction*, makes several demands before their marriage. Telling the hero that she knows he only wants a "brood mare" for a wife, she refuses to have sex with him before she is ready, and also demands that she be allowed to read anything she wants—including feminist tracts by Mary Wollenstonecraft. Strong women are not limited to the heroines. Lady Arbutthnot, in *Rendezvous,* is a former British Secret Agent, and continues her spying throughout the novel.

In addition, while heroines of romances written prior to the mid-eighties are at odds with other women, the women in newer romances tend to have and maintain friendships with other females. This must be compared to *The Flame and the Flower,* in which the heroine, Heather, is constantly subjected to the negative evaluating gazes of other women. At Heather's first introduction to her new community she elicits:

A few sneers and derogatory remarks . . . from the still-single maidens and their mothers, and from the men a complimentary silence. Bonneted heads came hurriedly together as the women whispered back and forth and grins broke wide on male faces. (Woodiwiss 253)

This is a structure in which the beautiful women are winners, while unattractive women are losers, ugly, and "unfeminine." The women's gazes as they "looked her up and down with anything but a friendly interest," are accompanied with unkind descriptions of their bodies, "The mother possessed broad heavy hips and narrow shoulders and other than dress and length of hair, she bore no resemblance to the gentler sex whatsoever" (253). Additionally, heroines such as Heather are often set against foils, who are usually depicted as sexually aggressive, vain, and greedy.

However, newer female-to-female relationships are supportive and generally noncompetitive. While occasionally a foil is inserted, the "rivalry" no longer gets in the way of the female friendship. For example, in Kinsale's *The Shadow and the Star,* Samuel believes himself to be in love with the beautiful Lady Kai. Far from portraying Kai negatively, or suggesting that Leda and Kai must hate each other, Kinsale shows Leda and Kai to be good friends. In Quick's *Deception,* Demetria, Jared's ex-fiancee and Olympia's apparent foil, is not a manipulative manhunter the male characters suppose her to be, but is instead devoted to a long-term relationship with her companion Constance. Olympia is never jealous of Demetria but befriends her.

In addition, there is often a strong theme of women joining together to protect each other from violence. In Quick's *Affair,* for example, Charlotte saves her sister from rape and later runs a business doing background checks for women on their prospective bridegrooms. In *Mistress,* Iphiginia helps her cousin Amelia, a rape victim, to exact revenge upon her attacker, and another major female character reveals that she killed her former husband when he was drunk and beating her—a move that is supported by other characters. Others of Quick's heroines, like Emily Farringdon or Iphiginia, use their business skills to help those less fortunate—for example, forming investment pools with widows, spinsters, and even servants.

Heroes

Just as characterizations of the heroine have changed since the mid-eighties with the incorporation of feminism into mainstream culture, heroes have altered drastically. Radway and Modleski described the hero as a silent, rugged man who is successful in the outside world, what Krentz has called the "alpha male," who functions as both hero and villain (107-08). The hero keeps his emotions hidden, except when he loses control in moments of violence or lust. However, in the decade since, the hero's presentation has changed. From the seventies to the nineties, the hero has become less silent, more emotional, and more overtly tender and caring, particularly in works by Kinsale and Quick. Perceived "masculine" strengths like autonomy, reserve, and lack of emotion are shown more and more to be a product of the hero's *lack* of mastery of the social world, rather than his power over it. Moreover, there has been a shift in narrative style that frequently changes identification from the female character to the male.

In typical novels of the seventies and early eighties, the romance hero was strong, always silent, and, if harboring any psychic pain, this pain was kept carefully hidden and only mentioned briefly. These men are experts in business and leaders of men. They are all presented as much more powerful than the female. Not only are they wealthier, with greater social power than the female, but they are firmly logical, and apparently emotionless, except when gripped with uncontrollable passion. Even their loving passion is depicted in terms of violence. For example, the hero's lovemaking often occurs as the result of a confrontation with the heroine, and his caresses are often described in brutal language.

The apparent strength of these heroes is to some extent caused by the fact that the reader is seldom allowed into the mind of the male. When we are allowed access, the man is usually shown to be thinking about the beauty of the female. Since the romance has long relied on a policy of "show, don't tell," the reader must read between the lines to discover the hero's motivations—i.e., he becomes angry because he loves the heroine. As Tania Modleski has observed, one of the main thrusts of the classic romance is to solve the masculine enigma. She notes that the mysteriousness of the hero seems to echo the ways that women have had to deal with men who are socialized to hide their feelings. Modleski argues that women have always had to rely on their ability to "read between the lines" to understand men and ensure their own survival. Romance novels merely repeat a social reality for many women (34).

In addition, the silent male character is inextricably linked to images of male violence, and violence is further linked to sexuality. Men assume the dominant position in regard to sexuality and the control of the female body. Just pages before the hero makes love to the heroine in *Moonstruck Madness*, he attempts to strangle her into submission:

He spoke softly and, reaching out, encircled her throat with his hand, his fingers rhythmically smoothing the downy-soft hairs at her nape as he continued, "It would be a pity for such a beautiful woman to choke and gasp as the rope tightened, taking away her breath, her eyes bulging in terror, the blood pounding in her head as she felt her little feet swing in the air, that petal-smooth skin mottled and purple. Not a pretty sight."

His fingers gradually stopped and began to tighten around Sabrina's neck. Her pulse was beating rapidly beneath his big thumb and as it continued to press she began to hear thundering in her ears, and, reaching up, grabbed frantically at his fingers, trying to prise them loose from her neck.

She stared into his eyes, which had turned almost black from his anger, disbelief in her face, when he suddenly loosened his grip . . . a cruel smile curved the Duke's mouth . . . "were you frightened?" he laughed heartlessly. (McBain 100)

In the typical romance of the seventies, the idea that men control women's bodies may be a temporary source of anger for the heroine, but it is also presented as inevitable and even desirable. In *The Flame and the Flower,* Heather meets her future husband when he rapes her. Later, Heather is nearly raped by another man. Saving her from this rape, Brandon follows with a sexual attack of his own.

His mouth swooped down hard upon hers, forcing her lips apart savagely as he thrust his tongue between them. Her lips were bruised as he kissed her hungrily. . . . Though she had thought herself saved from rape, she now feared she was headed for that same fate again. She had no will power to keep Brandon from taking what he wanted and what he had every right to. (Woodiwiss 345)

Brandon tells her "You are mine, Heather. No one will have you but me. Only I shall taste your body's joys. And when I snap my fingers, you will come" (345). Later Brandon tells her that he is prepared to "take you by force . . . for I can not go on living under the same roof with you and never finding my pleasure within your body. You may resign yourself to the fact that we will be sharing a bed" (349). At first outraged at Brandon's demands, Heather quickly realizes that "He is my husband and the father of my child. He owns me and I am the one without right to hold myself from him" (349). While alluding to the legal relationship between husband and wife at the time of the novel's setting, Heather's uncritical acceptance of this fact helps to naturalize for contemporary readers the heroine's subservient role in the relationship.

Such scenes clearly illustrate the reason that many feminists have been disturbed by the romance because they naturalize male violence and violence as part of sexuality. However, Radway's own research suggests that romance readers do not like violent scenes. Her readers go to great lengths to negotiate the meanings of such scenes and to throw a positive light on their occurrence. For example, this figuration of the hero is almost always interpreted positively by readers, who interpret male violence as a sign of the hero's uncontrollable passion for the heroine (140-44). Radway believes the negotiation between reader and violence in the text is a way for readers to resolve the contradictions of their lives in patriarchal society. Importantly, when the texts become too violent, Radway's readers can no longer negotiate them and they stop reading.

In the works of Kinsale and Quick, there is much less need for the reader to negotiate between male silence, male violence, and male passion. Heroes are far less physically violent and are actually presented as emotionally and even mentally weaker than the heroine. Most importantly, the heroines do not tolerate male violence or the assumption that the hero owns their bodies. Furthermore, heroines "own" their own desire; they have a more active role in sex, often initiating it.

Kinsale shifts the balance of power by making men vulnerable and destined to be radically changed by their sexual contact. In *The Shadow and the Star,* Leda muses that "Men were a mystery: formidable and comforting, elusive and forthright, full of strange passions and turnabouts" (264). At first glance, this appears to be another example of the masculine enigma observed by Modleski. However, there is also something else going on here. Readers do not have to read between the lines to justify male behavior; the explanation is already evident because of a growing movement to "tell" as well as "show" the hero's secrets. This exhumation of the hero's thoughts and feelings is crucial because it reveals that the hero is suffering because he is insecure and in need of the heroine's guidance, protection, and love.

Especially in the works of Kinsale, heroes are actually quite powerless. Although some heroes continue to be rich and powerful in the outside world, their social power is often threatened. Whereas the women of earlier romance are usually orphans or in dire economic circumstances, in Kinsale's novels the men are socially and emotionally disempowered. For example, Arden of *The Dream Hunter* was distanced form his emotionally abusive parents. Lord Ivaragh of *Uncertain Magic* saw his father murdered by his mother, suffers from blackouts, and is poor. Sheridan of *Seize the Fire* suffers from post-traumatic stress, an abusive father, a past life as a slave, and is poor. In *The Hidden Heart,* the hero witnessed the massacre of his family and is poor. In *Flowers from the Storm,* Christian, a wealthy and brilliant Duke, loses his ability to recognize words and speak, is imprisoned in an insane asylum, abused by villainous guards, and battles his backstabbing family who seek to take control of his title and his money. Partly paralyzed, he is unable to speak in complete sentences. S. T., the hero of *The Prince of Midnight,* is a famous highwayman and nobleman, forced to give up his title, money, and career due to a mysterious inner ear imbalance which causes him to fall over when he fights. Still another hero, Samuel, in *The Shadow and the Star,* is traumatized by his life as a child prostitute. Although Samuel grows up to be wealthy and a martial arts master, he lacks confidence and thinks of himself as dirty.

The contrast between the social status and perceived power of the male—most heroes are titled and/or rich—forms an achingly funny contrast with the heroes' emotional plights. Despite the fact that Kinsale's heroes are handsome, debonair, and "men's men," they are wounded men. While the writers of the seventies and eighties also depicted men with psychic wounds (for instance, Wolfgar in *The Wolf and the Dove,* who is scarred by his childhood as a bastard), it is important to note that the expression of these wounds has altered radically. The older novels only allude to the hero's pain. Readers are left to piece together a puzzle based on scraps of knowledge about the hero's past, building them into an understanding of the male—another example of the solving of "the secret underlying the masculine enigma" (Modleski 34). Kinsale's novels, however, emphasize masculine pain to such an extent that it seems inevitable. Her books leave the reader feeling that men suffer from an essential masculine lack.

Particularly in Kinsale's writing there is a focus on intense male suffering that is almost ritual in its repetition. In *The Shadow and the Star*, both hero and heroine are uncomfortable with their sexuality. Leda, a bastard raised in genteel poverty, must fight her sense of social unworthiness because she is "half-French." Yet her fears are as nothing compared to the experiences of Samuel, the former child prostitute. One is first introduced to his character, who is given no name in his introductory scene, in the midst of a Ninja ritual in which he "accepts emptiness." During the first half of the novel he is a cat burglar with an uncanny ability to disappear into the night. The idea that he is insubstantial counteracts most notions of romance heroes as solid. Further, the idea of male as illusive, vanishing, is played upon throughout the novel; Samuel first encounters Leda by hiding in her apartment at night; he regularly slips through the shadows. He even escapes a shark attack by his ability to be still and blend into the surroundings.

Samuel's need to hide (tellingly, Leda is able to find him in the dark) is explained by his background as child prostitute. The sense of the child behind the man is never far removed. The first time he is introduced by name, the reader sees him as a lonely boy meeting his adoptive parents for the first time. Samuel repeatedly chews his finger like an infant. He attempts to control this urge by placing his arm behind his back—a gesture he continues to make as an adult. While waiting to meet his adoptive parents he stands, "trying to be inconspicuous and conspicuous at the same time, and terrified that he had been forgotten" (20). Meeting his adoptive mother for the first time:

His feet in the pinching shoes took him forward, a step, and then a run, and he fell into her arms with a clumsy force which made him feel stupid and hot with shame. . . . The swelling in his throat hurt and throbbed as if something was trying to get out that couldn't. . . . "I'm sorry, Mum . . . I'm sorry . . . I didn't know—I didn't have nowhere else to go."

She closed her eyes. For a miserable moment he thought it was disgust, and he deserved it. He knew he must deserve it. He shouldn't have let those things happen to him; he should have done something; he shouldn't have been helpless and afraid. (20-21)

In addition to feeling intense shame, Samuel is often in physical pain, with pinching shoes, a painful swelling in his throat, and feelings of heat and stupidity. Such physical descriptors of male emotional turmoil are used repeatedly in the course of the novel. For example, when Samuel confronts his sexual feelings for the first time in his adult life, he is described in terms of fracture, uncertainty, and tremendous emotional vulnerability.

He could have evaded her. But his will and his action split apart from one another. He stood planted, with a lifetime of endurance fracturing, and allowed her to walk straight into him. . . . He had anarchy inside of him. . . . He did not know how to kiss a woman. He thought he should press his closed mouth to hers, but the contact disarmed him. (266-67)

When Leda asks him if he is lonely he thinks,

Lonely. God. So hot and intense and alone. . . . The sweetness of the embrace amazed him; he felt absurdly close to tears with the warmth of her against his face and beneath his hands. (268-69)

Similarly, in an exhaustive seven-page monologue at the conclusion of *Seize the Fire,* the hero relates the tale of his humiliating life as a Sultan's slave and his experience as a commander of a ship during a bloody battle in which he was responsible for killing 200 soldiers, as well as an entire town. During the flashback and monologue he feels himself "crumbling":

There was something crushing him, forcing his way the spreading cracks in his reason. . . . He sounded like a madman, yelling and sobbing and swearing. His hands were bleeding . . . he pressed his forehead to the wet stone, hiccuping, still whimpering curses under his breath. (444-45)

Again, the hero finds himself close to tears. He is described in physically painful terms as "fractured" and bleeding. He is childlike, sobbing, hiccuping, and whimpering. Adjectives like "crumbling," "crushing," and "cracked" depict him as broken and in need of fixing. This depiction of the broken hero is an interesting twist on the historical view of women's emotional "hysteria" as a sickness; in the romance novel, the male's inability to handle his emotions affects him like a sickness.

The revelation of male pain coincides with a greater availability of the male form to the female gaze. In *The Shadow and the Star,* for example, while one only knows the color of Leda's hair and eyes and no detail about her shape, Samuel's looks are very important. When he is introduced to Leda, Leda stares at his eyes that are "Silver and burning beautiful, utterly stunning in a face of masculine flawless inhumanity . . . perfect . . . perfect beyond anything but dreams" (Kinsale 23). In a reverse of the woman on a "pedestal," Sheridan Drake in *Seize the Fire* is introduced descending a staircase while the heroine watches:

The face belonged to an archangel from the shadows: a cool, sulky mouth and aquiline profile, and Satan's own intelligence in the assessing look he gave her. The candles behind him lit a smoldering halo of reddish gold around his black hair and turned each faint, frosted breath to a brief glow.

   He was not homely. He was utterly and appallingly beautiful. (Kinsale 15-16)

   The perusal of the male psyche and form is similar to the investigation of the female body found in earlier novels. Interestingly, psychoanalytic feminists have shown that the fetishizing gaze, which objectifies women's bodies, developed as a way to contain the threat of the women's lack of the penis. Similarly, I think that the fetishizing of male suffering points to a form of containment. Male suffering may be a way of containing the threat of male power. However, containment also underscores an essential *lack* on the part of the man: the lack of the woman who can take away his pain.

   The good woman who heals the wounded hero is a staple of romance fiction. The rugged man is always effectively socialized, transformed by novel's end into a gentle nurturer. However, the emphasis in these new novels is slightly different. While older heroes are softened so as to better take care of the heroine, Kinsale's heroes start soft and become stronger. Indeed they are so wounded that they are barely functioning; only their contact with the heroine allows them to survive. The women save the hero from self-destruction and social failure. For example, women are able to offer men a way of life that gives them emotional security. Men become psychically healthy and better people as a result of their contact with the women. Maddy protects Christian's inheritance, Zenia saves Arden's life in the desert and reunites him with his family, Leda helps Samuel overcome his childhood trauma. The result of this is that women are presented as healthier and emotionally stronger than men. The heroine saves the day because she is able to cope with the world better than the hero.

Mutuality

In the recent works of Kinsale and Quick, the greater strength of the heroine and the dependence of the male create a sense of interdependence. This is significant because it suggests a political and epistemological shift in regard to the traditional Western "masculinist" espousal of autonomy and male control through withdrawal. As Radway observed, despite the union of male and female at the end of older romances, a masculinist position is still maintained; men continue to be violent or rugged, women assimilate to male control and find their identity through marriage.

However, Quick and Kinsale maintain a sense of independent female identity by creating relationships between the heroes and heroines that are entirely mutual. Mutual emotional bonding often takes place before any sexual union occurs. For example, in *The Dream Hunter,* Arden and Zenia grow to know each other in the desert, where they each save each other's lives. In *The Shadow and the Star,* Samuel and Leda similarly share a close friendship before they become lovers, as do Maddy and Christian in *Flowers from the Storm.* The couples give each other unconditional emotional support as a prerequisite to sex.

The friendliness of such relationships breaks from the romantic tradition of opposites who seem to hate each other, but really love each other. Although there is always turbulence in the relationship, this turmoil is generally situational rather then stemming from hostility. The couples are always tender with each other and act as friends. Mutuality is at the heart of these relationships.

In fact, individualism is no longer shown as healthy. Heroes are unhappy, miserable, and ultimately weak because of their emotional isolation. Heroes are saved by acknowledging their need for other humans and entering into a relationship. Relationships are no longer based on sexuality and male dominance but on mutuality and equality. In turn, this emphasis on mutuality further changes the meanings of sexual relations, as well as gender and gender roles. This shift is political because it, in turn, suggests an epistemological stance that is based on theories of connection and inclusion rather than individualism and control. This framework is much more comfortable to the kind of feminist sensibility seen operative in the novels under discussion.

Sex

This framework of inclusion and connection is most eloquently expressed in the way that Kinsale and Quick depict sex. Sex in romance novels has historically symbolized the emotional/spiritual joining of the hero and heroine. However, I would argue that the manner in which sex is depicted radically alters the interpretation of that joining. Sex, as presented in novels such as those by Woodiwiss, reveals expectations about male dominance. For example, women in older romances are always placed as the object of the male gaze, as recipients of male sexual action. They are thus understood as essentially sexually powerless. In addition to removing female agency from sex, sex in the older framework is "male" in that it is decontextualized and separated from the world of the everyday. Rather than being seen as part of the process of a relationship, sex is the glue that holds it together. As in *The Flame and the Flower,* it does not matter whether the hero and heroine actually get along as long as the sex is good, and the sex is always good because there is only one kind of sex—sex that is male-dominated and disassociated from time, place, or emotional context. However, new romances have stopped treating sex as a cure for the differences between the hero and the heroine. Although sex does unite them, it is a joining that only further underscores an already satisfactory relationship. Furthermore, a growing contextualization of sex shifts our traditional understanding of the act itself, throwing into question mainstream ideas regarding sex and sexuality.

In older novels, focus on body parts and woman as object, discussed earlier, create the sense that sex is something done to a woman. The woman's body is described in intimate detail, while the man's body and face receive much less attention. Female parts are described in intimate, loving detail, with a wealth of adjectives informing readers that legs are "slender," and bosoms are "full." The emphasis on the visual in sex is masculinist, revealing that the bedroom is another place in which women must watch themselves even as they are being watched, and be aware of their effect upon a man.

In addition, sex is a separate, decontextualized experience in these earlier novels. It occurs in moments that are in some way removed in time or from the normal functioning of the universe. Even when the heroine is initially willing to have sex, she is generally swept away by her passions. The heroine in these moments is literally outside of herself, and often becomes something not quite human. For example, Shanna and Roark's sexual encounters often follow fits of rage or fear. In one scene Shanna, in terror of a thunderstorm, becomes like an animal:

Shanna cowered in the dark . . . tears streamed down her cheeks. She crouched as if she sought some den or lair away from the storm. As he took her in into his arms, she clawed at his chest and mewled. (Woodiwiss, *Shanna* 337)

The idea of female sexuality as a liminal state, outside of the everyday, is disturbing because it suggests that sexuality is part of a higher force and cannot be controlled by the heroine.

Thus, sex in a novel like 1972's *The Flame and the Flower* is "pornographic" in the sense that sex is something that is done to a woman, often against her will, as it is to Heather, who realizes she has "no right" to stop her husband. It is also noteworthy that these novels feature a highly masculine conception of sex, in that sex is goal-oriented, inevitably ending in a climax. Sex scenes detail body parts and the action of the body, resulting in one generalized sensation, of "magic, a stunning, beautiful, expanding bloom of ravaging rapture" (Woodiwiss, *Shanna* 136), a single, centralized explosion that is highly phallic in function. It does not reflect an "erotic" sensibility as defined by Luce Irigary in *The Sex That Is Not One*. An "erotic" scene, based on Irigary's notion of the eternally dialogic, eternally connected female body, would be conceived of as diffused, less goal-oriented, and more context driven. Such a scene would not focus on a single climax but would instead attend to a variety of sensual points and pleasures while acknowledging an ever-shifting range of emotions and sensations.

Kinsale and Quick's novels quite clearly possess an erotic aesthetic. Their descriptions of female body parts are less precise while the emotional components of sex become far more complex. While the men are always desirous of the women's body and individual parts are mentioned, there are no specific descriptors of those parts. For example, while limbs and bosoms may be "lovely" to the man, they are no longer necessarily "slender," or "full." Instead of perfection of individual body parts as an indicator of "good sex," good sex is dependent upon specific sexual *actions* and *situations.*

A clear requirement for "good sex" in these novels is consensual, non-coercive sex. Not only are more recent heroines able to "own" their own desire, often initiating sexual contact, as do Augusta in *Rendezvous* and Olympia in *Deception,* but there is an explicit lack of tolerance for male sexual violence. For example, in *The Shadow and the Star,* Samuel stops when Leda says no. Even though he knows that, "he could have conquered in an instant," he stops because:

in her face he saw doubt and faith and earnestness, a wholehearted dependence upon him . . . and a sweet, impossible bravery; the heroism of small defenseless creatures facing peril.

In her weakness, she defeated him. He could not go on. (Kinsale 271)

However, heroines do not simply rely on the kindness of men to protect them from sexual violence; they demand, and claim their right to sexual freedom through their own actions. For example, in Quick's *Seduction,* the hero breaks his promise of consensual sex when he orders the heroine into bed. Sophy responds by drugging his tea. She then pours an enormous amount of blood-red tea onto the bed to make him believe that he has had his way with her. When the hero awakens, he believes that he has been unbelievably violent to her and is horrified with himself. He stays away from her.

An "erotic" sensibility is also apparent in the way that sex is shown to be part of a process, itself composed of processes. Sex is no longer the "climax" of a relationship, but is part of an evolving relationship. Furthermore, within the act of sex itself, the emotional states of the hero and heroine are in a constant process of transformation. Sex is thus no longer a mere physical act, but is understood to be an expressive form of communication, signaling things that are outside of the physical act itself. For example, Kinsale's sex scenes show the heroine and hero experiencing not only love, but a myriad of often conflicting emotions during sex. Interestingly, although the sex is consensual and usually pleasurable for the women, there is often a large amount of psychic pain or turmoil involved in the event. It is never uncomplicated or without motivation.

A typical scene occurs in *The Dream Hunter*. Zenia, sure that Arden will desert her, has sex with him. The experience is one that is mixed with her surety that he will leave her, her desire for him to stay, her sexual desire for him, and her desire to have a baby. All these emotions are blended into a sex scene in which Zenia takes command. Sex becomes a way for her to negotiate a range of conflicted feelings as well as take out her aggression on the male. For example:

Zenia's position gave her control of him. It was when she moved, flexing her body and hips to find the source of her own pleasure, that he inhaled with swift ecstasy. She reveled in the deep ache of penetration. "You won't leave me," she said in a breathless hiss at the back of her throat. "You won't, you won't, you won't" . . . she could steal it. She could nurse his seed in her and take it with her and hold it to herself and keep it for her own, another child to love when he was gone. (322)

Yet this scene is not only one of passive-aggressive sexual use of the male, for Zenia finds emotional and sexual satisfaction in the sex. Part of her satisfaction comes from viewing sex as a way to have a child. Further, her physical pleasure comes not just from the climax, but from her pleasure in a range of tactile sensations:

A radiant shudder seemed to seize her, a bright joy as his life surged into her, permeating her again. She held him to her, clutched his head to her breasts while their bodies throbbed together.

Zenia clung to him, whimpering. Her mind was blank and yet full of energy, sliding from wonder back to the present, slowly regaining awareness of herself; of him; the sharp stretch of her legs, the tickle of his hair against her skin, the hard press of his body bearing her weight. (323)

It is clear here that sex is a form of power, an idea that appears in several other novels. In the one rape that occurs in any of the novels under discussion, *The Prince of Midnight,* the hero, S. T., declares his love for the heroine early in the book. Because she feels like she owes him for helping her, she offers to have sex with him. When he responds that he does not want to have sex without love, Leigh undresses and touches his body. The hero is unable to control himself and has sex with her. Although he experiences physical pleasure, he hates it emotionally. In a reverse of the usual rape scene, in which the woman watches distantly as she is raped, S. T. watches himself. Afterward he feels "furious and ashamed" that he took what Leigh offered "like a beggar." Putting his face in his hands he realizes that, "Some bastard had murdered her family, and all he could do was violate her. He was angry, humiliated, and lonelier than he had ever felt in his life" (Kinsale 81).

In this scene, sex is a commodity and a tool to gain power over others. It is noteworthy for several other reasons. First, this scene is the only one of all these books in which the woman is having sex without any sexual or emotional desire for the man. Further, although the rather masochistic way Leigh uses sex—as a passive-aggressive punishment of both S. T. and herself—is disconcerting, I feel that such a treatment of sex (especially when combined with more satisfactory visions of sex that occur later in the novel) does display a feminist consciousness because it problematizes the conception of sex as a context-free, natural act. Sex is no longer conceived of as something that is done to a woman or man, something outside of the hero and heroine or their personalities, emotions, and situations. Rather, sex is instead highly dependent upon the shifting range of emotions and sensations that come into being during the course of a relationship. Such scenes acknowledge the existence of the interplay between personal and interpersonal power during sex, as well as emotional and intellectual motivations that lay behind the sexual act. By revealing the way in which power relations are constructed and contested in sex, sex is politicized.

This linkage of sex and interpersonal violence does have the potential to eroticize violence; however, I do want to add that while Kinsale problematizes sex, there is nonetheless a strong sense throughout her novels that while the reality is often problematic, "good sex" is the utopian goal. "Good" sex involves love and tenderness and complete reciprocity of feeling between the hero and heroine. This is also the case in Quick's novels. For example, in 1994's *Mistress,* during their first sexual encounter Iphiginia and Marcus interact in a mutually playful nature.

She shivered in his arms and thrust her hands beneath the edges of his shirt. . . . "You feel wondrously fine, my lord," she breathed, awed by the feel of him. "Altogether magnificent. You remind me of a statue of Hercules that I once viewed in Venice."

Marcus gave a muffled laugh that quickly turned into a groan. "Be warned, I am no statue, madam, although at the moment a certain part of me is certainly as hard as stone."

"I am aware of that" . . . She knew if she wanted to stop this from going further, she must speak up now.

She smiled at Marcus and said nothing at all. (Quick 169-70)

These romances move away from depictions of male-dominated sex and show a female perspective on both the reality of sex, and sex as an expression of a utopian, reciprocal relationship.

Conclusion

While many older romances are about an unformed young woman's journey to adulthood whose experiences with the man mold her into a new being, the romances of Kinsale and Quick depict a journey by the hero. The heroine's identity remains stable, while the hero drastically changes. In addition to being less objectified physically, heroines are more often able to shape the world around their desires. Beginning from positions of greater security (economic and/or emotional), women act upon the social world as well as the private realm. Heroines voice overtly feminist stances, like the importance of women in history. They maintain friendships with other women, breaking the myth of female competition.

The greater stability and strength of the heroine means that while the narrative still depicts a journey, the journey is not about the necessity for female change, but rather the need for men to change. These new novels have moved the *necessity* of male transformation to the forefront, and, by doing so, challenge existing notions about cultural norms. While older romances showed feisty heroines as outside the norm and in need of men to make them "normal" wives and mothers, newer novels reveal that the "masculine" qualities of autonomy and control are often debilitating to men. Heroes are normalized by their association with the heroine.

Men are no longer implicitly guiding figures for the women, but are explicitly guided *by* women. Despite their social power, physical strength, or intelligence, men are depicted as essentially wounded and flawed and in need of fixing. Men need women in order to develop psychic strength. By emphasizing the change in the male, a feminist viewpoint, advocating the importance of caring relationships, emotional self-knowledge, weakness, and human frailty, is thus explicitly stated.

The shifting balance of power between the hero and heroine ultimately changes sexual relations between the genders. Sex is no longer the thing that naturally unites men and women. It is no longer the cure to a troubled relationship, but is part of a process in the development of a relationship. By changing sex to a process, the new romances denounce a view of sex which is decontextualized, visual, and pornographic. Sex in newer novels is eroticized in that it is viewed in context and as possessing many complicated elements. Further, there is a growing tendency to problematize the nature of sex, revealing it as an area in which power is deployed. Even though Kinsale and Quick highlight the inherent power battles in sexual relations, they maintain a focus on the utopian goal of good sex, which is always consensual.

I would like to conclude by saying that I do not believe that romance novels are feminist tracts in and of themselves. Many romances, with their focus on wealth and titles, still advocate capitalism and consumerism, which are based on competition rather than mutual care. Further, it must be noted that romances ultimately deal with the union of a man and woman. Romances thus ultimately espouse heterosexuality as the norm (although there is a greater inclusion of positive homosexual characters). While the epistemological push for connection, rather than autonomy, suggests the need for a new world order which is non-hierarchical, non-competitive, and mutually supportive, the importance of the male and the necessity of a man in a woman's life reinforces patriarchal norms. As Radway has earlier noted, women in romances are not expected to be autonomous, but must still perceive of themselves as selves-in relations (16). Furthermore, the feminist notions espoused in these romances are examples of essentialist feminism—women are validated based on naturally "feminine" abilities to heal and nurture. Given these considerations, I nevertheless suggest that romance novels have incorporated explicitly feminist themes into the basic structure of the genre. I see it as a sign of progress that this popular genre is at least beginning to construct messages that women have the right to succeed in the public realm and have the right to love without fear.

Works Cited

Cawelti, John G. *Adventure, Mystery and Romance: Formula Stories as Art and Popular Culture.* Chicago: U of Chicago P, 1976.

Irigary, Luce. "The Sex Which Is Not One." *The Second Wave: A Reader in Feminist Theory.* Ed. Linda Nicholson. New York: Routledge, 1997.

Jones, Ann Rosalind. "Mills and Boon Meets Feminism." *The Progress of Romance: The Politics of Popular Fiction.* Ed. Jean Radford. London: Routledge, 1986. 195-220.

Kinsale, Laura. "The Androgynous Reader: Point of View in the Romance." *Dangerous Men & Adventurous Women; Romance Writers on the Appeal of the Romance.* Ed. Jayne Ann Krentz. Philadelphia: U of Pennsylvania P, 1992. 31-44.

——. *The Dream Hunter.* New York: Avon, 1994.

——. *Flowers from the Storm.* New York: Avon, 1992.

——. *The Hidden Heart.* New York: Avon, 1986.

——. *The Prince of Midnight.* New York: Avon, 1990.

——. *Seize the Fire.* New York: Avon, 1989.

——. *The Shadow and the Star.* New York: Avon, 1991.

——. *Uncertain Magic.* New York: Avon, 1987.

Krentz, Jayne Ann. Introduction. *Dangerous Men & Adventurous Women; Romance Writers on the Appeal of the Romance.* Ed. Jayne Ann Krentz. Philadelphia: U of Pennsylvania P, 1992. 1-10.

——. "Trying to Tame the Romance: Critics and Correctness." *Dangerous Men & Adventurous Women; Romance Writers on the Appeal of the Romance.* Ed. Jayne Ann Krentz. Philadelphia: U of Pennsylvania P, 1992. 107-14.

McBain, Laurie. *Moonstruck Madness.* New York: Avon, 1977.

Modleski, Tania. *Loving with a Vengeance: Mass Produced Fantasies for Women.* New York: Methuen, 1982.

Mulvey, Laura. "Visual Pleasure and Narrative Cinema." *Contemporary Film Theory.* Ed. Antony Easthope. New York: Longman, 1993.

Quick, Amanda. *Affair.* New York: Bantam, 1998.

——. *Deception.* New York: Bantam, 1993.

——. *Mistress.* New York: Bantam, 1994.

——. *Rendezvous.* New York: Bantam, 1991.

——. *Scandal.* New York: Bantam, 1991.

——. *Seduction.* New York: Bantam, 1990.

Tompkins, Jane. *West of Everything: The Inner Life of Westerns.* New York: Oxford UP, 1992.

Woodiwiss, Kathleen. E. *The Flame and the Flower.* New York: Avon, 1972.

——. *Shanna.* New York: Avon, 1977.

——. *The Wolf and the Dove.* New York: Avon, 1974.

Postmodern Identity (Crisis):
Confessions of a Linguistic Historiographer
and Romance Writer

Julie Tetel Andresen

My name is Julie, and I write romances.

Over the years, I have sometimes felt like I am at an unofficial AA meeting where I must confess to my romance writing behavior. Other times, I have made it a political gesture to come out of the closet and admit it. As a member of the English Department at Duke University where I teach linguistics, I publish scholarly books and articles with titles like "The Behaviorist Turn in Recent Theories of Language" and "Signs and Systems in Condillac and Saussure." I also write historical romances with titles like *And Heaven Too*, *Simon's Lady*, and *Tangled Dreams*. I love linguistics, but I feel passionate about romance.

In 1994, I was invited by the Psychology Department at Western Michigan University, Kalamazoo, to give a series of lectures on the current state of evolutionary scripts for the development of human language in the species. When several psychologists at Western Michigan learned that I wrote (and actually published!) popular romances, I was asked to give yet another lecture, jointly sponsored by the creative writing program, where I would explain this unusual combination of writing interests: obscure linguistic theories and mass-market romance.

The psychologists at Western Michigan are known for their adherence to the work of the premier American behaviorist, B. F. Skinner (1904-90). For decades, Skinner has been known to the linguistics community primarily as an outcast, in large part because Noam Chomsky (b. 1928), the premier American linguist of his day, published an excoriating review of Skinner's *Verbal Behavior* (1957) in the major linguistics journal, *Language*, in 1959. After that review, Skinner's account of verbal behavior was pretty much dead in the linguistics community. In the late 1980s, I, as a linguistic historiographer (that is, someone who studies the historical record of linguistics), decided to take a look at Skinner's book, since it formed such an important part of recent American linguistic history. Upon reading it, I discovered that I liked quite a bit of it, and I saw the need to rehabilitate some of Skinner's views on verbal behavior in several articles that I published. To my surprise, I found myself instantly embraced by the behaviorist community and was invited to speak all over the country.

The psychologists at Western Michigan were the first and only group—before the "Rereading the Romance" conference in 1997—to be interested in the intersection of my academic writing and my romance writing. Behaviorists are, after all, curious about all kinds of behavior, particularly the odd combinations. As I began to formulate an explanation of my own odd combination of writing behaviors for these psychologists, I was struck both by the difficulty and by the delight of the experience. I was also struck by how just plain strange it was, because I experienced the attempt to explain my own behavior to myself as an intriguingly not-so-novel novelty. It is the not-so-novel novelty of that experience which I hope to explain in the course of the present exposition.

The story of my dual and divergent writing behaviors begins like this:

In the past fifteen years, I have had increasing occasion to speak about my life and work as a romance writer. I have given newspaper and radio interviews, and I have spoken before reading groups and library associations. Until very recently, I have had no opportunity to address questions concerning my particular writing craft. Until very recently, all of my explanatory efforts have been devoted entirely to perfecting the gentle art of my verbal self-defense of the entire genre of romance fiction. That is, the majority of my public efforts to articulate my thoughts on the subject of my romances have been directed at finding effective answers to the standard and inevitable questions that interviewers and "just plain folk" alike find themselves unable *not* to ask a romance writer: 1) How much money do you make? 2) When are you going to write a real book? 3) How come you write under a pen name? Are you ashamed of what you're writing? 4) Do you let your children read your books? 5) What about all those rape scenes in historical novels? 6) How do you do your research (wink, wink, snicker, snicker)? 7) What is a linguist at a respected university like you doing writing romances? And my personal favorite: 8) Is it true that romances are written by sexually frustrated housewives?

Similarly, in the past fifteen years, I have had occasion to speak about my research field of linguistic historiography. These occasions have taken the form of discussions with my colleagues in both the English Department and the Department of Cultural Anthropology (where I have a joint appointment), as well as with students, fellow linguists, behavior analysts, other psychologists, and regular old, random people.

Most recently, I have had to present myself in relationship to my research field in the form of that wretched but challenging genre known as "Statement of Purpose for Tenure."

My point is that, over the years, I have had to account for bits and pieces of myself in bits and pieces, but until the psychologists at Western Michigan invited *both* of me to speak, I had not been asked to account for *all* of myself at once.

At first, I experienced this attempt to account for the whole of myself as something new, even puzzling. I was frankly stymied for several weeks, wondering if there was anything intelligible I could possibly say to explain why one person could be engaged in such apparently disparate activities as writing esoteric, neck-up, high-minded linguistic historiography for an extremely small audience of scholars (most of whom could be counted on my ten fingers and ten toes), and, at the same time, writing accessible, determinedly neck-down narratives of heterosexual love relationships for a potentially huge audience of millions. I was tempted to say that having these two writing interests was odd, even cognitively dissonant at times—and leave it at that. But that would be explaining nothing, because it was this very supposed oddness of one person engaged in the two activities that prompted the psychologists to invite me to account for myself.

The more I thought about it, the more I realized that I had never experienced the two writing activities, one or the other of which I engage in on a day-to-day basis, as odd or even at odds with one another. My self-description of the two activities has always been that they are, in fact, mutually energizing. And how new, after all, could the explanatory experience be in light of the accountings I routinely give of myself, albeit in bits and pieces? The newness was only that of finding myself in the position of having to articulate what I had felt all along at some unarticulated level, namely that the perception of oddity or disparity between my two writing activities is not a function of some chopped up set of sensibilities inside of me but is rather produced by evaluative categories and institutionalized practices that exist outside of me.

Because I was born into a world in which the romance genre and the discipline of linguistics were already well-constituted discourses, I understand that I have been formed by the evaluative categories and institutionalized practices that maintain them as much as I have resisted the logic that separates them. I understand as well that my pragmatic challenge to the logic that separates them, in my day-to-day exercise of one or the other, necessarily reforms those categories and practices, however minimally, whether I want or intend to reform those categories and practices or not. (I am not sure that I do.) I would go so far as to say that it is precisely when someone like me—that is, someone with my socioeconomic background and education—comes along and discovers that she does not like the kind of literature that she is either supposed to like or that most people of a similar demographic profile *do* like that the evaluative categories and institutionalized practices become exposed and available for examination and then, possibly, reorganization. If I were engaged in writing high-level syntactic analyses of exotic languages and, say, recognizably consciousness-raising post-feminist fiction or even cerebral murder mysteries, certain categories and practices would be confirmed rather than contested, and the perception of dissonance between my two activities would not be as wide. If I were that person, I might not have been asked to give an explanation of why I write what I write, because it would have been obvious.

I have identified four personal characteristics, constitutive of the organization of my inner sensibilities, that make coherent and continuous my inclinations and interests as a romance writer and as a linguistic historiographer. In other words, here are the reasons why the two different writing activities don't seem so different to me:

#1) I am not a minimalist. I am tempted to avoid the negative self-description and call myself a maximalist. However, that would still be self-definition by opposition to someone else's primary term, so I think I will call myself an extravagantist.

Take, for instance, the novels of Ann Tyler. I admire her work greatly, but her writing is not to my taste. I do not bring up Ann Tyler to put her down. I do not valorize my work by devalorizing hers. I bring her up because her work strikes me as being at an esthetic polar opposite from mine. Her characters and their relationships are, in a word, bony. Now her craft is great, and in the German sense of *Kraft*, she has power to bring a very particular world into existence. To my eye, her stories are like finely etched engravings. I have read many of her stories and appreciated them and even enjoyed them, but *they are not to my central reading taste.*

My taste is for flesh, lots of it. I do not like those painfully skinny Giacometti statues. I certainly like the corpulent men and women (especially the women) in the paintings of Fragonard, Watteau, and Titian. I like things round, lush, and colorful—in other words, I respond well to the esthetic dimensions of the romance, in particular, the historical romance. Fifteen years ago, I experienced something of a relief when, while working on my dissertation, a friend lent me Georgette Heyer's *Cotillion* as a diversion, and I ate it up, finding that historical romances, specifically romanticomedies, seemed to satisfy my reading taste for physical, emotional, and verbal extravagance. Soon thereafter, I began to write my first romance. I set it in the thirteenth century, and I recall taking intemperate pleasure in describing a medieval feast and in spreading the tables with food. No authorial anorexia for me.

My esthetic and authorial tastes are intimately bound with my conception of myself, which can be understood, in part, in terms of the consequences of being born a baby girl in the 1950s and becoming a woman in the culture in which I have lived for the past 45+ years. My sense of my bodily self is—curiously, given the culture in which I live—the opposite of the wisdom articulated by the diet guru, Richard Simmons, who has said that inside every fat woman is a thin woman trying to get out. Inside of me, by way of contrast, I am aware of a fat woman trying to get out, and I let her out as often as I can. If I could sing (which I cannot), I would not be a romance writer, I would be a torch singer of operatic proportions.

So, then, what could have been my response as a graduate student in the 1970s upon encountering Chomskyan linguistics, that most svelte of language theories? I think I experienced, quite simply, cognitive distaste for this emaciated theory of language. Chomskyan linguistics is based on the linguistic analysis of single, monologic sentences occurring in isolation. I do not say that these sentences are "uttered" in isolation, because they never issue forth from any particular speaker's mouth; and I call them monologic (versus dialogic) because they are never a response to another utterance, nor do they, in turn, ever provoke responses. Chomskyan linguistics was first built around an elegant set of rules to explain its monologic sentences and is now built around an exquisitely abstracted set of principles and parameters. Either way, it is thin to the vanishing point, for in its very conceptualization, language is theorized to be a thoroughly disembodied entity.

So, fifteen years ago, I was a graduate student in search of a theory of language that I could respond to positively, and in order to increase the possibilities of finding such a theory, I turned to the historical record of the discipline and began to hunt around. I am happy to report that I have found many theories to my taste, Skinner's account of verbal behavior being one notable, full-bodied example. In *Verbal Behavior,* bodies speak, bodies move, they interact with one another, they affect one another, they laugh, argue, and have fun. No wonder I took so readily to Skinner and preferred him to Chomsky's world of hushed, bodiless, streamlined analyses.

#2) Although I have set up an esthetic pole where Ann Tyler is at one end and I am at the other, I do not believe in any similar emotion/

intellect continuum, such that the farther one is toward the emotional end, the farther away one is from the intellectual end, and vice versa.

I suppose I should tell you that I was a girl who did pretty well in school, and I suppose that I should also tell you that I was the girl who consistently got a "check minus" on her report card in the category: "ability to control emotions." I must have been crying, laughing, or generally emoting in school, but it was primarily crying. In any case, I was not behaving within the emotional norms preferred by the public schools—and my inner child still rages at the thought of not only having been graded on my emotions but also *having been graded down* for them, as if they were some wild part of me that I either needed to tame or kill. Come to think of it, my adult self rages, too, at the thought of either taming or killing my emotions. I *like* living life at a high emotional pitch, or perhaps I can live only at this pitch. I don't think I can even tell it is a high pitch, for it seems normal to me. Yet the clues are all around me that I do emote more strongly than the norm, and sure enough, I still get an occasional "check minus" from my husband and two sons in the category: "ability to control emotions."

I probably do not need to belabor the point that the romance genre is a likely candidate for satisfying my desire and need for emotional charge, both in my reading and writing experiences. (Writing romance is, in fact, emotionally regulatory for me.) Certainly all literature is expressive, but it seems to me that romance foregrounds emotionality— makes it its subject matter. In the romance, the central problem is the working through of the emotional relationship between hero and heroine. The central problem is not, say, the solving of a murder as it is in a mystery novel or the creation of a parallel universe as it is in a science fiction novel. I do not insist on differentiating romance from other genres on the basis of its foregrounding of emotionality. I will, however, insist that it is not built into the genre that an emotionally charged love story will insult your intelligence or, alternatively, will have no appeal to the intellect. Let's face it: some romances are dumb, but some are not, and I like to read and write emotionally compelling stories that satisfy the (intellectual? technical? literary?) demands of plot, character development, historical specificity, thematic elements, style, and imagery.

Turning back to linguistics, the logical premise of the Chomskyan theory of language is that syntactic structures and "knowledge of language" can be successfully analyzed as autonomous objects—that is, objects studied apart from particular contexts and apart from the particular beliefs, needs, desires, emotions, idiosyncrasies, historical circumstances, etc., of particular speakers. I have either always refused or am constitutionally unable to undertake such an autonomously conceived analytic task. It is a fundamentally alien notion to me to think that I—or anyone else—could utter a sentence apart from any beliefs, needs, desires, emotions, etc. So, when I was a graduate student, it was difficult for me to wring any emotional transport out of (or even see the sense of analyzing) such classic sentences as "Flying planes can be dangerous" or "Seymour cut the salami with a knife" which were left to float in white space on a textbook page, without a context, without a speaker, without a listener, and without a purpose, emotional or otherwise.

So there I was, a graduate student, faced with the Chomskyan model of language that assumed that communication does occur and proceeded to explain *how* it occurs but saying nothing of *why* it occurs. The "why" seemed the more interesting question to me, along with the "why" of why Chomsky was making the kinds of assumptions he was making about language. So I backed up through the historical record of linguistics and came to a stop at the 18th century. There I discovered that both the *grammairiens philosophes* and Chomskyan linguists were working from an inherited Cartesian epistemology/psychology. I was able to see Chomsky as a most recent and prominent purveyor of the dichotomization of intellect (*raison*) and emotion (*passion*) formalized by Descartes and inherited by Condillac, perhaps the most influential *grammairien philosophe*, who continued to separate understanding (*entendement*) from will or willful desire (*volonté*). Rousseau, Diderot, and even Condillac had problematized the intellect/emotion dichotomy under the influence of an imported Lockean sensualism. Still, the traditional master narrative of intellectual history established the commonplace that the cool rationalism of the Enlightenment was followed, in serial fashion, by the heated passion of Romanticism, as if intellect and emotion could not coherently co-occur at any given time, in any given philosophy.

But, of course, intellect and emotion do interpenetrate in the work of, say, William Dwight Whitney (1827-1894) and William James (1842-1910), and it pleases me to think that American pragmatism, in a certain sense, did not "buy into" the intellect/emotion dichotomy. Or, perhaps, it is that Whitney and James understand understanding to be so thoroughly *embodied* that they cannot help but discuss it in terms of the ever-situatedness of individually, historically circumstanced bodies interacting in specific contexts. On discussing the faculty of memory, for instance, James writes in *Principles of Psychology*: "Evidently, then, *the faculty does not exist absolutely, but works under conditions*, and *the quest of the conditions* becomes the psychologist's most interesting task" (3). This "quest of conditions" defines my various projects: from understanding the historical and otherwise contingent conditions that shape a given theory of language at a given period of time; to understanding the historical and otherwise contingent conditions that shape the characters in my romances as they, in turn, shape a certain historical and otherwise contingent plot played out in the "theater of my mind"; to understanding the historical and otherwise contingent conditions that shape any given instance of verbal behavior.

#3) I have already told you that I cannot sing. I also cannot paint or sculpt. That's okay, because I love language. I love new words. I love old words. I love to talk, and I love people to talk to me. My preferred genre in film is the Hollywood romanticomedy. My preferred genre in television is the situation comedy. I loved *I Love Lucy* as a kid. I think *Home Improvement* is funny now. The romanticomedy and the situation comedy are genres that are dialogue-intense, and the best, from my point of view, are hallmarked by witty repartee.

My point is this: the center of the center of my romances is animated by the dialogue between the hero and heroine. If you do not have good dialogue, you do not have good romance. Dialogue is "where the action is" as far as the romantic chemistry between the two characters is concerned. Dialogue is the verbal sculpture of the characters, and their dialogic interactions sculpt their chemistry. If what the characters are saying is not interesting and if their dialogic interactions are not interesting, then I do not care how beautiful and sexy they are, their love relationship will not interest me.

Let me re-invoke Ann Tyler. I have said that her characters and their relationships are bony. I would like to add that her dialogues are consistently about miscommunication. Her dialogues go like this. (Fingers on both hands spread and turned away from one another, fingers not meshing.) I, on the other hand, like my hero-heroine dialogues to go like this. (Fingers on both hands spread, facing one another, and now interlocking.) There can be serious misunderstandings between the hero and heroine—and there often are—but it is the possibility of entangling, then clearing them up that is tantalizing to me. Hero and heroine have to be talking to each other, verbally engaged with each other, even if they are talking at cross-purposes. No matter how serious in tone or theme, romances are comedies. Romances are premised on the possibility of communication and happy resolution and a satisfying love relationship. In a romance, the hero's answer to the heroine's question: "What's bothering you?" is *never:* "I don't want to talk about it."

As a graduate student, I could make absolutely nothing out of those poor, lonely, emotionless, theoretically unprovoked, and defiantly unresponsive utterances of the type "Seymour cut the salami with a knife." I think I was even resentful that these lone, fully finished, seemingly transparently interpretable sentences could be the centerpiece of linguistic inquiry. So, when I encountered the work of V. N. Volosinov, a Soviet linguist of the 1920s, about five years ago, I immediately recognized a kindred spirit. Let me quote a passage from Volosinov's *Marxism and the Philosophy of Language:*

The actual reality of language-speech is not the abstract system of linguistic form, not the isolated monologic utterance, and not the psycho-physiological act of its implementation, but the social event of verbal interaction implemented in an utterance or utterances.

Thus, verbal interaction is the basic reality of language.

Dialogue, in the narrow sense of the word, is, of course, only one of the forms—a very important form, to be sure—of verbal interaction. But dialogue can also be understood in a broader sense, meaning not only direct, face-to-face, vocalized communication between persons, but also verbal communication of any type whatsoever. A book, i.e., a *verbal performance in print*, is also an element of verbal communication. (94-95)

To this, all I can say is: "Sounds right to me."

#4) This is where I will try to explain why I experienced this attempt to account for the whole of myself as a not-so-novel novelty. This is also where I pretty much sum up my view of everything.

Romance writing and linguistic historiography share, to my way of thinking, two characteristics: they are both and at once adventuresomely iconoclastic and irrevocably traditional. It is as if they both "hedge my bets" in similar ways.

When I struck out to do linguistic historiography in the late 1970s, it was not a recognized or even recognizable subdiscipline of linguistics in the United States. It is hardly more recognized today (that is a different story), but it is fully recognizable, at least to me and other international scholars, if to no one else. When I began to imagine linguistic historiography, I was engaging in relativist heresy: I was not accepting Chomskyan linguistics as a set of true statements about language. I was not believing that Chomskyan linguistics was describing an immediately available object, "language." Rather, I suspected that the shape of that object, "language," was forcefully determined by often unstated and unquestioned presuppositions concerning, among other things, the nature of the mind and of society. I also suspected that the shape of that object, "language," at any given time might well be the result of unquestioned presuppositions about that object uncritically inherited from a preceding theory of language, no matter how much, at times, one theorist might disclaim his connection with a preceding theory. I was interested to read the historical record of linguistics in order to gain a broad understanding of the theoretical range and presuppositional structures of the variously configured objects called "language," and I wanted that broad understanding to serve as a method—although not the cheapest and easiest method, surely—for producing a new understanding of that object.

I admit that the relativist heresy gave me a thrill. It also gave me some long-term unemployment, but that period of unemployment was productive for the exercise of my romance writing craft. At the same time that I was enjoying my heresy (in splendid poverty, I might add), I was also enjoying a certain ironic awareness that my activity of rummaging around in the dusty old texts in the university library, assimilating a vast historical learning, could hardly be more traditionally, recognizably academic. For a long time, it was my private joke that I was alone among American linguists in my ability to quote linguists who were dead but that my field was too innovative for me to find employment.

The same blend of the innovative and the traditional in the romance genre apparently appeals to my creative writing imagination. The romance genre is either 800 years old or 200 years old, depending on how you count it, but either way you count it, it is a venerable literary form. The central problematic—that of establishing a long-term heterosexual love relationship that usually involves marriage and reproduction—could hardly be any more traditionally grounded. At the same time, the conventions of the romance novel fall so far outside the pale of traditional definitions of "real" literature that the adjective "trashy" flies, magnet-like, to the term "romance" as easily as "dumb" precedes "blonde." It has always struck me as deliciously ironic that this most traditional genre could be so reviled and by some of the most traditional sectors in our culture.

Now I admit to getting a heretical thrill from skirmishing on the borders of the magic circle surrounding "real" literature as well. My challenges to those borders, my insistence on the respectability of the romance genre have been variously perceived as outrageous, pretentious, deluded, untenable, a slap in the face at "real" literature written by "real" writers with "real" talent, a quirky, campy start, or "just a phase." (This last is my mother's position. It's like: "Julie can't be serious. She's too smart to be serious about this.")

So either way I have been turning in the past fifteen years, I have been the Barbarian at the Gate. Go figure.

Well, actually, I *can* figure. The ways I have been turning have been directed by my ways of knowing that seem similar to the ways of knowing of American behaviorism. I admit to liking, once again, the heretical thrill that I as an American linguist could feel in taking up the cause of defending Skinner's *Verbal Behavior*. Or at least I could say that the prospect of further heresy held no terrors for me. However, I could not have taken up that heretical cause if I had not also responded to the account of verbal behavior that Skinner was offering and that was so consonant with my backward-looking ways of knowing and the lessons I had learned from reading the historical record of linguistics, namely: a) that any given theory of language and any given instance of verbal behavior is the product of the history of the reinforcements of the situated, historically circumstanced variables at hand; b) that some of those situated, historically circumstanced variables will prove useful or powerful enough to recur, thus making for a high degree of repetition and formularization in every "new" thing we say or say about language; and c) that in particular historical circumstances, it might be perceived as "new" to point out the repetitive, formulaic nature of our verbal behaviors.

As for my romance writing, I believe that the romance is neither more nor less formulaic than any other kind of fiction, and having said that, I hasten to add that I am completely comfortable with its repetitions and formularization. I have repeatedly encountered the objection to romance fiction that it has "a predictable happy end." To my way of thinking, the happy end is not a conclusion but a premise of the genre, and the question for a reader opening the first page of a romance novel is not *whether* the romance will end happily but *how* it will achieve its happy end, just as the person who turns on *Home Improvement* at 8:00 is not wondering *whether* Tim will solve his problem with Jill and his kids by 8:29 but *how* he will resolve it, usually with the aid of Good Neighbor Wilson. Criticizing a romance novel for its "predictable happy end" is, to me, the equivalent of criticizing a high-culture Renaissance painting of the Madonna and Child for depicting, well, a Madonna and Child. A love relationship is a fine and venerable topos. It is an "institutionalized something" to write about, just as the Madonna and Child is an "institutionalized something" to paint about.

My view of language, my view of linguistic historiography, and my view of the romance genre have been mutually reinforcing, enough so that my various writing behaviors have maintained themselves under long-term aversive conditions. The most sustained and publicly aversive conditions have pertained to my romance writing behavior, and I rehearsed at the outset the questions routinely encountered by romance writers, each of which carries a densely-packed load of negative prejudice. The current conditions for my various writing behaviors are no longer so aversive, and I am amazed (and yet not so amazed) that recent, more positive reactions to my various writing behaviors are not immediately welcome to me. The simple reason is that they create for me the problem of establishing new responses, ones that are not defensive and argumentative but instead explanatory. In writing these pages, I have been trying to move through explanatory territory in order to stimulate new behavioral responses, but I have to admit that it is easier for me to walk through the old, familiar territory of simply defending myself against attack.

The compressed lessons of linguistic historiography, romance writing, and Skinnerean behaviorism all exemplify for me the notion of "intentionless invention of regulated improvisation" as elaborated by the French sociologist, Pierre Bourdieu. In his terms, the human *habitus*— that is, embodied or forgotten history—is the active presence of the individual's whole past which continues to produce history on the basis of history, thereby ensuring the permanence in change. The individual— constantly carrying and carried by, constantly possessing and possessed by institutional practices—finds in discourse the triggers for further discourse, finds in instituted means of expression further instituted means of expression, finds in behavior further behavior, which goes along, as Bourdieu says, like a train laying its own rails. The clever person—and we are all clever people, in our own ways—constantly improvises within the regulatory range of possibilities that institutionalized practices necessarily imply.

The way our verbal interactions work, the way a good story works, the way the entire world works is, I believe, like a train laying its own rails. What can be said, imagined, or produced in the future is an *inevitably* contingent product of what was said, imagined, and produced in the past, and how what was said, imagined, and produced was reinforced. And yet what is said, imagined, or produced is always unexpected because the resources of our institutionalized practices are never exhausted and because new and different clever people come along every day. I came along and recognized in the full (even fat) bodied, emotionally saturated, dialogue-intense genre marketed as romance fiction an institutionalized practice whose resources are extremely rich for me, given my tastes, inclinations, and personal history. I do not now envision an end to my ability to improvise within the regulatory range of the genre. I came along and, with my love of language at various levels, felt the desire to recover the *habitus* of thought about language, that full and rich body of forgotten history that is an active presence in the discipline of linguistics. I felt the desire to "write the cross-generational dialogue" created by linguists over the centuries. I have always been aware that that dialogue was open-ended, yet also aware that the historian always "cheats," always get to look ahead to see "what happens next." I hope that my work, whether it is linguistic historiography or romance fiction, always strikes as much by its unpredictability as by its retrospective necessity, like a good joke or a pun.

I cannot resist quoting William James again, this time with a passage that should be engraved on my key chain:

Our minds thus grow in spots; and like grease-spots, the spots spread. But we let them spread as little as possible: we keep unaltered as much of our old knowledge, as many of our old prejudices and beliefs, as we can. We patch and tinker more than we renew. The novelty soaks in; it stains the ancient mass; but it is also tinged by what absorbs it. Our past apperceives and co-operates; and in the new equilibrium in which each step forward in the process of learning terminates, it happens relatively seldom that the new fact is added *raw*. More usually it is embedded cooked, as one might say, or stewed down in the sauce of the old. (*Pragmatism* 113)

This passage summarizes what I find so delightful and compelling in the work of this first great naturalist psychologist to write in the wake of Darwin, and I used it in my talk at Western Michigan to set up my subsequent lectures on the evolutionary scripts for language. James understood that evolution does not produce novelties from scratch and that even in the development of our mental processes—whether phylogenetic or ontogenetic—the action of natural selection/experience works on what already exists. I can telescope James's passage to read like an aphorism: "Fresh experience grafted onto old knowledge makes new knowledge." Or, reverse angle: "Old habits die hard." You see, my taste for formularization runs deep.

The James quote also serves my purposes by explaining rather beautifully—and this image of grease-spots spreading is deeply satisfying to me esthetically—the sense of the unexpected and the inevitable that I experienced in this accounting for the whole of myself. The exercise has felt new to me—which it is, because my grease-spot of self-understanding has spread. It has also felt as if I have thought all this before—which I have, because my grease-spot of self-understanding was already there. I have been standing at the intersection of these two writing activities all these years, looking either down one lane or down the other, but I had never bothered—never been *asked*—to describe what the intersection itself looked like.

By inviting both of me to speak, the psychologists at Western Michigan, generally in tune with what I am "up to" concerning verbal behavior, must have guessed that there would be some reason why I do what I do and that it would have everything to do with my personal history and the places I fit and do not fit within the evaluative categories and institutionalized practices of the culture that shapes me and that I, like it or not, shape in return. I am not saying that the psychologists could have guessed what they would hear, for I, at least, had never said it before, but I hope they heard this unexpected and inevitable account of myself and thought, just as you might be thinking: "Sounds right to me."

Works Cited

James, William. *Pragmatism*. 1907. New York: Meridian, 1969.
——. *Principles of Psychology*. 1890. 2 vols. New York: Holt, 1918.
Volosinov, V. N. *Marxism and the Philosophy of Language*. 1929. Trans. Ladislav Matejka and I. R. Titunik. Cambridge, MA: Harvard UP, 1973.

Hero, Heroine, or HERA:
A New Name for an Old Problem

Anne K. Kaler

Waiter. Waitress. Waitperson.
Actor. Actress. Actperson.
Hero. Heroine? Heroess? Heroette? Female Hero?

Wait a minute. What do we call a female character when she is the center of action and does the job of the hero? A man who is the principal male character in literature is called a "hero." However, when a woman who is listed in the dictionary as "a heroic woman in literature" or a "central female character" is called merely a "heroine," I have serious problems with the terminology.

Often the male version of a word controls and defines the art and the action: thus, the male term of "actor" or "poet" or "hero" becomes the standard by which the art is judged. Language restricts a female who practices an art to being an "actress" or a "poetess" or a "heroine." But the use of "ine" or "ess" weakens the core word by suggesting that the "ine" or "ess" person is somehow an afterthought to the art or activity.[1] Somehow she is reduced to being a dilettante requiring a tacked-on, made-up term to describe her. Notice that many dictionaries do not list the word "actress" or "poetess" separately; a "waitress," however, has a separate listing, perhaps because it reflects a service area rather than an art.[2]

Perhaps my reluctance to use the word "heroine" comes from its association with the Hero and Leander story. As you remember, the beauty of Hero, a priestess of Aphrodite (and therefore a sacred prostitute), causes the otherwise undistinguished young Leander to swim the Hellespont nightly; unfortunately, he drowns in the rough waters one night and she kills herself. These actions can be viewed from several perspectives. Does this mean that Hero tempts the fine young man to lose his life? Or is the lovesick Leander just a poor swimmer? My feminist complaint is that the mythical Hero is acted upon; she never acts on her own volition. She is a heroine, a passive prize to be won. After all, what choice did she have? She had a father who forbade her the lover of her choice, a lover who risked all for a moment of pleasure, and a story-

187

teller who expected her to throw herself in the sea. More likely, she drowned in tears of frustration and boredom. Shakespeare's heroine Hero in *Much Ado about Nothing* has a similar fate; she allows herself to be acted upon by all the characters, even to faking her own death. Despite their names, these Heros are not "heroes" but passive "heroines."

In antiquity, while the male heroes cavorted about with the goddesses, the women stayed at home. Even in that women-riddled tale of the *Odyssey,* all the women are working and waiting—Helen is darning Menelaus' socks; Nausicca is doing her brothers' laundry; Penelope is weaving her father-in-law's shroud and fending off suitors; and, even when the goddess Circe is not spinning spells, she is busy at her loom. These sedentary womanly occupations preclude journeying: the heroes journey, the heroines sit and sew. That's fine for classical literature but hardly an acceptable agenda for feminists who want a name for the work that they do. For example, what term are we going to give the four women in the television show *The Golden Girls* or *Designing Women*? Heroes? But they are not men. Heroines? When there is no consistent male for them to depend on? Heroesses? When they control their own destiny? Female Heroes? Descriptive but awkward.

Here, then, is the crux of the problem. There is no word, no name, no clear-cut genderless identification of the act of being heroic. But it doesn't have to be so. Just because the term "hero" is presently limited to the male of the species should not hinder the female hero from finding or developing her own term. But rather than inventing a new term, we need only to explore the original word "hero" to uncover what we've been overlooking all these years.

Ironically we discover that Hera, the chief female deity in the Greek theogony, is the source of the word "hero." A "hero" was a term attached to any brave man who did great deeds in honor of Hera, in any one of her representations as the Great Goddess who nourishes and slaughters her sons or lovers or husbands. The most famous of these "Hera's boys" is Herakles (also known as Hercules) whose name means "the glory of Hera." Their relationship, however, is stormy because, as the legal wife and sister of Zeus, Queen Hera upheld the sacredness of marriage and persecuted the mortal maidens whom Zeus impregnated, one of whom was Herakles' mother Alcmena. Although Hera was tricked by Athena into nursing the infant to make him immortal, she opposed him throughout his existence by cursing him with periodic madness. As strong as he was, Herakles' rash and impetuous deeds led him into constant conflict with the Queen Hera and, indeed, with all women. Like the blind seer Teresias who was changed into a woman for seven years by Hera, Herakles is auctioned off for a year's service to Omphale, the Lydian queen who forces him to adopt woman's dress and occupations to teach him humility. (Today we'd call it "getting in touch with his feminine side.") Because Omphale was also considered a symbol of the *omphalos* or navel of the world through which a hero must pass, Herakles assumes the role of the sacrificed son/husband of the Great Goddess which Omphale represents. When he reconciles with Hera as the Great Goddess in a *hierogamos* or sacred marriage, he does so by marrying her substitute, her daughter Hebe.

So the term "hero" won't do, since it is restricted to a man's endeavors. Surely the English language must have a word for the woman who controls her own destiny, who is autonomous, who goes outward on her own quest for identity (the masculine myth) and who goes inward on her spiritual journey toward awakening (the feminine myth). So if neither "hero" not "heroine" will fit, what term exists to define the "hero" who is a female?

The word is HERA.

HERA is derived from Hera, the mother/wife goddess, the equal to Zeus, the queen of the gods, the seat of power, and a vital member of the triad of goddesses. (To emphasize the importance of the term, I've used caps when speaking about the new term HERA.) Like Annie Oakley, a HERA can "do anything better" than a hero. She already does the same things as a hero: she represents her country's virtues, dresses for battle, exhibits bravery. As the chief female character who undertakes her journey toward self-identity just like any hero described by mythologists, the HERA experiences a call to action; she has companions and mentors; she is given sacred weapons; she crosses thresholds of death, has underworld adventures, and returns from death to bring new hope.

Defining the HERA should not disparage or displace the "hero." What the HERA adds is her own particular quest of the feminine journey toward awakening. Her strongest ability is the power to reconcile opposing elements, to balance her universe, to restore herself and others to holistic health. Because her inward journey often precedes her outward quest, the HERA's nurturing nature and survival instincts appear in mythology as aspects of the Great Goddess. For example, in the movie *Aliens,* the main character destroys the spider mother and her eggs to protect the young girl she has rescued. But she saves the young of her species only by killing the young of another species. When Scarlett O'Hara admits to Rhett that she could survive without him if she had to, she weighs the fact that eleven people are dependent upon her. Her answer exhibits so much of the HERA's survival instinct that she loses his love. These are not the actions of a "heroine" who wait patiently for a man to rescue her.

The HERA is not a heroine.

The HERA has existed in earlier literatures as a bawd, courtesan, thief, rogue, wanderer, con artist, and picara, the feminine form of the wandering rogue or picaro. Just as Hera predates Herakles, the Spanish bawd Celestina predates the picaro Lazarillo des Tormes. Just as Daniel Defoe's Moll Flanders may be a picaresque wandering rogue who reacts to society's forces around her, his Roxana is an autonomous, feisty picara, a HERA. As the *Roxana: or The Fortunate Mistress* of the title, she raises the question whether a mistress can be fortunate or does a mistress create her own fortune.[3]

A HERA acts; she is not acted upon. A HERA does not sit around and wish that she were somewhere else having adventures—she goes out and causes adventures. She is autonomous even when it offends. In literature, which tends to split women into the patronizing duality of heroines—those who inspire like Mary and those who tempt like Eve—the HERA is an abomination because she incorporates both ends of the spectrum. Her frank sexuality offends the Puritanical; her aggressiveness distresses the social mores; her direct manner outrages the conservative.

The HERA develops most easily in action-adventure genres such as science fiction, fantasy, and mystery because those genres combine the masculine power of reason with the feminine power of intuition. The brain is a greater equalizer than the computer or the typewriter and the interaction between the brain's two lobes produces the non-gender-specific appeal of the mystery. Miss Marple is no less efficient than Hercule Poirot, whose name (Herakles, again) and description are startlingly feminine. Jessica Fletcher is no less clever than Perry Mason, who has to have a feminine backup, a younger male, and an old buddy in the District Attorney's office to function. V. I. Warshawski and Kinsey Milhone are no less gutsy than Sam Spade or Mickey Spillane and Cagney and Lacey are as good at police work as Starsky and Hutch.

Science fiction also equalizes. "Hard" science fiction abounds with stories about males adventuring into space but the ships they travel in have such strong feminine components that they are often named after women. Fantasy, long the realm of the male Inklings, has now become a "soft" genre dominated by women writers who create male and female heroes and HERAS equally well.

Early category romances presented heroines who waited for heroes to rescue them. But rebellion came early. Jane Eyre is a HERA strong enough to resist illicit love but also strong enough to disregard society's prohibitions when Rochester's call touches her compassion. When the category romance had to change to reflect real life, the "heroine" became the autonomous engineer of her own destiny. The demands of the reading public now force authors to construct strong women, whose identities are not dependent upon a hero's rescuing them from dicey situations or threatening dragons: Terese Ramin's characters often rescue the hero and Elizabeth Lowell's ladies are equal scientists with the males. In the historical romance, the HERA takes on all time periods and all comers.

The contrast between a hero and a HERA is most easily seen in the *Star Wars* films where Luke Skywalker is a hero and his sister, Princess Leia, is a HERA. Luke's journey toward identity takes him down the familiar path of the outward quest through his mentors Obi Wan Kenobi and Yoda toward the final acceptance of the inward quest when he refuses to destroy his father. Leia's journey is the reverse of Luke's. Her meditative inward journey is completed before the action begins. She knows who she is—Princess of the Empire, daughter of a Jedi knight. What she needs to prove is her masculine mettle which she does repeatedly, slogging into battle with the best of them. That she falls in love with Han Solo does not detract because she never lets that love distract her from her goal. In fact, her love proves that her balanced personality can incorporate all relationships so that she becomes the ruler—autonomous, matured, completed. In contrast her twin brother goes on his inward journey toward more spiritual affairs.

The HERA fights when she has to. As a fighter, she sings of "arms and the man," not the kitchen and the bed. Barbara Hambly's HERAS are aggressive and feisty, battle-scarred and battle-trained. So are Marion Zimmer Bradley's Free Amazons and Jo Clayton's Aleytys, Skeen, and Terrillian. So are Janet Morris's Estri and C. L. Moore's Jirel of Joiry.

The HERA is not stupidly brave. She takes all the help she can to get out of a bad situation. Wonder Woman uses her bracelets, not as symbols of feminine slavery or as attractive baubles to entice a man, but as defensive weapons to deflect bullets. When she uses her golden lasso as a truth-binding device, she is employing the magic weapon of a hero. Sheena, Queen of the Jungle, uses her jungle animals to her advantage just as Becky Sharp knits her green net bag to entice Joseph Sedly and Scarlett O'Hara alters her drapes into a dress to lure Rhett Butler.

Not every HERA is a warrior. Indeed, the history of the woman warrior is at times too imitative of the male hero's penchant for gore, violence, and self-aggrandizement. The wise HERA avoids conflict when she can, seeking to be a peace weaver instead. In *Twelfth Night,* Viola's refusal to fight when she does not know how shows her good sense; her personal courage, however, is shown when she offers to die rather than to bring harm to her lover, Duke Orsino.

The HERA wears sensible clothing. Are soft clothes a sign of a soft mind and a weak body? A HERA like Modesty Blaise uses both work clothes and fancy clothes to disguise the deadliness of her "weaker sex." Conversely, a preference for velour jogging suits does not weaken Modesty's partner Willie Garvin any more than lace on the sleeve of an eighteenth-century fop prevented him from being excellent swordsmen. The lace on Scarlett's petticoat does not interfere with her scheming practices, and Mata Hari probably got more information in her negligee than Joan of Arc did in her armor. Laura Holt in the Remington Steele series dresses in slacks because they are practical togs for a woman who has so many physical chase scenes. A HERA therefore dresses in working clothes—armor, jeans, camouflage, or sequins.

One example of the HERA is found in Vonda McIntyre's Snake in *Dreamsnake* where the healer in a primitive post-nuclear society has been given three snakes with which to work—Mist, an albino cobra, indicative of her courage; Sand, a diamondback rattlesnake, a sign of her reason: and Grass, a dreamsnake, her fantasy ability. When she loses Grass to the frightened parents of a child she is healing, she undertakes a quest to find the illusive off-world dreamsnakes. Her quest brings her to many adventures: she adopts an abused stablehand as a daughter, she convinces an impotent man that he is fully a man, she cures horses and people and herself. She solves her problem without the help of anyone else: her lover Arevin and daughter Melissa appear only in a secondary way because she has integrated her own personality, has reconciled her opposing forces into a workable world, and has faced death and won.

Yes, indeed and in deeds, the HERA will do nicely as a term for the autonomous woman on her double mythic journeys. Language should be brought into line with literary reality and the independent woman should be called by her rightful name—HERA, "the glory of Hera."

Notes

1. The *American Dictionary of the English Language,* 3rd ed., derives the ending "ess" from Middle English "esse" and Latin "issa" and states that "differentiation based on gender may be legitimate: acting, for example, is an occupation in which the parts one can play may in fact depend on one's sex." *Webster's Third New International Dictionary* claims that an "actor plus ess" is its second definition of "a female actor." It also mentions an obsolete meaning of "actress" as a "woman who takes part in any affair."

2. *Webster's New Collegiate Dictionary,* 2nd ed., and the *Random House Dictionary,* for example.

3. See my book, *The Picara: From Hera to Fantasy Heroine* (Bowling Green, OH: Bowling Green State University Popular Press, 1991).

Contributors

Julie Tetel Andresen is from the Chicago suburb of Glenview, Illinois. Since 1976, she has lived in Durham, North Carolina, with her husband and two sons. She has a B.A. in French from Duke University, an M.A. in French from the University of Illinois, Urbana, and a Ph.D. in Linguistics from the University of North Carolina, Chapel Hill. She is an associate professor in the Department of English at Duke University and has a joint appointment in the Department of Cultural Anthropology. She is also the Director of the Duke University–University of Bucharest, Romania faculty exchange. She is the author of numerous scholarly articles and a scholarly book, *Linguistics in America 1769-1924: A Critical History* (Routledge 1990, 1995).

In addition to her career in academics, Andresen has published fifteen historical romances under the name Julie Tetel with commercial presses such as Warner Books, Fawcett, and Harlequin. She has recently started her own publishing company, Helix Books, dedicated to romance fiction. Visit her at: www.helixbooks.com

Amber Botts has an M.A. in English from Pittsburg State University and a B.A. from Washburn University in Topeka. She lives in southeast Kansas and teaches American Literature and A.P. composition. She has been reading romance as a fan since high school and began studying it while in graduate school.

Carol Breslin is a professor of English at Gwynedd-Mercy College. Although her specialty is Chaucerian studies (her doctoral dissertation treated justice and law in selected *Canterbury Tales*), Carol teaches a variety of courses including the freshman writing course and journalism as well as Chaucer and his Contemporaries. Current research interests range from the representation of the Vietnam War in American literature to post-modern critical appraisals of the works of Pearl S. Buck.

Her reading and interpretation of popular romance novels has been under the guiding hand of Dr. Anne Kaler, a colleague at Gwynedd-Mercy, who persuaded her that along with some excellent stories these works might offer some interesting treatments of themes, conventions, and character types found in more "literary" writing. As promised, she has often found much to delight in—authentic medieval landscapes, historical accuracy, a spiritual emphasis, a portrayal of women as strong, compassionate human beings, and an optimistic view of life and the possibility of happiness that just won't quit.

Diane Calhoun-French holds a Ph.D. in English from the University of Louisville. She is currently professor and Dean of Academic Affairs at Jefferson Community College-SW in Louisville, Kentucky. Her teaching and research interests include writing, Victorian literature, popular culture, and women's studies. She is Executive Secretary of the Popular Culture Association in the South, past President of the National Association for Women in Education, and editor of NAWE's journal, *Initiatives*. She regularly publishes and presents papers on such subjects as women's romance fiction, mystery fiction, daytime serials, and images of women in popular culture. She lives with her husband, one dog, and nine cats on a farm near Lebanon Junction, Kentucky.

Dawn Heinecken is a Ph.D. candidate in American Culture Studies at Bowling Green State University. She holds a B.A. in Theater and Dance from Amherst College and a M.A. in Mass Communication from the University of Wisconsin-Superior. A former sports writer, her current research interests include female action heroes in popular culture.

Rosemary Johnson-Kurek is an academic platypus with a Ph.D. in Educational Technology, an M.A. in Popular Culture, and a B.A. in Communications, but is currently teaching English at the University of Toledo where she feels fortunate to be in a cutting edge computer classroom. When she is needed, she also tutors at the Writing Center, teaches film theory, produces low-budget video, and instructs for the Department of Developmental Education at Owens Community College. To compensate for years of writing and reading the behavioral prose common in the field of education, she began reading romances in massive quantities after finishing her doctorate. Dr. Johnson-Kurek organized the 1997 ReReading the Romance symposium held at Bowling Green State University.

Anne K. Kaler, currently a professor of English at Gwynedd-Mercy College, serves as area chair of the Romance Writers and Writing panels for the national PCA/ACA Conference and Mid-Atlantic PCA/ACA. She is a member of the Romance Writers of America, Valley Forge Chapter. Presently, she is editing an issue of *Clues* on romance in mystery and a collection of critical essays on Ellis Peters's twelfth-century Benedictine detective, entitled *Cordially Yours, Brother Cadfael.* Her publications include *The Picara: From Hera to Fantasy Heroine* and articles in *The Culture of Celebrations, Heroines of Popular Culture* from Bowling Green State University Popular Press, and in *Andrew Greeley's World* (Warner) and in *Chocolate: The Food of the Gods* (Greenwood), along with articles in various journals.

Pamela Marks coordinated the Writing Center at the University of Rhode Island's College of Continuing Education in Providence, where she also taught American literature. During the summer, she teaches Business Communication at Harvard University. She received her B.Ed. in English at the University of Hawaii at Manoa, and her M.A. and Ph.D. in 19th Century American Literature from URI at Kingston. Her essays have appeared in *Moreana* and the *Providence Journal*. She has conducted panels on Death and Dying in Film, Literature and Culture for the national PCA/ACA conference.

Jennifer Crusie Smith began studying romance fiction as research for her dissertation on the politics of love in Western literature. Inspired by that research, she also began to write romance fiction and has since sold seven novels to Harlequin/Silhouette as Jennifer Crusie. She currently teaches as a graduate assistant in the Department of English at Ohio State University.

Abby Zidle is completing her doctoral work in English at University of California/Davis. Both her bachelor's (Stanford) and master's (Davis) are also in English. Her dissertation is entitled "Secret Formula/Formula Secrets: Popular Feminism and the Romance Genre." She spent the 1997-98 academic year as a visiting lecturer teaching American Literature at the University of Bordeaux, France.

CPSIA information can be obtained
at www.ICGtesting.com
Printed in the USA
FFOW04n1403081116
29082FF

9 780879 727789